Carnegie Commission on Higher Education
Sponsored Research Studies

AMERICAN HIGHER EDUCATION:
DIRECTIONS OLD AND NEW
Joseph Ben-David

A DEGREE AND WHAT ELSE?
CORRELATES AND CONSEQUENCES OF A
COLLEGE EDUCATION
*Stephen B. Withey, Jo Anne Coble, Gerald Gurin,
John P. Robinson, Burkhard Strumpel, Elizabeth
Keogh Taylor, and Arthur C. Wolfe*

THE MULTICAMPUS UNIVERSITY:
A STUDY OF ACADEMIC GOVERNANCE
Eugene C. Lee and Frank M. Bowen

INSTITUTIONS IN TRANSITION:
A PROFILE OF CHANGE IN HIGHER
EDUCATION
(INCORPORATING THE 1970 STATISTICAL
REPORT)
Harold L. Hodgkinson

EFFICIENCY IN LIBERAL EDUCATION:
A STUDY OF COMPARATIVE INSTRUCTIONAL
COSTS FOR DIFFERENT WAYS OF ORGANIZING
TEACHING-LEARNING IN A LIBERAL ARTS
COLLEGE
Howard R. Bowen and Gordon K. Douglass

CREDIT FOR COLLEGE:
PUBLIC POLICY FOR STUDENT LOANS
Robert W. Hartman

MODELS AND MAVERICKS:
A PROFILE OF PRIVATE LIBERAL ARTS
COLLEGES
Morris T. Keeton

BETWEEN TWO WORLDS:
A PROFILE OF NEGRO HIGHER EDUCATION
Frank Bowles and Frank A. DeCosta

BREAKING THE ACCESS BARRIERS:
A PROFILE OF TWO-YEAR COLLEGES
Leland L. Medsker and Dale Tillery

ANY PERSON, ANY STUDY:
AN ESSAY ON HIGHER EDUCATION IN THE
UNITED STATES
Eric Ashby

THE NEW DEPRESSION IN HIGHER
EDUCATION:
A STUDY OF FINANCIAL CONDITIONS AT 41
COLLEGES AND UNIVERSITIES
Earl F. Cheit

FINANCING MEDICAL EDUCATION:
AN ANALYSIS OF ALTERNATIVE POLICIES AND
MECHANISMS
Rashi Fein and Gerald I. Weber

HIGHER EDUCATION IN NINE COUNTRIES:
A COMPARATIVE STUDY OF COLLEGES AND
UNIVERSITIES ABROAD
*Barbara B. Burn, Philip G. Altbach, Clark Kerr,
and James A. Perkins*

BRIDGES TO UNDERSTANDING:
INTERNATIONAL PROGRAMS OF AMERICAN
COLLEGES AND UNIVERSITIES
Irwin T. Sanders and Jennifer C. Ward

GRADUATE AND PROFESSIONAL EDUCATION,
1980:
A SURVEY OF INSTITUTIONAL PLANS
Lewis B. Mayhew
(Out of print, but available from University Microfilms.)

THE AMERICAN COLLEGE AND AMERICAN
CULTURE:
SOCIALIZATION AS A FUNCTION OF HIGHER
EDUCATION
Oscar Handlin and Mary F. Handlin

RECENT ALUMNI AND HIGHER EDUCATION:
A SURVEY OF COLLEGE GRADUATES
Joe L. Spaeth and Andrew M. Greeley
(Out of print, but available from University Microfilms.)

CHANGE IN EDUCATIONAL POLICY:
SELF-STUDIES IN SELECTED COLLEGES AND
UNIVERSITIES
Dwight R. Ladd

STATE OFFICIALS AND HIGHER EDUCATION:
A SURVEY OF THE OPINIONS AND
EXPECTATIONS OF POLICY MAKERS IN NINE
STATES
Heinz Eulau and Harold Quinley
(Out of print, but available from University Microfilms.)

ACADEMIC DEGREE STRUCTURES,
INNOVATIVE APPROACHES:
PRINCIPLES OF REFORM IN DEGREE
STRUCTURES IN THE UNITED STATES
Stephen H. Spurr

COLLEGES OF THE FORGOTTEN AMERICANS:
A PROFILE OF STATE COLLEGES AND
REGIONAL UNIVERSITIES
E. Alden Dunham

FROM BACKWATER TO MAINSTREAM:
A PROFILE OF CATHOLIC HIGHER EDUCATION
Andrew M. Greeley

THE ECONOMICS OF THE MAJOR PRIVATE
UNIVERSITIES
William G. Bowen
(Out of print, but available from University Microfilms.)

THE FINANCE OF HIGHER EDUCATION
Howard R. Bowen
(Out of print, but available from University Microfilms.)

ALTERNATIVE METHODS OF FEDERAL
FUNDING FOR HIGHER EDUCATION
Ron Wolk
(Out of print, but available from University Microfilms.)

INVENTORY OF CURRENT RESEARCH ON
HIGHER EDUCATION 1968
Dale M. Heckman and Warren Bryan Martin
(Out of print, but available from University Microfilms.)

The following technical reports are available from the Carnegie Commission on Higher Education, 2150 Shattuck Ave.,
Berkeley, California 94704.

RESOURCE USE IN HIGHER EDUCATION:
TRENDS IN OUTPUT AND INPUTS, 1930–1967
June O'Neill

MAY 1970:
THE CAMPUS AFTERMATH OF CAMBODIA AND
KENT STATE
Richard E. Peterson and John A. Bilorusky

MENTAL ABILITY AND HIGHER EDUCATIONAL
ATTAINMENT IN THE 20TH CENTURY
Paul Taubman and Terence Wales

AMERICAN COLLEGE AND UNIVERSITY
ENROLLMENT TRENDS IN 1971
Richard E. Peterson

PAPERS ON EFFICIENCY IN THE MANAGEMENT
OF HIGHER EDUCATION
Alexander M. Mood, Colin Bell, Lawrence Bogard,
Helen Brownlee, and Joseph McCloskey

AN INVENTORY OF ACADEMIC INNOVATION
AND REFORM
Ann Heiss

ESTIMATING THE RETURNS TO EDUCATION:
A DISAGGREGATED APPROACH
Richard S. Eckaus

SOURCES OF FUNDS TO COLLEGES AND
UNIVERSITIES
June O'Neill

TRENDS AND PROJECTIONS OF PHYSICIANS IN
THE UNITED STATES 1967–2002
Mark S. Blumberg

NEW DEPRESSION IN HIGHER EDUCATION—
TWO YEARS LATER
Earl F. Cheit

PROFESSORS, UNIONS, AND AMERICAN HIGHER EDUCATION
Everett Carll Ladd, Jr. and Seymour Martin Lipset

A CLASSIFICATION OF INSTITUTIONS OF HIGHER EDUCATION

POLITICAL IDEOLOGIES OF GRADUATE STUDENTS: CRYSTALLIZATION, CONSISTENCY, AND CONTEXTUAL EFFECT
Margaret Fay and Jeff Weintraub

FLYING A LEARNING CENTER: DESIGN AND COSTS OF AN OFF-CAMPUS SPACE FOR LEARNING
Thomas J. Karwin

THE DEMISE OF DIVERSITY?: A COMPARATIVE PROFILE OF EIGHT TYPES OF INSTITUTIONS
C. Robert Pace

TUITION: A SUPPLEMENTAL STATEMENT TO THE REPORT OF THE CARNEGIE COMMISSION ON HIGHER EDUCATION ON "WHO PAYS? WHO BENEFITS? WHO SHOULD PAY?"

THE GREAT AMERICAN DEGREE MACHINE
Douglas L. Adkins

AN OWL BEFORE DUSK
Michio Nagai

DEMAND AND SUPPLY IN UNITED STATES HIGHER EDUCATION: A TECHNICAL SUPPLEMENT
Leonard A. Miller and Roy Radner

The following reprints are available from the Carnegie Commission on Higher Education, 2150 Shattuck Ave., Berkeley, California 94704.

ACCELERATED PROGRAMS OF MEDICAL EDUCATION, *by Mark S. Blumberg, reprinted from* JOURNAL OF MEDICAL EDUCATION, *vol. 46, no. 8, August 1971.**

SCIENTIFIC MANPOWER FOR 1970–1985, *by Allan M. Cartter, reprinted from* SCIENCE, *vol. 172, no. 3979, pp. 132–140, April 9, 1971.**

A NEW METHOD OF MEASURING STATES' HIGHER EDUCATION BURDEN, *by Neil Timm, reprinted from* THE JOURNAL OF HIGHER EDUCATION, *vol. 42, no. 1, pp. 27–33, January 1971.**

REGENT WATCHING, *by Earl F. Cheit, reprinted from* AGB REPORTS, *vol. 13, no. 6, pp. 4–13, March 1971.**

COLLEGE GENERATIONS—FROM THE 1930s TO THE 1960s, *by Seymour M. Lipset and Everett C. Ladd, Jr., reprinted from* THE PUBLIC INTEREST, *no. 25, Summer 1971.**

WHAT'S BUGGING THE STUDENTS?, *by Kenneth Keniston, reprinted from* EDUCATIONAL RECORD, *American Council on Education, Washington, D.C., Spring 1970.**

THE POLITICS OF ACADEMIA, *by Seymour Martin Lipset, reprinted from David C. Nichols (ed.),* PERSPECTIVES ON CAMPUS TENSIONS: PAPERS PREPARED FOR THE SPECIAL COMMITTEE ON CAMPUS TENSIONS, *American Council on Education, Washington, D.C., September 1970.**

*The Commission's stock of this reprint has been exhausted.

INTERNATIONAL PROGRAMS OF U.S. COLLEGES AND UNIVERSITIES: PRIORITIES FOR THE SEVENTIES, *by James A. Perkins, reprinted by permission of the International Council for Educational Development, Occasional Paper no. 1, July 1971.**

FACULTY UNIONISM: FROM THEORY TO PRACTICE, *by Joseph W. Garbarino, reprinted from* INDUSTRIAL RELATIONS, *vol. 11, no. 1, pp. 1–17, February 1972.**

MORE FOR LESS: HIGHER EDUCATION'S NEW PRIORITY, *by Virginia B. Smith, reprinted from* UNIVERSAL HIGHER EDUCATION: COSTS AND BENEFITS, *American Council on Education, Washington, D.C., 1971.**

ACADEMIA AND POLITICS IN AMERICA, *by Seymour M. Lipset, reprinted from Thomas J. Nossiter (ed.),* IMAGINATION AND PRECISION IN THE SOCIAL SCIENCES, *pp. 211–289, Faber and Faber, London, 1972.**

POLITICS OF ACADEMIC NATURAL SCIENTISTS AND ENGINEERS, *by Everett C. Ladd, Jr., and Seymour M. Lipset, reprinted from* SCIENCE, *vol. 176, no. 4039, pp. 1091–1100, June 9, 1972.*

THE INTELLECTUAL AS CRITIC AND REBEL, WITH SPECIAL REFERENCE TO THE UNITED STATES AND THE SOVIET UNION, *by Seymour M. Lipset and Richard B. Dobson, reprinted from* DAEDALUS, *vol. 101, no. 3, pp. 137–198, Summer 1972.*

THE POLITICS OF AMERICAN SOCIOLOGISTS, *by Seymour M. Lipset and Everett C. Ladd, Jr., reprinted from* THE AMERICAN JOURNAL OF SOCIOLOGY, *vol. 78, no. 1, July 1972.*

THE DISTRIBUTION OF ACADEMIC TENURE IN AMERICAN HIGHER EDUCATION, *by Martin Trow, reprinted from* THE TENURE DEBATE, *Bardwell Smith (ed.), Jossey-Bass, San Francisco, 1972.*

THE NATURE AND ORIGINS OF THE CARNEGIE COMMISSION ON HIGHER EDUCATION, *by Alan Pifer, based on a speech delivered to the Pennsylvania Association of Colleges and Universities, Oct. 16, 1972, reprinted by permission of the Carnegie Foundation for the Advancement of Teaching.*

AMERICAN SOCIAL SCIENTISTS AND THE GROWTH OF CAMPUS POLITICAL ACTIVISM IN THE 1960s, *by Everett C. Ladd, Jr., and Seymour M. Lipset, reprinted from* SOCIAL SCIENCES INFORMATION, *vol. 10, no. 2, April 1971.**

THE POLITICS OF AMERICAN POLITICAL SCIENTISTS, *by Everett C. Ladd, Jr., and Seymour M. Lipset, reprinted from* PS, *vol. 4, no. 2, Spring 1971.**

THE DIVIDED PROFESSORIATE, *by Seymour M. Lipset and Everett C. Ladd, Jr., reprinted from* CHANGE, *vol. 3, no. 3, pp. 54–60, May 1971.**

JEWISH ACADEMICS IN THE UNITED STATES: THEIR ACHIEVEMENTS, CULTURE AND POLITICS, *by Seymour M. Lipset and Everett C. Ladd, Jr., reprinted from* AMERICAN JEWISH YEAR BOOK, *1971.**

*The Commission's stock of this reprint has been exhausted.

THE UNHOLY ALLIANCE AGAINST THE CAMPUS, *by Kenneth Keniston and Michael Lerner, reprinted from* NEW YORK TIMES MAGAZINE, *November 8, 1970.**

PRECARIOUS PROFESSORS: NEW PATTERNS OF REPRESENTATION, *by Joseph W. Garbarino, reprinted from* INDUSTRIAL RELATIONS, *vol. 10, no. 1, February 1971.**

. . . AND WHAT PROFESSORS THINK: ABOUT STUDENT PROTEST AND MANNERS, MORALS, POLITICS, AND CHAOS ON THE CAMPUS, *by Seymour Martin Lipset and Everett C. Ladd, Jr., reprinted from* PSYCHOLOGY TODAY, *November 1970.**

DEMAND AND SUPPLY IN U.S. HIGHER EDUCATION: A PROGRESS REPORT, *by Roy Radner and Leonard S. Miller, reprinted from* AMERICAN ECONOMIC REVIEW, *May 1970.**

RESOURCES FOR HIGHER EDUCATION: AN ECONOMIST'S VIEW, *by Theodore W. Schultz, reprinted from* JOURNAL OF POLITICAL ECONOMY, *vol. 76, no. 3, University of Chicago, May / June 1968.**

INDUSTRIAL RELATIONS AND UNIVERSITY RELATIONS, *by Clark Kerr, reprinted from* PROCEEDINGS OF THE 21ST ANNUAL WINTER MEETING OF THE INDUSTRIAL RELATIONS RESEARCH ASSOCIATION, *pp. 15–25.**

NEW CHALLENGES TO THE COLLEGE AND UNIVERSITY, *by Clark Kerr, reprinted from Kermit Gordon (ed.),* AGENDA FOR THE NATION, *The Brookings Institution, Washington, D.C., 1968.**

PRESIDENTIAL DISCONTENT, *by Clark Kerr, reprinted from David C. Nichols (ed.),* PERSPECTIVES ON CAMPUS TENSIONS: PAPERS PREPARED FOR THE SPECIAL COMMITTEE ON CAMPUS TENSIONS, *American Council on Education, Washington, D.C., September 1970.**

STUDENT PROTEST—AN INSTITUTIONAL AND NATIONAL PROFILE, *by Harold Hodgkinson, reprinted from* THE RECORD, *vol. 71, no. 4, May 1970.**

COMING OF MIDDLE AGE IN HIGHER EDUCATION, *by Earl F. Cheit, address delivered to American Association of State Colleges and Universities and National Association of State Universities and Land-Grant Colleges, Nov. 13, 1972.*

MEASURING FACULTY UNIONISM: QUANTITY AND QUALITY, *by Bill Aussieker and J. W. Garbarino, reprinted from* INDUSTRIAL RELATIONS, *vol. 12, no. 2, May 1973.*

PROBLEMS IN THE TRANSITION FROM ELITE TO MASS HIGHER EDUCATION, *by Martin Trow, paper prepared for a conference on mass higher education sponsored by the Organization for Economic Co-operation and Development, June 1973.**

Ph.D.'s and the
Academic Labor Market

Ph.D.'s and the
Academic Labor Market

by *Allan M. Cartter*

Professor of Education and Economics
University of California, Los Angeles
and Vice-President
Higher Education Research Institute

112364

A Report Prepared for
The Carnegie Commission on Higher Education

McGRAW-HILL BOOK COMPANY
New York St. Louis San Francisco
Auckland Düsseldorf Johannesburg Kuala Lumpur London
Mexico Montreal New Delhi Panama Paris
São Paulo Singapore Sydney Tokyo Toronto

*The Carnegie Commission on Higher Education,
2150 Shattuck Avenue, Berkeley, California 94704,
has sponsored preparation of this report as part
of a continuing effort to obtain and present
significant information for public discussion.
The views expressed are those of the author.*

PH.D.'S AND THE ACADEMIC LABOR MARKET

This book was set in Palatino by University Graphics, Inc.
It was printed and bound by The Maple Press Company.
The designer was Elliot Epstein. The editors were Nancy Frank
and Michael Hennelly for McGraw-Hill Book Company and
Verne A. Stadtman for the Carnegie Commission on Higher Education.
Audre Hanneman edited the index. Milton J. Heiberg supervised the
production.

Library of Congress Cataloging in Publication Data

Cartter, Allan Murray.
Ph.D.'s and the academic labor market.

Bibliography: p.
Includes index.
1. Doctor of philosophy degree. 2. Teachers—Supply
and demand—United States. I. Carnegie Commission on
Higher Education. II. Title.
LB2386.C37   331.1'26   75-38700
ISBN 0-07-010132-9

123456789MAMM79876

Contents

Foreword

There are few more effective ways for a college or university president to influence institutional quality than by paying very close attention to the adequacy of the number and the ability of individuals appointed to his or her faculty. It is important, therefore, for leaders of higher education to become intimately familiar with the factors that influence the availability of persons qualified for academic employment, and with the dynamics of the academic market place. Such knowledge is particularly essential if presidents and trustees are to determine when they will have chances to introduce new blood, when they can improve the balance of teaching and research across departments, or when they can enrich their manpower commitment to either a single discipline or the institution generally.

Young men and women who are at the threshold of their preparation for postgraduate study and academic careers also need to know as much as they can about faculty demand and supply for reasonable periods into the future. The investments they will have to make may not yield a return for up to six years after they commence their preparations, and it is tragic to encounter new Ph.D.'s who started working for their degrees when their subject fields were booming only to finish them when the market for their training had all but disappeared.

It is also important to understand the trends and behavior of academic employment in order to shape national higher education policy. Responses to temporary depressions of demand in certain fields should not be hasty or wholesale, and efforts to introduce costly graduate programs in subjects of timely, but perhaps short-run, popularity could be foolhardy. Decisions to economize in overall institutional operations by prematurely, or unnecessarily, dismantling effective graduate programs in a time of financial stringency could be cause for deep regret at some future date.

It is easier to say that more sophisticated academic manpower forecasting is needed, however, than it is to provide it. Basically, such activity concerns the future—which is notorious for holding back vital data essential for unlocking its secrets. For all the work that has been done in forecasting future enrollments and academic manpower needs, especially in recent years, the finest efforts have yet to achieve scientific certainty.

But we know a lot more now than we did fifteen years ago, and Allan Cartter, who has written this report for the Carnegie Commission on Higher Education, has long been recognized as the one pre-eminent leader in efforts to improve our understanding of the subject. In this book, he shares his analyses, his reservations, and his conclusions about academic manpower forecasting with clarity and thoroughness. He also indicates what needs to be done by institutions, professional associations, and the government to help improve the forecasting process. The result is a welcome and useful addition to the Commission's series on higher education.

Clark Kerr
Chairman
Carnegie Commission
on Higher Education

January 1976

Preface

In 1970 Clark Kerr first asked if I would undertake a detailed study of academic labor markets under the auspices of the Carnegie Commission. However, a year's leave of absence from university administrative duties, necessary for such a project, was not possible in that year or the following year. Finally in 1972 I resigned as chancellor of New York University and took up duties as senior research fellow at the Commission, assisted by a Guggenheim Fellowship. Involvements with Commission staff delayed serious work on the project for nearly a year, but the Commission generously extended support for an additional year spent at UCLA. Some two years later than originally anticipated, the task is completed, with some measure of relief to both sponsor and author.

In many ways the delay was advantageous, for the scene has changed considerably since the study was first contemplated. Population projections for the late 1980s and 1990s appear quite different today from what they did in 1972; post-Vietnam adjustments in college attendance patterns are now more fully revealed, and the representation of women in graduate education has increased significantly. I feel more confident today about the outlook for the academic labor market in the 1980s than I did two years ago.

Over the last several years I have had capable assistance from three research assistants. During my year at the Commission, Ralph Purves worked on the original enrollment projections, drawn on in the final Carnegie Commission report. Wayne Ruhter, now assistant professor of economics at the University of Texas (Dallas), assisted me for a year and was especially helpful with the materials in Chapter 9. We drew on these findings in a jointly authored monograph, *The Disappearance of*

Sex Discrimination in First Job Placement of Ph.D.'s (1975). During the past year John M. McDowell aided in the computations and analyses in Chapter 8. Some of this material also appears in an essay we jointly authored in *Assuring Academic Progress Without Growth* (Cartter and McDowell, 1975). It was a pleasant experience to have these mentor/apprentice relationships with Ruhter and McDowell evolve into professional collaboration, and I am indebted to both.

My wife and children are pleasantly surprised that the book is completed; for too long they have seen the manuscript take first priority on evenings and week-ends. Their joy may be short-lived, however, for several colleagues and I have now embarked upon a two-year intensive study of the future labor market for Ph.D.'s in the humanities.

Although a number of professional colleagues have read parts of the manuscript, the author must accept responsibility for any sins of commission or omission. In a study that purports to project enrollment and faculty hiring levels 15 years ahead, the perils are great, and one's own intuition should be credited or blamed for the results. Nonetheless, I have benefited significantly from suggestions and criticisms from numerous colleagues and students, and I appreciate their contributions.

In a subject area that has received so little attention, and where the data and methodology are still in a rather primitive stage, a work such as this must be considered speculative. I have no doubt but that several years hence the projections will need substantial revision. Although I hope to keep abreast of changing demographic and labor market conditions, it is to be hoped that many other researchers will be attracted to these areas. If the author's prognosis is even approximately correct, the 1980s will require the creative talents of many educators, administrators, and public policy-makers to ease the adjustment problems.

Allan M. Cartter

Ph.D.'s and the Academic Labor Market

1. Projecting Academic Demand

Over the last 15 years, the labor market for persons trained at the Ph.D. level has come under increasing scrutiny. This is partly because in the post-Sputnik world the nation became more conscious of the need to have an adequate supply of highly trained scientists and engineers and partly because, since World War II, the Ph.D. has come to be considered the necessary credential for most teachers in four-year colleges and universities. Perhaps of equal importance, labor market imbalances have arisen during the decade, thus focusing public attention on the shortage or surplus of Ph.D.'s.

Between 1957 and 1967, higher education enrollments grew at the average rate of 7¾ percent annually, while research funding of universities grew nearly 10 percent annually in real (constant dollar) terms. Demand for personnel trained at the doctoral level rose rapidly, seemingly far outstripping the number of new Ph.D.'s being awarded by the nation's major universities. Since 1967 enrollment growth has been more moderate, at approximately 4 percent annually, and university research funds have remained almost constant in real dollars. In addition, after a lag in supply adjustment, the number of doctorates awarded increased by 70 percent between 1967 and 1973. Thus, as the popular press has reported it, the academic labor market shifted from "boom" to "bust" conditions within several years.

In fact, neither the shortage nor the surplus of Ph.D.'s was as marked as press reports made them out to be, and today most observers have come to accept the view that the market for highly educated persons works reasonably well in adjusting the supply to changing demand conditions.

Several points have clearly emerged from the experience of the last 15 years and its analysis. First, as has always been

1

obvious but sometimes forgotten in public-policy debates, the educational equivalent of the economists' "period of production" is approximately six years. That is, on the average it takes six years from entrance to graduate school to completion of a Ph.D.[1] Elapsed time from baccalaureate degree to doctorate averages 8.2 years, and if one considers that a student's critical decision whether or not to pursue an advanced degree is ordinarily made while he or she is still an undergraduate, one could say that a six- to ten-year lag time in supply adjustments must be expected under normal conditions.

Second, the academic demand for college teachers has many of the same characteristics that one finds in the demand for investment goods in the economy as a whole. It is largely a "derived demand," depending on the rate of change in the total number of students attending college. Thus, if the ratio of students to faculty remains constant at, say, 15 to 1 and total enrollment moves from 5,000,000 to 5,150,000, one can expect that about 10,000 new teachers will be required to handle the additional students. However, if instead of a 3 percent increase in enrollment there is a 6 percent increment, the total number of new teachers required to handle new enrollments would rise by 100 percent. Therefore, like the case of investment goods, small changes in the demand for final products (the education of students) produces an exaggerated change in the demand for investments inputs (college teachers). Fairly significant swings in the demand for new academic personnel must be expected in the academic labor market. These swings may be moderated in the short run by changes in retirement practices (for example, the common resort to overage appointments in the 1960s, the attention being given today to early retirement), changes in hiring standards (for example, the more frequent hiring of teachers at the M.A. or uncompleted-dissertation stage in the mid-1960s), and variations in student-faculty ratios (such as changes in faculty teaching loads and class size), or by greater or lesser reliance upon adjunct and junior instructors. However, in the longer run there is a reasonably high degree of stability in these factors.

Third, it is now commonly accepted that we need to improve

---

[1] About 5.5 years in the sciences, 5.6 years in the social sciences, and 6.3 years in nonscience fields (National Research Council, 1974).

our reporting of current labor market data, the information and search mechanisms for bringing jobs and people together, and our ability to predict future needs. The professional societies, as well as the U.S. Employment Service, have been active in recent years in trying to make the market function more perfectly, and improved forecasts and forecasting methods have been sought in an attempt to reduce time-lags evident in the system.

This book is largely devoted to this last task. It attempts to project future faculty needs, based on a careful analysis of recent trends, and to explore the likely supply responses of the academic labor market to changing demand conditions. If the market outlook for the last quarter of this century indicated relatively stable conditions, this might be only an intellectual exercise. But the view that emerges in this study suggests that radical changes in conditions lie ahead that will tax the ingenuity of faculties, academic administrators, and public officials. While the 1970s appear to be reasonably stable, the 1980–1995 period, due to demographic conditions, promises to be unlike anything we have faced before. Such a period—popularly described as a "steady state" because no growth (in fact, some contraction) is anticipated in the 18- to 21-year-old population—may be "steady" in terms of number of institutions and total academic employment, but, because of the similarity of the graduate schools to the capital goods sector, it promises to be anything but steady for the new doctorate holders entering the academic labor market.

As the analysis suggests, if college attendance patterns follow past trends and the instructional process remains pretty much as we know it today, 1980 to 1995 will be a lean period as far as job opportunities in academia are concerned. But this kind of stress upon the higher education system may be just the kind that will induce desirable change. A seeming misfortune on the one hand often opens up new opportunities on the other. Entirely new markets may be discovered as doctorates increasingly seek employment in government, industry, and commerce, and as educators and government officials discover that with only little extra effort the goal of a lifelong-learning society can be realized. A projected surplus of both facilities and instructional personnel in the 1980s may be just the trigger to finally bring about the long-predicted (but long-delayed) revolution in recurrent education. (See, for example, Carnegie Commission on Higher Education, 1973c; and Cartter, 1973.)

In this respect it may be that this book will serve as an early warning mechanism. The author's earlier articles on teacher supply and demand, written in the mid-1960s, projected that academic employment would decline modestly in the early 1970s just as Ph.D. output had caught up with demand levels of the 1960s. It was predicted, however, that the real problem would emerge about 1980, as the size of the traditional college-age group began to contract. If anything, the outlook for the 1980s and early 1990s looks somewhat worse from today's vantage point, for the last several years have seen a decline in high school graduation, college attendance, and graduate school entry rates. While these may be temporary adjustments in the wake of the Vietnam War, they have dampened enrollment estimates for the next decade or two. The projections in Chapters 3 through 6 are considerably more optimistic than those of the U.S Office of Education today,[2] but considerably less rosy than even this author's projections of three or four years ago.

Over the last several years, there has been an emerging debate over the adequacy of projections based on a fixed-coefficients model of manpower flows. The alternative is to construct a more complex recursive model that allows for market responses. The choice between them depends partly on one's time frame and partly on whether one wishes to forecast actual behavior or to project current trends to highlight critical points where policy changes may be required. Most Ph.D. labor market projections up to 1970 (including this author's) were of the fixed-coefficients type. In an earlier essay I noted that projections attempting to influence policy judgments are frequently self-denying if they are taken seriously.

Thus one should draw a careful distinction between projections and predictions; the former may illustrate the consequences of current trends and thus serve to alter the course of events. In a meaningful sense, successful projections may be those that turn out to be poor predictions of actual events. My projections of 1964 and 1965 that the academic labor market would reverse itself in 1969 and 1970 and

[2]See U.S. Office of Education (1974). Only an 8 percent increase in total degree-credit enrollment is predicted between 1972 and 1982, and only a 9 percent increase in FTE faculty.

become a surplus labor market could be called unsuccessful in the sense that few persons took them seriously, thus permitting them to become accurate predictions. Today, with wide attention focused on the apparent oversupply of Ph.D.'s in many fields, it is likely that projections indicating even more marked imbalances in the late 1970s and early 1980s will be at least partially countered by adjustments in enrollment patterns over the next few years (Cartter, 1974, pp. 282–283).

Richard Freeman's book, *The Market for College-Trained Manpower* (1971), forcefully argued that market responses work effectively even in the case of doctoral supply and demonstrated that the characteristics of "cobweb" market behavior were evident in the Ph.D. labor market. The cobweb model (so named because the diagrammatic representation of the adjustment path resembles a cobweb) illustrates how time-lags in supply adjustments produce cyclical behavior around an equilibrium.

The position taken in this volume is that fixed and variable coefficients are each appropriate at various levels of education. At the high school and college undergraduate level, the non-economic factors seem to prevail. While choice of major in college is reasonably responsive to changes in career opportunities (for example, the reaction of engineering enrollments over the last 10 years), college entrance and persistence appear to be little affected by prospective opportunities for college-educated personnel. (However, full-time college attendance is moderately responsive to current job market conditions, largely as a reflection of variations in parental ability to pay.) Thus, in Chapters 3 and 4, fixed (although not necessarily constant) coefficient techniques are used to project likely ranges of high school graduation and undergraduate enrollment.

Postbaccalaureate education, on the other hand, appears to be much more market responsive. Therefore, although Chapters 5 and 6 make first approximation projections of graduate enrollments and advanced degrees utilizing predetermined coefficients, Chapters 7 and 8 relax these assumptions and allow for feedback effects in response to market conditions. Unlike the situation at the undergraduate level, where students commonly decide on postsecondary education and only secondarily (and frequently much later) select a major area of study, graduate or advanced professional students usually continue their education beyond the B.A. only if they have a professional interest in a specific field. At the margin there is a degree of substitutability between, say, law and social science, medicine and life science, business and public administration, and the like, but the elasticity of substitution is not nearly so great as in the upper-division collegiate years.

A recursive, market-responsive, model is a closer approximation to the real world at advanced levels of education than is a fixed-coefficients model. If it faithfully reflects behavior in the real world it obviously is a better predictive, or forecasting, technique than a model that merely highlights emerging imbalances by projecting trends. It also is a more useful learning device in understanding the workings of specialized labor markets, and over a long period of time one can begin to correct errors of perception or response and bring the model closer to reality. By contrast, about all one learns in the long run from fixed-coefficients models is that some projectors have been more accurate (or luckier) than others.[3]

This volume, therefore, takes a middle view—that there is a place for both approaches and that different levels of education and career preparation call for different methods of estimation. A market model is no more appropriate for predicting enrollment in second grade or in the Army War College than would a fixed-coefficients model be for predicting enrollment in proprietary schools of cosmetology.

The debates over appropriate forecasting techniques sometimes obscure a deeper and more philosophical issue: How should the universe of higher education adapt to changing demand conditions for highly educated personnel? At the risk of gross oversimplification, one might generalize that the persons who tend toward mechanical projections of current trends are often those who would prefer to see more centralized planning for education. They tend to look toward federal agency or state superboard leadership and would encourage improved data collection to facilitate better manpower budgeting. At the other extreme, some who favor market models do so from a position of advocacy, believing that the market is not only capable of making adequate self-adjustments but that freedoms of individual and institutional choice are more important than

---

[3]An excellent essay on forecasting techniques has recently been published by The National Board on Graduate Education. See Freeman and Breneman (1974).

personal or institutional dislocations resulting from erratic market behavior. Having created two straw men, it is easy to take a middle stand between these positions. It takes only cursory review of the past two decades to recognize that had we believed and acted on our projections in a centralized-planning manner we would have made things worse more often than not. Our national record of response timing has not been encouraging, and the lag between changing conditions and legislative and administrative response has often exacerbated, rather than moderated, fluctuations.

On the other hand, those who would leave all adjustments to market responses frequently concern themselves only with input and output magnitudes, ignoring the fragility of the institutions that perform the transformation function and discounting the human costs involved when an oversupply of highly specialized talent is insufficiently utilized.

Events of the last several years have provided a modest foretaste of the adjustment problems that graduate education and doctoral labor markets may experience in the period 1980–1995. As Chapters 5 and 6 indicate, the demand for academic personnel in the 1980s is likely to be only a small fraction of the level we have been accustomed to in the last 15 years. While growth in nonacademic demand will probably offset the academic decline for fields like engineering and natural and social sciences, those disciplines that rely primarily on placements in college teaching are likely to experience the most severe adjustment problems. Thus a major reason for attempting to improve manpower projections and forecasting techniques is to minimize time-lags by providing the best possible information as to likely market conditions five to ten years ahead.

Beyond five to ten years, the uncertainties become greater, and the likelihood that the form and organizational structure of higher education will remain unchanged diminishes. Educational goals and aspirations are not fixed, and they respond over time to the changing constraints of what is possible. "Universal access" has become a commonly accepted objective at least in part because this is the first decade in which it has appeared to be an attainable goal. Given the demographic pattern and the likely supply of highly trained personnel that the next decade or two appear to present, other goals— unrealizable in the past—now move into the realm of the possible. For the first time since World War II, shortages of adequately trained teachers are no longer the critical constraint. If the projections of Chapters 3 through 6 are even approximately correct, then the educational process could be significantly enriched. By 1990 average student-faculty ratios could be reduced by at least one-third; postsecondary educational opportunities could be extended to all adults who have missed this experience; lifelong recurrent education could become a reality.

Whether or not we shall take this bold step toward a real "learning society"[4] depends upon how society orders its priorities, not upon whether there is manpower available to undertake the task. On the one hand, the very fact that youth will represent a declining fraction of the population over the last quarter of the century means that the financial burden on society of traditional education will be somewhat lightened and that enrichment of the educational process may rightfully claim greater attention. On the other hand, the recognition of other pressing social needs and the emergence of higher societal aspirations in areas of health, housing, mass transportation, environmental protection, energy, and so on may suggest that higher education will not be able to maintain its share of support from public funds.

The economist is perhaps more aware than most of the distinction between needs, in the abstract, and needs as expressed by the willingness of individuals, institutions, or public bodies to pay. Several years ago, the author addressed a meeting of the American Psychological Association on the possibilities of having too many Ph.D.'s in relation to job opportunities in the coming decade. One discussant heatedly argued that the shortage of clinical psychologists would continue unabated because at least 5 percent of society needed attention and only 1½ percent were receiving treatment. Need, in this case, however, was not being expressed by lines in waiting rooms or patients being turned away, but by a value concept of what a healthy society might desire if money were no object. Similarly, in the case of higher education, it is one thing to view the opportuni-

---

[4]The options are discussed in greater detail in the Carnegie Commission report *Toward a Learning Society* (1973c).

ties for enrichment that a plentiful supply of highly qualified college teachers make possible and quite another to assure that sufficient resources are forthcoming to take advantage of these opportunities. In the last several years there have been more cases of faculty terminations and discontinuance of programs than moves to smaller class size and diminished student-faculty ratios.

For educational enrichment to occur, either in the improvement of traditional forms of education or through the extension of educational opportunities to new audiences, there will have to be a rising societal demand and adequate institutional response. Several encouraging developments have appeared within the last several years. Colleges and universities have begun to take much greater interest in the part-time student, in the adult out-of-phase student, in nontraditional forms of learning and instruction, in variously packaged programs for advanced recurrent education, and the like. In most cases, institutions have been rewarded with the discovery of new audiences who have previously been outside the mainstream of higher education. The growth of nondegree collegiate enrollment, doubling over the last six years, and of external degree programs suggests that this is merely the beginning of a new area of expansion. To an extent, supply creates its own demand; the development of programs and institutions especially designed to reach out to a broader cross section of the community tends to encourage and awaken new social demands for further education.

The enrollment and faculty projections in this book take these possible developments only partly into account. Insofar as such trends are already evident, they are reflected. To the extent that lifelong learning and recurrent education may represent a quantum jump in the development of higher education in the future, they are only matters for speculation in this and the concluding chapter.

The evidence presented here, however, is perhaps the best testament that such developments should be given thoughtful consideration, for the 1980–1995 period is one in which considerable talents and educational resources will be underutilized if postsecondary education merely maintains its traditional outlook and service function.

In the format of this book we move from the past to the present and to the future. Chapter 2 reviews the manpower outlook for persons trained at the doctoral level in the 1950s and 1960s and tries to determine why the record for projecting future academic labor market conditions has been so poor. Chapters 3 through 5 then carefully analyze recent trends and project enrollments based on fixed coefficients. Chapters 6 and 7 show what this outlook is likely to mean to the market for new college teachers and add the refinement of market response to supply and demand adjustments in the academic labor market. Chapter 8 analyzes faculty flows and attempts to see what various market or policy-determined responses may mean for the age distribution of college faculties. Chapter 9 reviews data on the first job placement of new Ph.D.'s since 1967 and provides insights on demand behavior under rapidly changing market conditions. Of particular interest is the comparative analysis for men and women in the several years before and following the new emphasis on affirmative action. Finally, Chapter 10 reviews the findings and explores some of the policy options that face higher education during the last quarter of the century.

2. A Retrospective View

In the wake of World War II, the returning GIs flooded the college campuses, and every institution was pressed to the limit to accommodate student demand. The amassed numbers partly represented the deferred demand of many who would have attended college in any event, but it also represented other thousands who found the door opened to them by the liberal education benefits of the first "GI Bill." As late as 1950, there were still 1 million veterans in college out of a total enrollment of 2.7 million. In those halcyon days every possible college teacher was pressed into service, and no one was unduly concerned with degree credentials.[1]

In the mid–1950s, however, even the Korean War veterans were declining in number, and the college-age population was shrinking, reflecting the low birthrates in the depression years of the 1930s. A rising college population could be predicted a decade ahead, due to the high number of post-World War II births, but the 1950s were uneasy years for higher education. Some colleges discussed a moratorium on promotion to tenure, fearing declining enrollments. A number of poorly endowed private universities suffered financial reverses and sought absorption into developing public systems (for example, Buffalo, Louisville, Omaha, Kansas City). Academic freedom had suffered from continuing attacks from the political right—Kenneth Galbraith described the period as "days of saliva tests for loyalty." The remuneration of college teachers had declined significantly from the 1920s and 1930s in real terms, and aca-

---

[1]The author, after 3½ years of military service in Europe and because of a shortage of qualified teachers, was pressed into duty as an instructor in economics in the last semester of his senior year and continued for two additional years before entering graduate school.

demic careers attracted only a small percentage of college graduates.

Perhaps the pervasive pessimism of college educators in the mid-1950s partly explains their willingness to believe that the quality of higher education was in danger of serious deterioration, for one of the most widely repeated myths was that the quality of college teaching staffs (as measured by degree credentials) was steadily deteriorating.

Looking back, it is clear that in fact teacher quality has improved steadily since World War II, with the possible brief exception of 1964–1967. It was widely believed at the time, however, that the proportion of full-time college teachers with doctorates declined throughout the 1950s and early 1960s and that the situation would progressively worsen for several decades ahead. Facing a very different set of academic labor market conditions today, it may be worth inquiring how the academic community was so mistaken in its outlook 10 or 15 years ago. The backward look is more than a purely academic question, for one may learn something from that experience that is relevant to today's problems. Some contemporary observers believe that the pendulum has swung so far in the other direction that we may seriously underestimate the needs of the future by looking only at immediate conditions and short-run trends.

Reviewing the literature of the period, and with some power to recollect how it seemed when one was living through those years and shared the popular outlook, it seems appropriate to distinguish between at least three different points of view. First, there were those researchers and policy influencers who reasonably foresaw that future needs would not be met by a mere continuation of current practice or trends and who wished to emphasize that change would be required. Second, there were those researchers who convinced themselves through incorrect analysis of data that things were deteriorating and who thus popularized the myth. And third, there were those who believed the researchers, frequently not distinguishing between the first and second categories, and believed both that things were currently bad and would get progressively worse. As one who began with the third outlook, then gradually realized that we were suffering from insufficient (or misleading) information and finally moved to the first position, it is possible to have some sympathies for those in each of these categories. However, those in the second category, the author among them if he has drawn incorrect inferences from limited data, are perhaps more to blame for policy inadequate to cope with emerging problems.

The first position identified above—those who hoped to influence policy by pointing up the incongruity between current trends and projected needs—is perhaps best illustrated by Dael Wolfle and the work of the first Commission on Human Resources and Advanced Training. In *America's Resources of Specialized Talent,* Wolfle (1954, pp. 43, 136) noted:

If the trend relating the number of doctors' to the number of bachelors' degrees continues into the future, and if bachelors' degrees follow the projections given [above], about 6,600 doctors' degrees can be expected in 1960 and 12,000 in 1970. [Actual figures were 9,829 and 29,866.] . . . It will be impossible to meet all the demands stated above by hiring new college graduates. Shortages there are, and serious ones too. . . . When it is possible to foresee shortages stretching ahead for some years into the future, efforts to increase the supply are completely justified. In the meantime, the situation provides a sobering reaffirmation of the importance of securing the best possible utilization of those who have the ability and education for work in the specialized fields.

More or less in the same vein—and the bible for new graduate deans in the late 1950s and early 1960s—was the essay by the Committee of 15, *Graduate School, Today and Tomorrow* (Strothmann, 1955). This report, financed by the Ford Foundation, concentrated on the projected needs for 1970. In retrospect, its estimates of total faculty needs for 1970 were reasonably accurate, but its assumption that supply responses would be minimal proved incorrect. The Committee of 15 argued that:

. . . between now and 1970 only about 135,000 doctorates will be awarded. . . . Even if all these new Ph.D.'s were to become teachers, we would, by 1970, need approximately 350,000 more college teachers than we shall probably train in our doctoral programs. . . . To expect that by 1970 the proportion of college teachers holding the Ph.D. degree will have declined from the present 40 percent to 20 percent is not statistical hysteria but grassroots arithmetic (ibid., p. 7).

The evocative simplicity of the final sentence, supported by the compelling logic of the remainder of the report, affected the thinking of graduate deans for a decade (this author included).

The report of the Committee of 15, however, did not emerge from thin air—it was not baseless fantasy. It apparently reflected the findings of a major study undertaken by the Research Division of the National Education Association (NEA) at the request of its Association for Higher Education.[2] The Committee of 15 report was a publication of The Fund for the Advancement of Education, which also supported the NEA effort. The first NEA report, *Teacher Supply and Demand in Colleges and Universities* (1955), was based on a major survey of college faculty in 1953–54, followed up by surveys of new teachers in 1953–54 and 1954–55. The 1955 report was the first of a biennial series that continued until 1965 and had a marked effect on higher education policy for 15 years. With the single exception of Berelson's *Graduate Education in the United States* (1960), no major voice disputed the NEA findings for a decade. (And, in Berelson's case, the problem of numbers and projected doctoral needs in the future was almost a tangential issue discussed rather summarily in the corpus of a much broader study of the nature of graduate education.)

To summarize the NEA conclusions as to the degree credentials of college teachers, the 1953–54 survey had found that 40.5 percent of all full-time teachers in senior colleges and universities possessed the doctorate. By contrast, of *new* teachers hired in 1953–54 and 1954–55 only 31.4 and 28.4 percent, respectively, possessed the doctorate. These findings were based on a survey of 656 four-year institutions in the former year and 827 in the latter year—a number representing three-fourths or more of all senior institutions. In view of the considerable data amassed by the NEA, it seemed logical to conclude that: "this evidence . . . strongly suggests that the American institutions of higher education are fighting a losing battle. The proof seems conclusive that recently employed full-time teachers are steadily reducing the general level of preparation of the entire corps" (National Education Association, 1957, p. 20).

Successive NEA studies bore out the earlier conclusions; the percentage of new teachers with the doctorate declined to 23.5 percent in 1956–57 and then remained between 25 and 28 percent for the next eight years. "The quality of the newly

[2]The forerunner of today's independent American Association for Higher Education.

employed group is deteriorating year by year," proclaimed the 1957 report. "Complacence—almost outright indifference—is much in evidence," stated the 1963 report; educational institutions are "unable to compete in the open market for new talent being produced; . . . universities and colleges find themselves more embarrassed day by day," it concluded (National Education Association, 1963, p. 9).

The first three columns of Table 2-1 reproduce the 12-year NEA series, meticulously collected biennially from nearly 900 colleges and universities. The conclusion seemed well documented that the marginal percentage of new teachers with the doctorate was far below the average of 1953–54 and thus was evidence of a steady deterioration in the quality of college faculties. One may fault the NEA Research Office for turning the text of the biennial reports into a near boiler-plate report of

TABLE 2-1 *Additions to college teaching staff and to doctorates in teaching, 1953–1965*

Year	Total new teachers annually (1)	New teachers with doctorate (2)	Ratio of new teachers with doctorate to new teachers (3)	Continuing teachers receiving doctorate (4)	Ratio of new doctorates in teaching to new teachers (5)
(Total staff in 1953–54)	(58,719)	(23,768)	(.405)		(.405)
1953–54	4,232	1,329	.314	n.a.*	n.a.
1954–55	4,694	1,333	.284	822	.460
1955–56	6,337	1,695	.267	856	.403
1956–57	8,308	1,953	.235	1,528	.419
1957–58	9,293	2,354	.253	1,529	.418
1958–59	9,100	2,254	.238	1,825	.448
1959–60	10,221	2,650	.259	1,894	.447
1960–61	11,184	2,886	.258	1,987	.436
1961–62	10,439	2,851	.273	2,115	.476
1962–63	12,186	3,092	.254	2,334	.445
1963–64	13,562	3,833	.283	2,732	.484
1964–65	16,059	4,361	.272	3,084†	.463†

*Not available.

†Estimated.

SOURCES: Columns (1) through (3) are from National Education Association (1965, table 2); column (4) is computed from National Education Association (1965, Table Y) and from comparable tables in earlier reports in the NEA series. Column (5) = [columns (2) + (4)] ÷ column (1).

previous editions—but the data collection effort between 1953 and 1965 far surpasses anything that the federal government or other agencies have ever dared to undertake.[3]

In 1963 and 1964 this author became interested in the question of the adequacy of the supply of college teachers, and the deeper he probed, the more puzzled he became with the NEA findings and the commonly accepted view of quality erosion. No college or university he was familiar with was experiencing a decline in the quality of its faculty, and yet everyone seemed to accept decline as proven fact. On several occasions in early 1964, it was proposed that the Commission on Plans and Objectives for Higher Education of the American Council on Education seriously study the subject—and each time the request was voted down as being "low priority." The 20 distinguished college and university presidents who made up the commission membership were agreed that everyone knew there was a crisis that would continue for another 20 years . . . "let's study something we can do something about."

In the summer of 1964, during a slack period in ACE affairs, a secretary was assigned to spot-check a random sample of institutions that had reported faculty degree distributions in successive editions of *American Universities and Colleges* (published every four years by ACE). In every case the percentage of faculty with the doctorate rose between 1950–51 and 1962–63. Soon thereafter, despite commission disinterest, a review of all four-year institutions reporting data in each of the editions of *American Universities and Colleges* was undertaken. Table 2-2 reproduces the findings of this endeavor for 781 four-year institutions (Cartter, 1965, p. 270). The reported percentages are for all faculty (including part-time) and are therefore lower than those reported by NEA for full-time faculty. In 1954–55, the ACE data indicated 31.6 percent of college professors and 40.4 percent of university professors held the doctorate, compared with 40.5 percent for all full-time faculty in the 1953–54 NEA survey.

These data, somewhat incomplete and sometimes reported

[3]The U.S Office of Education undertook one major effort in 1962–1963, but the results were completely counter to the NEA findings and no major faculty survey has been conducted since 1963. See discussion of the COLFACS study on p. 18.

TABLE 2-2 *Percentage of total faculty with the doctorate, private and public colleges and universities, 1950–51 to 1962–63*

Category of institution	1950–51	1954–55	1958–59	1962–63
Four-year colleges				
Private	29.7	32.5	33.7	35.4
Public	23.2	30.1	32.0	33.5
Total, colleges	27.3	31.6	33.0	34.5
Universities				
Private	37.3	40.0	40.7	43.8
Public	36.0	40.7	41.7	44.9
Total, universities	36.6	40.4	41.3	44.5

SOURCE: (Cartter, 1965*b*, table 2, p. 270).

improperly by institutions, suggested that the percentage of professors with the doctorate had increased in each four-year interval for each type of senior institution. These conclusions were so contrary to the NEA surveys that they seemed to call for a much closer scrutiny of the NEA findings.

The NEA surveys had been two-pronged: institutions were surveyed to determine the number and characteristics of new hires [as in columns (1) and (2) of Table 2-1]; graduate schools were queried as to where new doctorates found employment. The two data sets were reported separately, but had never been put together. A careful review of the latter series indicated that while about 30 percent of new doctorate recipients entered college teaching (and thus were also reported as "new hires" by the employing institutions) a number over two-thirds as large received their doctorate after being appointed and "continued in college teaching." And those who took teaching positions before completing the degree never showed up in the NEA doctoral-hire series. Upon discovering this discrepancy, the author calculated columns (4) and (5) of Table 2-1 and quickly concluded that the NEA data were in fact consistent with the view that faculty quality was rising, not deteriorating. As column (5) of Table 2-1 indicates, the ratio of new doctorates in teaching to newly hired teachers (a more meaningful comparison than just observing how many had completed their doctorate *prior to* assuming teaching duties) hovered between 0.40 and 0.48 in the late 1950s and early 1960s, suggesting that the average doctorate-faculty ratio had in fact been rising.

Just at this moment, some preliminary tables from the U.S. Office of Education College Faculty Survey (COLFACS) were shared with the author, and all the pieces fit together. The COLFACS survey, intended to replicate the NEA survey of all faculty in 1953–54, indicated that in 1962–63 50.6 percent of senior college full-time faculty possessed the doctorate. The recast NEA series were consistent with this finding, particularly when one recognized that a higher percentage of nondoctorate faculty members drifted out of education employment over the years.[4] Thus it suddenly appeared that, indeed, higher education had been undergoing *enrichment* of its faculty for a dozen or more years while most educational observers were convinced that the reverse was true. This finding, partially presented in "A New Look at the Supply and Demand for College Teachers" (Cartter) in early 1965, was followed by a somewhat more sophisticated statistical presentation by the author before the American Statistical Association (Cartter, 1966c) and a popularized version at the 1965 ACE annual meeting (Cartter, 1966b). In retrospect it would be fair to say that the author became a missionary for what then seemed like a radical point of view.

In a paper for the American Association of Higher Education in 1971 I have recounted the tribulations of the next several years. Surprise and initial disbelief were quite understandable reactions; even criticism of theory or interpretation were expected responses. Unexpected were accusations of damaging higher education or the refusal to look at the facts. At issue was the relevance of this reinterpretation to the current and future status of the academic labor market, for if the recent past was much better than previously thought, the conclusion that the graduate education expansionist policies of the 1960s would

---

[4]The COLFACS survey indicated that in the one year surveyed, 3.1 percent of faculty members with doctorates left higher education, while 7.1 percent of faculty without doctorates departed from the teaching sector. In addition, the difference in doctorates by rank suggested a differential attrition rate. In 1962–63, only 42 percent of assistant professors held doctorates, but 61 percent of associates and 78 percent of full professors had that highest degree (Cartter, 1965b, p. 275).

lead to a likely surplus of Ph.D.'s in many fields by 1970 was a logical corollary.

Supporting the viewpoint that the academic labor market would shortly shift from a seller's to a buyer's market was the emerging demographic pattern of the college-age population. The market for college teachers has many of the characteristics of the capital goods industry in the broader economy. A relatively stable component of the demand for capital goods is replacement need; in the human capital market this is the need to replace faculty who die or retire. A much more erratic demand component is the need to expand or contract productive capacity when consumer demand rises or falls. If, for example, replacement needs in a stationary state are 5 percent annually, and then consumer demand begins to grow at a 5 percent rate, the demand for investment goods doubles. If consumer demand continues to grow, but drops to only a 2 percent growth rate, the demand for investment goods can be expected to absolutely decline by 30 percent (that is, 5 percent replacement plus only 2 percent for expansion instead of 5 percent). Thus the demand for capital goods tends to respond in exaggerated fashion to modest changes in the demand for consumer goods.

In the academic analogy, the demand for college teachers is investment demand (albeit in human capital) and college enrollments represent consumer demand. Slight changes in the latter invoke substantial changes in the hiring of college teachers.

Even in the early 1960s it was clear that the size of the traditional college-age population would expand much more slowly in the 1970s than in the 1960s. The early concerns of the author about the future demand for college teachers were based primarily on the slower growth rate of the 18- to 21-year-old population beginning in 1969—not on an expectation that there would be an absolute decline in the pool of college eligibles in the 1980s. By 1965, however, the Bureau of Census projection (Series B) thought most likely to occur indicated a decline in the 18- to 21-year-old population of about 2 million (12 percent) between 1980 and 1987, preceding another sharp increase of almost 50 percent during the last 15 years of the century. The anticipated rise was predicated on the larger number of young women who would reach child-bearing age in the 1970s. Series

B estimates, made in 1965, for the first time raised the possibility of a brief no-growth period in college enrollments, making the outlook for faculty hiring in the 1980s rather gloomier. By 1968, with the continuing sharp decline in birthrates, it had become clear that the post-1980 drop in the college-eligible population would be a longer and deeper trough than previously believed. The birthrate experience of the last five years has now brought us to the sober conclusion that the end-of-the-century 18- to 21-year-old population is likely to be 5 to 10 percent smaller than it is today. Thus, rapid growth in the college-age cohort, which has been the dominant influence on educational growth over the past two decades, is soon coming to an end to be replaced by conditions closer to that of a stationary state.

Right up until 1969, when the first signs of a weakening job market for college teachers began to emerge in a number of disciplines, it was difficult to get either educators or federal government officials to take seriously the likelihood of an over-supply of Ph.D.'s in the foreseeable future. Federal policy, until about 1968, under the National Defense Education Act and the Higher Education Facilities Program, stressed expansion and developing graduate programs. Testimony before congressional committees by successive commissioners of education emphasized the need for an ever-larger number of college teachers at the doctoral level. As late as the fall of 1968 the U.S. Office of Education office concerned with graduate education, in a memorandum to the graduate deans, was predicting a cumulative deficit of more than 120,000 doctorates by 1974. Biennial reports of the National Science Foundation (NSF) on the supply and utilization of doctoral scientists predicted shortages for the 1970s in their 1967 and 1969 reports; only in 1971 did the possibility of modest surpluses emerge (National Science Foundation, 1967; 1969; 1971). The 1970 edition of the U.S. Office of Education *Projections of Educational Statistics* (1971, Table 39, p. 74) predicted a demand for college faculty averaging 71,000 annually in the 1975–1980 period, slightly higher than in 1965–1970.

Judging from the actions of state legislatures and public universities in developing new graduate programs and expanding existing ones, they, too, shared the optimism of the federal establishment. Between 1968, when the demographic configuration for the 1980s and early 1990s became clear, and 1974, doctorates awarded grew by 10,600 (46 percent) and first-year enrollments in graduate programs expanded by 155,000 (34 percent); the number of universities awarding the doctorate grew by more than 40 between 1968 and 1974, and many additional doctoral programs were initiated that had not yet awarded a degree by 1974.

On the job market front, both physics and mathematics began to experience some difficulty in placing new Ph.D.'s in 1967 and 1968. Economics first became aware of a changing market in 1969, but that could be partly attributed to the exodus of economists from Washington with the change in administrations. In 1970, the popular press began to pay attention to emerging doctoral placement problems when the Modern Language Association meeting in the fall was nearly disrupted by the many hundreds of graduate students seeking jobs who could not even find a job interview to attend. At about this time, cut-backs in the aerospace industry began to affect engineers and scientists, and the slowdown in federal research and development expenditure began to be severely felt. Economic recession, beginning in some areas of the economy in 1971, and worsening by 1973, brought the full impact of supply and demand imbalances home to the scientific community.

Only in the last year or two, however, has it become commonly accepted that the imbalance problem is more than a temporary one—that it may last for the next 20 years. The discouraging demographic trends noted earlier now predict an 18- to 21-year-old population in the year 2000 about 10 percent smaller than in 1975. Economic seers, who once projected real growth in the gross national product at 3 to 4 percent annually, now more commonly project long-term growth rates at 1½ to 2 percent. The last refuge of optimists is that we are about to experience a revolution in adult continuing education.[5] Nondegree enrollments in higher education increased fourfold between 1967 and 1973 and are predicted by the U.S. Office of Education to grow by another 50 percent by 1983. However, even in that case they would account for only 14 percent of FTE enrollment (U.S. Office of Education, 1975, Tables 9–12). More importantly, less than 4 percent of teachers in nondegree

---

[5]See, for example, Weathersby (1974), in his paper presented at the NCHEMS national invitational seminar.

curricula are doctorate holders today (Cartter & Salter, 1975) —perhaps 1,400 out of some 35,000. Further complicating the reading of trends is the fact that today's nondegree enrollments are still swollen by veterans on the GI Bill.

It is difficult to be optimistic about a dramatic (as opposed to a gradual) increase in adult participation in higher education unless there is some radical change in public policy that would assume income maintenance during an adult's reentry into higher education. The author (1973) has made such a proposal, drawing on the creative ideas of a 1973 OECD Conference on Changing Patterns in Working Time,[6] but he is less than optimistic that the concept of lifetime educational "drawing accounts" will be enacted within the next 10 or 15 years. In the absence of a national policy providing an incentive for recurrent education, adult participation is likely to remain principally a casual leisure-oriented pastime for moderately high socioeconomic-status groups, rather than a savior for traditional degree enrollment programs in higher education.

Looking ahead, therefore, it seems wise counsel to assume that collegiate enrollments will decline moderately (at best) in the 1980–1994 period, perhaps significantly if potential students are quite sensitive to declining rates of return. If this is the case, the demand for new college teachers is likely to continue to decline over the next decade, and the capacity of today's graduate education enterprise is likely to be underutilized for some years ahead.

Looking backward, it seems evident that this emerging problem could (and should) have been recognized by public-policy makers a decade ago. True, the magnitude of the decline in birthrates after 1965 was not then clear, but the mere likelihood of deceleration should have given sufficient advance warning. By 1969 or 1970 it had become quite clear that the 1980s were going to be years of contraction for higher education—yet it has only been in the last year or two that the message has finally sunk in for thoughtful educators. Even today many faculty believe that the worst is past, and judging from graduate school entrance rates in humanities and social science disciplines, too few students are fully aware of the decline in potential academic job prospects.

[6]See particularly the provocative background paper by Rehn (1972).

Perhaps there will be a revolution in the financing of recurrent education; perhaps humanists will successfully uncover vast new job opportunities in alternative career lines; perhaps some quantum technological leap will occur that will dramatically increase federal and industrial research and development expenditure; perhaps public concern for higher education will reemerge so that we will enter upon a new era of educational enrichment. Perhaps—but perhaps not.

In this volume, the author has taken a more cautious approach, assuming only modestly improving trends in educational participation rates. His outlook, once considered radically pessimistic, now appears to be moderately optimistic in comparison with that of many of his scholarly colleagues.

The succeeding chapters attempt to carefully review the pattern of likely educational growth and to assess the implications for new doctorates hoping to enter the academic labor market in the last quarter of the century. It is also, implicitly, a plea for more serious thought and research on the issue of projected market conditions for that most precious resource—human talent and educational wealth. Despite the effort that has gone into this study, it is only a speculative first step toward a much better understanding of human capital markets. We can ill afford the mistaken judgments and optimism of the 1960s—nor is today's pessimism a compensating antidote. Perhaps some parts of this research effort will lay the foundation of much improved analyses and policy guidance for the future.

3. Demographic Factors Affecting College Enrollment

Over 97 percent of college a.1d university students are 18 years of age or older—thus one would think that projecting the pool of college eligibles at least 18 years ahead would be a common and uncontroversial practice. During the great growth period for higher education in the 1960s, however, this was rarely done, and some of the disequilibrium problems now facing, or soon to face, higher education can be attributed to shortsightedness.

Several reasons for the failure to look far enough into the future in higher education planning are apparent. First is the legitimate reason that projecting beyond cohorts already born may be risky if birthrates are changing. Demographers distrust attributing too much weight to current data on birthrates if they are counter to trends of the last five to ten years, for fear that the most recent year or two may represent merely a normal fluctuation around a more clearly established long-term trend. The upturn in births in 1942–43 and again in 1946–47 were initially viewed with caution as possible short-term deviations from prewar norms, and it was not until about 1952 that it became clear that the birthrate itself had climbed to a new plateau about one-third higher than in the 1930s. Similarly, the decline in the birthrate beginning about 1960, reflected in the absolute number of live births several years later, was not confidently viewed as a trend until the late 1960s. Even today, the precipitous decline in the fertility rate since 1970 is only just beginning to be accepted as a harbinger of a new pattern sharply changing the outlook for college enrollments in the 1990s.

Perhaps more importantly, however, educational planners usually place mid-range limits on their forward projections of not more than five to ten years. ("Long-range planning" in colleges and universities usually means 10 years.) While this may be understandable for institutional planners who are concerned primarily with faculty, facilities, and programs for a single institution, it is less defensible for those concerned with the development of statewide systems or for federal agencies viewing the national scene. The Office of Education, for example, for a decade or more, has issued each year a volume on *Projections of Educational Statistics* with a time horizon always of 10 years into the future.[1] While it is true that the farther into the future one projects enrollments or degrees, the greater the margin of error is likely to be, the age-eligible cohort can be predicted ahead nearly 20 years with a high degree of accuracy. Setting an artificial 10-year limit on the horizon meant that the decline in the 18- to 21-year-old population after 1980, which has been predictable since the early 1960s, was not reflected in Office of Education official projections until 1972.

Similarly, the biennial studies by the National Science Foundation on science and engineering doctorate supply and utilization have been cast in a 10-year time horizon, thus ignoring the likely sharp shift in demand conditions in the academic marketplace in the early 1980s until their 1972 edition.

While census data on births and projected age distribution of the population are published regularly, the fact that information about the size of the college population 15 to 25 years ahead was not readily available in education projections publications has contributed to a regrettable shortsightedness. In periods of relatively constant birthrates one can afford to be indifferent about an intermediate or long-range projection, for growth patterns are not likely to change dramatically; however, given the sharp increase and then decline in birthrates since 1946, failure to look far enough ahead has exacted a price. The public school system in the 1950s and early 1960s, and the colleges between 1964 and 1969, were faced with critical shortages of facilities and personnel without adequate advance planning. Now the situation is reversed. First grade classes in 1977 will be 12.6 percent smaller than in 1975, which in turn will be 14

---

[1]Actually, the volumes come out approximately one year after the close of an academic year and, in the case of enrollment data, refer to data in the fall of the preceding academic year; so, in effect, the projections stretch only eight years into the future.

percent below 1966. Adding 12 years gives one an inkling of the response higher education may have to make in the 1980s.

TRENDS IN BIRTH AND FERTILITY RATES Birthrates indicate the number of live births per 1,000 population; fertility rates express births per 1,000 women aged 15 to 44. Table 3-1 shows fertility rates since 1930. To set the beginning date for these series in perspective, the fertility rate, which was 89.2 in 1930, had been 117.9 in 1920 and 126.8 in 1910. (Prior to 1910 only rates for whites are available: for example, 130 in 1900, 194 in 1850, and 278 in 1800.) The rise from a depression low of 75.8 to 122.7 in 1957, and the drop to 72.6 in 1973, are the sharpest historical movements in this nation's history. The 1973 fertility rate was below the 1936 depression trough, and, for the first time, equalled the zero-population-growth rate.

Ideally, for projections more than a few years ahead, one would like to know the "completed fertility rate"—that is, the number of children born to a cohort of 1,000 women upon completion of childbearing. As in the case of the World War II fluctuations in birth and fertility rates, year-to-year variations can be caused by decisions to postpone having children even though the size of the completed family may be unchanged. Wartime is an obvious period when postponement is common—either because of temporary separation or because of a

TABLE 3-1
Fertility rates since 1930

Year	Fertility rates
1930	89.2
1931	84.6
1932	81.7
1933	76.3
1934	78.5
1935	77.2
1936	75.8
1937	77.1
1938	79.1
1939	77.6
1940	79.9
1941	83.4

TABLE 3-1 *(continued)*	

Year	Fertility rates
1942	91.5
1943	94.3
1944	88.8
1945	85.9
1946	101.9
1947	113.3
1948	107.3
1949	107.1
1950	106.2
1951	111.3
1952	113.5
1953	114.7
1954	117.6
1955	118.0
1956	120.8
1957	122.7
1958	120.1
1959	120.1
1960	118.0
1961	117.2
1962	112.1
1963	108.5
1964	105.0
1965	96.6
1966	91.3
1967	87.6
1968	85.7
1969	86.5
1970	87.6
1971	82.3
1972	73.4
1973	72.6
1974	68.5*

*Provisional.

SOURCES: For 1930–1973, U.S. Bureau of the Census (*Historical Statistics of the U.S., 1960; Current Population Reports,* ser. P-25, various years). For 1974, U.S. Department of Health, Education, and Welfare (*Monthly Vital Statistics Report,* 1975).

positive decision to wait until more normal lives could be led. Similarly, in the 1930s, depressed economic conditions contributed significantly both to postponement and to smaller completed families.

The recent decline in birth and fertility rates, particularly the steady decrease since 1961, cannot be explained away by unusual external events. Several minor recessions have occurred, and the Vietnam War contributed to some general uneasiness in the 1967–1972 period, but the birthrate continued to fall throughout 1973. Indeed, in the eight months between November 1971 and July 1972, the 17 percent decline in seasonally adjusted fertility rates was the sharpest drop we have ever experienced. A contributing factor to the decline over the last decade has been the widespread acceptance of oral and intra-uterine contraceptive devices that have sharply reduced the number of unplanned children. Although accurate national data are not available, the legalization of abortions in a number of states has also contributed significantly to the decline in the birthrate. Attitudes of young men and women clearly reflect a change in expectations both as to marriage and to bringing children into the world.

It would be easy to reach the same conclusion that many observers of the 1950s reached—to merely extrapolate present birthrate trends into the future. However, just as student attitudes in so many other areas of social and political concern have begun to swing back to norms of a decade or two ago, it seems probable that attitudes toward childbearing also will be modified over the next few years. At the least, it is likely that the rate of decline in birthrates will diminish; more probable is a leveling off or a slight reversal over the next decade.

The Bureau of the Census has had to continually change its projections series over the last 10 years to keep up with current trends. At the present time, the most likely projections series seem to be its Series E, developed as a "low" series in 1970 and already 6 percent too high in predicting 1973 births, or the Series F developed in late 1972, which approximates the actual experience of 1974 births.

Figure 3-1 illustrates the birthrate assumptions of Bureau of the Census Series E and F projections. Series E is based on an assumed 2.1 completed family births per woman, and Series F assumes a 1.8 completed fertility rate. The birthrate per 1,000

FIGURE 3-1 *U.S. Bureau of the Census Series E and F birthrate projections to 2000*

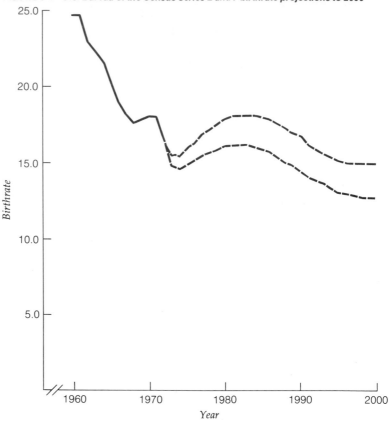

SOURCE: U.S. Bureau of the Census (1972).

women fluctuates even under the constant completed fertility rate due to variations in the size of the 15- to 44-year-old female cohort. By the year 2000 the birthrate decreases to 14.8 under Series E assumptions and to 12.7 under Series F.

Table 3-2 shows actual births from 1952 to 1973 and projects births under the two series to 1982. Columns 5 and 6 show the number of young persons 18 years old associated with births in the left-hand two columns. Beginning in 1973 the number attaining 18 years of age assumes a survival rate of .9675 and a continued immigration rate nationally of 400,000 per year (U.S. Bureau of the Census, 1972, Tables A-1 & A-5). Based on 1972 experience, this immigration rate would add 132,700 persons to the age cohort by age 18.

	Births				Age 18	
TABLE 3-2 *Actual and projected births, 1952–1982, and age-18 population, 1970–2000 (in thousands)*	*Series E*	*Series F*	*Year of birth*	*Year attained age 18*	*Series E*	*Series F*
	3,913		1952	1970	3,703	
	3,965		1953	1971	3,847	
	4,078		1954	1972	3,926	
	4,104		1955	1973	4,030	
	4,218		1956	1974	4,057	
	4,312		1957	1975	4,168	
	4,313		1958	1976	4,187	
	4,298		1959	1977	4,204	
	4,279		1960	1978	4,207	
	4,350		1961	1979	4,344	
	4,259		1962	1980	4,254	
	4,185		1963	1981	4,182	
	4,119		1964	1982	4,120	
	3,940		1965	1983	3,945	
	3,716		1966	1984	3,728	
	3,608		1967	1985	3,625	
	3,520		1968	1986	3,550	
	3,567		1969	1987	3,597	
	3,660		1970	1988	3,690	
	3,705		1971	1989	3,735	
	3,407		1972	1990	3,437	
	3,191		1973	1991	3,221	
	3,269	3,075	1974	1992	3,296	3,108
	3,401	3,168	1975	1993	3,423	3,198
	3,529	3,255	1976	1994	3,547	3,282
	3,654	3,339	1977	1995	3,668	3,353
	3,773	3,417	1978	1996	3,783	3,440
	3,885	3,490	1979	1997	3,892	3,510
	4,073	3,608	1981	1999	4,073	3,624
	4,142	3,649	1982	2000	4,140	3,663

SOURCE: See Table 3-1.

The largest number of annual births in the United States occurred in 1961, when the total reached 4,350,000. In 1973, births were 28.4 percent lower than in 1961. According to both Series E and F the absolute number of births will rise again during the next decade, climbing by 33 percent or 17 percent respectively.[2] Correspondingly, the age-18 population can be expected to peak in 1979 and then decline until 1991 or 1992, increasing modestly again to the end of the century.

THE POOL OF POTENTIAL COLLEGE STUDENTS

Traditionally, 18 has been the most common age for college entrance, and the 18-to-21 cohort has been thought of as "the college-age group." In fact, in 1972 only 51.3 percent of all college freshmen were aged 18 (although 72.7 percent were 17 to 19), and 67.9 percent of all undergraduate students were between 18 and 21 (72.1 percent were not over 21). Thus, 18 to 21 is an age range that includes more than two-thirds of undergraduate students, but by no means describes the age boundaries.

The age distribution of undergraduates between approximately 1964 and 1970, however, was somewhat distorted by the fact that a significant proportion of young men continued their education to postpone draft eligibility, and the distribution has been skewed in the opposite direction since 1970 by the entry (or reentry) of many veterans. In making any long-term projection it will be useful to try to eliminate this effect from the recent data on student age.

For 1972 the Veterans Administration reports 1,064,513 veterans enrolled in institutions of higher learning.[3] This was 11.4 percent of all students in higher education, and 20.5 percent of male enrollees. Of this number, an estimated 150,000 were enrolled in postbaccalaureate study; of the remaining, approximately one-third are assumed to have been in vocational and occupational training programs of a nondegree nature (primarily in two-year colleges).

[2]By the end of the century, the Series E birth projection is 3,906,000, while Series F is 3,166,000. Thus no increase can be expected in the college-age population in the first 20 years of the next century, and under Series F it would decline by approximately 12 percent after the turn of the century.

[3]See Carnegie Commission on Higher Education (1973*a*, Table A-15, p. 163) from a special compilation reported by the Veterans Administration to the Commission.

TABLE 3-3 *Age distribution of male college undergraduates and likely veterans status, fall 1972*

Age		First	Second	Third	Fourth	Total	Total distribution (percent)
Under 18	A	138	1	1		140	3.5
18		590	108	1		699	17.6
19	B	154	435	73	3	665	16.7
20		50	167	349	84	650	16.3
21		39	59	125	274	497	12.5
22	C	33	42	63	130	268	6.7
23		55	70	52	47	224	5.6
24		26	63	34	46	169	4.3
25–29	D	95	146	129	117	487	12.2
30–34	E	33	62	34	54	183	4.6
TOTAL		1,213	1,153	861	755	3,982	100.0

SOURCE:, U.S. Bureau of the Census (1973*b*, p. 22).

Data are not available indicating the age distribution of veterans in college, but it can be assumed that the average veteran was approximately two years older than his male nonveteran counterpart. Table 3-3 provides the basis for a rough approximation of the number of veterans by age and year of college.

Table 3-3 is divided into five lettered areas, and we can estimate the probability of veterans falling into each of these areas. Area A is likely to contain no veterans, for the indicated ages for each year preclude the likelihood of prior military service. Area B is likely to contain a small number of veterans who served less than two years in the military services. A high proportion of area C male students, who are two to five years older than the customary student, are likely to be veterans, as are a somewhat smaller proportion of older students in areas D and E.

In Table 3-4 the distribution of male students in each category is shown. Column (2) shows an assumed likelihood that students in each category had previously had military service, and column (3) produces an estimated number of veterans that is a reasonable fit with the estimate that about two-thirds of prebaccalaureate veterans were enrolled in degree-credit programs.

Returning to each of the cells in Table 3-3, one can adjust the

	Student category*	Total number of males	Estimated percentage of veterans	Estimated number of veterans
	A	2,057	0	0
	B	576	5	29
	C	679	50	340
	D	487	40	195
	E	183	20	37
TOTAL		3,982		601

TABLE 3-4 Male undergraduates enrolled in fall 1972 by estimated veterans status (in thousands)

*As determined in Table 3-3.

SOURCE: See Table 3-3.

number of students to reflect the age distribution if none of the men had had military service. Our rule of thumb procedure shifted two-thirds of the presumed veterans in each cell back two years in age, and one-third back one year. This division was to allow for some proportion who were discharged in less than two years. (It was assumed arbitrarily that young men who were interested in attending college did not reenlist—an over-simplification.)

Table 3-5 shows the resulting age distribution of all under-graduates (male and female) as reported by the Bureau of the Census for fall 1972, and the adjusted estimate intended to eliminate the effects of the presence of a significant number of veterans in college. The adjusted distribution, even though a rough measure, is probably closer to a typical peacetime age distribution. If nothing else, the exercise is a reminder that the apparent gradual increase in the proportion of undergraduates who are 25 or older is partly a temporary aftereffect of the Vietnam War. The 1970 census reported 14 percent in this upper-age category; the 1972 sample census of undergraduates reports 14.4 percent; but the adjusted distribution in Table 3-5 indicates 13.4 percent.[4]

How good a proxy is the 18-to-21 age group in indicating the pool of potential college entrants in normal peacetime years?

[4]For 1960, however, the Bureau of the Census (1963, pp. 1-377–1-378) reported 16.1 percent between the ages of 25 and 34. In 1960–61 the Veterans Administration reports 209,973 veterans receiving college benefits, approximately 7 percent of all enrollees (see footnote 3).

TABLE 3-5 *The age distribution of college undergraduates, as reported by the Bureau of the Census, and adjusted to offset the presence of veterans, fall 1972*

| | Total undergraduates (in thousands) | | Percentage distribution | |
	Census	Adjusted	Census	Adjusted
Under 18	293	293	4.1	4.1
18	1,424	1,455	20.4	20.8
19	1,255	1,292	18.0	18.5
20	1,150	1,185	16.4	16.9
21	916	962	13.1	13.8
22	407	416	5.8	6.0
23	310	251	4.4	3.6
24	229	203	3.3	2.9
25–29	692	636	9.9	9.1
30–34	316	299	4.5	4.3
TOTAL	6,992	6,992	100.0	100.0

SOURCE: For census data, see Table 3-3. Adjustments are the author's.

Table 3-6 shows the census-reported age distribution of undergraduates by type of institution and year of study. The median ages fit the general 18-to-21 pattern, although it is apparent that 18 to 21 is a better proxy for estimating the pool from which students are drawn into four-year colleges than it is for the two-year college. Table 3-7 shows the percentage of students in each year of college who fall within the 18-to-21 age range as reported by the Bureau of Census and as adjusted in the preceding paragraphs to eliminate the effect of veteran enrollments.

If a significant fraction of undergraduates are drawn from ages over 21, then in periods when there is a rapid change in the 18-to-21 age group there will be a tendency to under- or overestimate enrollment changes.

We can test how well the 18-to-21 population serves as a proxy for "the college-age group" by comparing the number of eligibles in that four-year age range with a composite four-year cohort weighted to reflect actual college attendance (from Table 3-6). In 1972, when the 18-to-21 age group numbered 15,096,-000, such a weighted composite four-year age group was 14,-

TABLE 3-6
Age distribution of college undergraduates, fall 1972 (in thousands)

| Age | All colleges | | | | | |
| | Total under-graduate enrollment | Percent of enrollment by age | Year | | | |
			1	2	3	4
14	1	0.0	1	0	0	0
15	4	0.0	4	0	0	0
16	23	0.3	22	1	0	0
17	265	3.8	255	8	2	0
18	1,424	20.4	1,191	226	5	2
19	1,255	18.0	242	850	157	6
20	1,150	16.4	83	247	676	144
21	916	13.1	62	112	191	551
22	407	5.8	62	68	85	192
23	310	4.4	88	79	72	71
24	229	3.3	46	78	46	59
25–29	692	9.9	173	196	172	151
30–34	316	4.5	89	102	47	78
Total	6,992	100.0	2,318	1,967	1,453	1,254

NOTE: Figures may not add to totals due to the rounding of numbers.
SOURCE: U.S. Bureau of the Census (1973, p. 22).

325,000, or 5.1 percent smaller. This reflects the fact that when the 18-to-21 group is growing rapidly, the long tail on the age distribution of college students is drawn from older and smaller age cohorts. Thus, one may tend to overestimate enrollments by focusing just on the 18-to-21 range. Conversely, when the actual 18-to-21 cohort is contracting, a weighted college-age cohort will be larger by an equivalent amount.

One way to minimize the possible error is to use a broader age range, such as 18 to 24, for projecting future enrollments. As Table 3-6 indicates, such an expanded age group encompasses about 81 percent of undergraduates, compared with 68 percent for 18 to 21, and thus somewhat improves the base from which enrollment can be predicted. However, there is an advantage in using a four-year age group—real or composite—as a yardstick. The majority of undergraduate students engage in a four-year program of study (for example, as indicated in the next chapter, total full-time-equivalent, or FTE, undergraduate enrollment is

2-year colleges			4-year colleges					Type of school not reported
	Year			Year				
Total	1	2	Total	1	2	3	4	
0	0	0	0	0	0	0	0	1
0	0	0	0	0	0	0	0	4
8	8	0	9	8	1	0	0	5
71	68	3	158	153	5	0	0	37
469	412	57	914	744	163	5	2	41
334	118	216	893	108	634	145	6	27
212	55	157	914	28	129	613	144	23
121	31	90	780	25	40	164	551	13
91	41	50	302	15	28	67	192	15
98	44	54	196	31	35	59	71	16
79	30	49	143	15	31	38	59	6
295	111	184	382	54	51	126	151	16
133	58	75	164	18	31	37	78	21
1,911	976	935	4,855	1,199	1,148	1,254	1,254	225

3.6 times FTE first-time enrollment), and one is more conscious of the constraints on the college attendance rate if one compares actual enrollment with a four-year age cohort. In addition, use of a weighted college-age cohort makes it somewhat less risky to slip into expressing enrollment rates as percentages of an age

TABLE 3-7   *Percent of enrolled undergraduates from the 18-to-21 age group, fall 1972*

	Year of college				
	Total	First	Second	Third	Fourth
Two-year colleges	57.9	60.0	55.6*		
Four-year colleges	72.1	75.4	84.1	73.9	56.1
All undergraduates	67.9	68.0	73.0	73.9	56.1
Adjusted for veterans	69.6	69.5	75.2	77.3	57.9

*Includes some two-year college students enrolled for the third year.

SOURCE: Calculated from Table 3-6; adjusted percentages based on Table 3-5.

cohort, for such rates more nearly reflect the percentage of an age group who ever enroll in college.

Table 3-8 gives a historical picture of the size of the 18-to-21 population and of the weighted composite four-year cohort since 1950, projecting under Series E and F birth assumptions out to the year 2000. Up through 1992 the size of the 18-to-21 age group is known; these potential students were born by 1974. For the 1995 projection, about one-fifth of the 18-to-21 group, but over two-fifths of the weighted composite cohort, represents persons born prior to 1974; thus the age-group projection for 1995 will probably prove correct with a margin of several percentage points. The year 2000 is based on projected births between 1979 and 1988 and is therefore riskier. Figure 3-2 diagrams the age-group series and suggests the range within

	18-to-21 age group		Weighted composite college-age group	
Year	*Series E*	*Series F*	*Series E*	*Series F*
1950	8,946		9,153	
1951	8,741		9,006	
1952	8,514		8,839	
1953	8,416		8,740	
1954	8,384		8,674	
1955	8,443		8,679	
1956	8,636		8,758	
1957	8,746		8,831	
1958	8,909		8,933	
1959	9,190		9,109	
1960	9,498		9,329	
1961	10,234		9,861	
1962	10,710		10,229	
1963	11,002		10,493	
1964	10,990		10,596	
1965	12,094		11,454	
1966	12,904		12,121	
1967	13,784		12,766	
1968	13,766		12,929	

TABLE 3-8
The size of the college-age population: actual 1950–1973 and projected 1974–2000 (in thousands)

	18-to-21 age group		Weighted composite college-age group	
Year	Series E	Series F	Series E	Series F
1969		14,094		13,307
1970		14,371		13,752
1971		14,684		14,062
1972		15,096		14,325
1973		15,506		14,649
1974		15,860		15,333
1975		16,181		15,555
1976		16,442		15,808
1977		16,616		16,032
1978		16,766		16,241
1979		16,942		16,461
1980		17,009		16,622
1981		16,987		16,703
1982		16,900		16,690
1983		16,501		16,466
1984		15,975		16,151
1985		15,418		15,793
1986		14,848		15,372
1987		14,500		15,088
1988		14,462		15,031
1989		14,572		14,996
1990		14,459		14,812
1991	14,132	14,005	14,535	14,447
1992	13,738	13,423	14,203	13,982
1993	13,426	12,886	13,962	13,584
1994	13,536	12,731	13,948	13,385
1995	13,934	12,941	14,098	13,378
1996	14,421	13,273	14,358	13,492
1997	14,890	13,585	14,686	13,665
1998	15,332	13,874	15,025	13,870
1999	15,737	14,145	15,244	13,969
2000	16,094	14,368	15,484	14,040

TABLE 3-8 (continued)

SOURCE: Computed from reported data in U.S Bureau of the Census, ser. P-20 (various years) and ser. P-25, no. 493 (1972).

FIGURE 3-2 *Size of the college-age population to 2000 (in hundreds of thousands)*

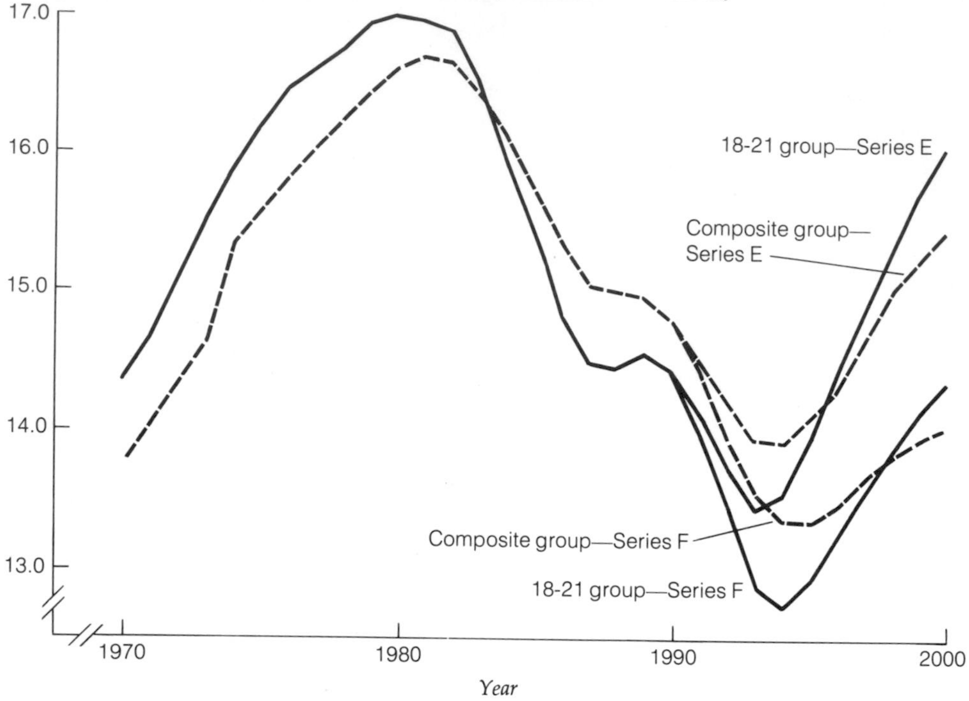

SOURCE: See Table 3-8.

which this population is likely to fall—a range between Bureau of Census Series E and Series F projections.

The most striking conclusion one draws from Figure 3-2 is that 1981 is the highest point on the horizon in terms of the projected size of the college-age group. Under the higher of the two population projections, the size of the cohort in 2000 would be about 6 percent below the early 1980s peak, and under Series F we would complete the century nearly 15 percent below 1981. If we had carried the Series E and F projections out to A.D. 2020, as the Bureau of the Census does, we would see that in that latter year the projected size of the college-age group would be 5 percent below A.D. 2000 for Series E and nearly 12 percent lower for Series F. Thus, in the lifetimes of present educators we cannot expect population growth to add to the growth of college enrollments beyond what will happen over the next several years. The great expansion of the 1958–1978 years is unlikely to occur again in the next 40 to 50 years.

4. Projecting Undergraduate Enrollments

For the greater part of this century a fairly constant proportion of high school graduates have continued their studies at the collegiate level (Campbell & Siegel, 1967). For example, in the first decade of this century total college enrollments averaged 2.36 times the number of high school graduates; in the 1960s it averaged 2.54, and only in the last three years of the decade did it surpass the 1900–1910 average. The ratio dipped in the depression and war years and rose briefly as GIs returned to complete their education, but the long-term trend has indicated a surprising constancy.

Table 4-1 indicates the ratio between high school graduation and the awarding of baccalaureate degrees four years later from 1920 to the present; this series also reveals a relatively stable relationship except for war and depression periods. It is important, therefore, to look closely at high school graduation rates before turning to college enrollment projections.

TABLE 4-1
High school graduates in selected years, and college graduates four years later (in thousands)

Year	High school graduates (t)	B.A. degrees (t + 4)	Ratio column (1)/column (2)
1910	156	41	.264
1920	311	77	.248
1930	667	127	.190
1940	1,221	117	.096
1950	1,200	271	.226
1960	1,864	466	.250
1965	2,665	728	.273

SOURCES: For 1910 through 1950, U.S. Bureau of the Census (1960); for 1960 and 1965, U.S. Office of Education (1973b).

**HIGH SCHOOL
GRADUATION
RATES** Between 1870 and 1970 the percentage of young persons graduating from high school in the United States rose from less than 3 percent to more than 75 percent. The most dramatic increases were in the 1920–1940 period, when secondary school attendance became nearly universal. In the post-1945 period, the graduation rate increased steadily but modestly at about one percentage point per year. Figure 4-1 gives an overall picture of the long historical trend.

The last 10 years, however, have been somewhat abnormal. Beginning in the mid-1960s the military draft became an important factor in the consideration of young men deciding whether or not to continue their education beyond the legal school-leaving age. The educational exemption for those who remained in full-time student status affected both high school completion rates and college enrollment rates. Up through 1965

FIGURE 4-1 *High school graduates as a percentage of 18-year-olds, 1900-1970*

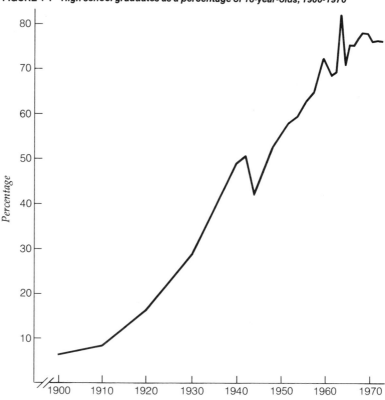

SOURCES: U.S. Bureau of the Census (1965; 1970); U.S. Office of Education (1973*a*, p. 55).

draft calls averaged only about 100,000 a year—or about 7 percent of the number turning 18 each year. In the 1966–1968 years, however, draft calls jumped to about 300,000, dropping back to about 250,000 annually for the next two years. The lottery system did not go into effect until December 1969, so students who dropped out or interrupted their education were subject to draft through most of the 1969–70 school year.

Table 4-2 shows high school graduates in relation to the age-18 population since 1950. Now, from the vantage point of 1973 data, it appears that the peak graduation rate years of 1968, 1969, and 1970 were abnormally high, and it can be presumed that 1972 and 1973 are somewhat more representative of the long-run trend. College enrollment projections of only a year or two ago largely ignored the effect of the draft on high school

TABLE 4-2 *Relationship between high school graduates and 18-year-old population, 1950– 1973 (in thousands)*			

Year	*18-year-old population*	*High school graduates*	*Graduation rate*
1950	2,164	1,200	.555
1952	2,058	1,196	.581
1954	2,135	1,276	.598
1956	2,244	1,415	.631
1958	2,307	1,506	.653
1960	2,569	1,864	.726
1961	2,832	1,971	.696
1962	2,794	1,925	.689
1963	2,802	1,950	.696
1964	2,780	2,290	.824
1965	3,743	2,665	.712
1966	3,528	2,632	.746
1967	3,527	2,679	.760
1968	3,504	2,702	.771
1969	3,606	2,829	.785
1970	3,703	2,896	.782
1971	3,847	2,943	.765
1972	3,926	3,006	.766
1973	4,030	3,037	.754

SOURCES: Column (1), U.S. Bureau of the Census (1965 & 1970); column (2), U.S. Office of Education (1973*a* and *Projections of Educational Statistics,* various years).

completion rates (although graduation was the key to college admission and thus continued deferment), believing that the observed trends were principally the result of broader social forces. The National Center for Educational Statistics (NCES), for example, in its *Projections* series, indicated as late as the 1972 edition that they assumed that the 1972–1982 high school graduation experience would follow the 1961–1971 trend (U.S. Office of Education, 1973*b*, p. 47, fn. 4). Earlier Cartter projections, up to 1972, assumed that high school graduation rates would rise by one percentage point per year, leveling off at .90 in 1982 (Cartter, 1974). By that arithmetic high school graduates should have numbered 3.26 million in 1973 rather than the NCES figure of 3.04 million—a difference of 220,000, or 7 percent. Projected into the future, that degree of error could become substantial.

The 1973 edition of the NCES *Projections* significantly reduces the estimated number of high school graduates for the 1970s and early 1980s. Two years ago, NCES projected 3,298,000 high school graduates for 1981; last year the projection had dropped to 2,960,000. This downward revision would appear to be too drastic, for it assumes a continuing decrease in the high school graduation rate from .754 in 1973 to .670 in 1981.

Reviewing Figure 4-1 and Table 4-2, it is apparent that the graduation rate cannot be expected to continue to increase in a linear fashion. Such an assumption may be appropriate for a short-term forecast, but as the rate approaches 100 percent it must obviously slow down. Several years ago it seemed reasonable to assume that the rate would increase fairly steadily for another decade or so and then plateau out. With the experience of the last two or three years in evidence, it now seems possible—although not necessarily probable—that we have nearly reached the maximum rate under current school-leaving laws.

Reflecting on the data, it seems wisest to posit three alternative paths—a high, medium, and low assumed growth path. Accordingly, Table 4-3 shows three possibilities for the years 1973 through 1990—the period for which the size of the 18-year-old population is now known. The "high" graduation rate projection assumes a 90 percent asymptote, leveling off in A.D. 2000. The "medium" assumption is an 85 percent asymptote reaching its zenith in 2000. The "low" assumption levels off at 80 percent in 1985. Viewing the history of the last decade or

TABLE 4-3 *Projections of high school graduates, 1973–1990 (in thousands)*

Year	Number age 18	High school graduates			Graduation rates		
		High	*Medium*	*Low*	*High*	*Medium*	*Low*
1973	4,030	3,037	3,037	3,037	.754	.754	.754
1974	4,057	3,111	3,103	3,103	.772	.770	.770
1975	4,168	3,251	3,234	3,230	.780	.776	.775
1976	4,187	3,299	3,270	3,266	.788	.781	.780
1977	4,204	3,346	3,304	3,296	.796	.786	.784
1978	4,207	3,378	3,328	3,315	.803	.791	.788
1979	4,344	3,519	3,458	3,436	.810	.796	.791
1980	4,254	3,476	3,407	3,378	.817	.801	.794
1981	4,182	3,446	3,367	3,329	.824	.805	.796
1982	4,120	3,420	3,333	3,288	.830	.809	.798
1983	3,945	3,298	3,207	3,152	.836	.813	.799
1984	3,728	3,139	3,046	2,979	.842	.817	.799
1985	3,625	3,074	2,976	2,900	.848	.821	.800
1986	3,550	3,028	2,925	2,840	.853	.824	
1987	3,597	3,086	2,975	2,878	.858	.827	
1988	3,690	3,184	3,063	2,952	.863	.830	
1989	3,735	3,242	3,111	2,988	.868	.833	
1990	3,437	2,997	2,873	2,750	.872	.836	.800

SOURCE: Projections by the author. Estimates of the 18-year-old population from Table 3-2.

two, these three projected rates seem to provide a range within which the likely growth path will occur.

Given these three projected series for graduation rates, the number of high school graduates will probably increase from 3.04 million to a high point in 1979, roughly 360,000 to 440,000 above 1973. Between 1979 and 1986 there would follow declines of from 500,000 to 600,000, succeeded by three years of modest increase before dropping again in 1990. Under any of the three assumptions, high school graduates in 1990 would be fewer than in 1973.

A somewhat slower rate of increase in high school graduation rates in the last quarter of the century seems likely. The differential between rates for male and female graduates finally disappeared in 1972—no longer, as was true 20 years ago, is the rate for males about 10 percent below that for females. Secondly, in many of the relatively affluent areas or states, rates have about reached their maxima; thus improvements in the national rate must come largely from a limited number of areas that have lagged behind the national average. Third, the lowest graduation rates today are found in inner-city and in rural areas, where a variety of social and economic factors make it difficult to raise retention and graduation rates. Thus, it seems likely that future progress will be slower than in the past, when relatively full employment and rising parental aspirations helped to raise the graduation rate quite apart from any public-policy efforts to raise educational attainment levels.

The selection of the three projection paths probably indicates to the reader that the author's intuition or insight favors the medium growth rate assumption. This represents a significantly slower growth in the graduation rate than was assumed in previous enrollment projections, but one which the experience of the last several years seems to suggest.

Beyond 1990, the size of the 18-year-old population is speculative, although, as was indicated in Chapter 3, Bureau of the Census Series E and F projections seem to be reasonable expectations. Table 4-4, therefore, carries the high school graduation projections through the last decade of the century based on these two population projections. The range of alternative growth paths becomes much wider when two sets of alternative assumptions are overlayed.

1972 and 1973 experience would strongly suggest that the Series F projection is the most likely—in fact, if one projected the *trend* in birth and fertility rates of the last three or four years, a new lower "Series G" would have to be developed. Viewing Series F high, low, and medium graduation rate projections, it appears that the number of high school graduates (which Table 4-3 suggested would begin to decline again after 1989) would fall to a low point in 1992 of between 2.49 million and 2.74 million and then rise again from 400,000 to 560,000 by the year 2000. (It might be recalled from Chapter 3 that Series F projections to the year 2020 suggest that there would be a decline again of about 12 percent in the 18-year-old population in the first two decades of the next century.)

Viewed in the longer perspective, the Series F projections for the end of the century would indicate a high school graduation class exactly the same size as in 1974 (medium assumption),

TABLE 4-4 Projections of high school graduates, 1990–2000 (in thousands)

Year	Number age 18		High school graduates						Graduation rates		
			High		Medium		Low				
	Series E	Series F	Series E	Series F	Series E	Series F	Series E	Series F	High	Medium	Low
1990	3,437	3,437	2,997	2,997	2,873	2,873	2,750	2,750	.872	.836	.800
1991	3,270	3,143	2,865	2,753	2,740	2,634	2,616	2,514	.876	.838	
1992	3,296	3,108	2,900	2,735	2,769	2,611	2,637	2,486	.880	.840	
1993	3,423	3,198	3,023	2,824	2,882	2,693	2,738	2,558	.883	.842	
1994	3,547	3,282	3,143	2,908	2,994	2,770	2,838	2,626	.886	.844	
1995	3,668	3,353	3,261	2,981	3,103	2,837	2,934	2,682	.889	.846	
1996	3,783	3,440	3,374	3,068	3,204	2,914	3,026	2,752	.892	.847	
1997	3,892	3,510	3,479	3,138	3,300	2,976	3,114	2,808	.894	.848	
1998	3,989	3,571	3,574	3,200	3,387	3,032	3,191	2,857	.896	.849	
1999	4,073	3,624	3,658	3,254	3,458	3,077	3,258	2,899	.898	.849	
2000	4,140	3,663	3,726	3,297	3,519	3,114	3,312	2,930	.900	.850	.800

(Low graduation rate is constant at .800 from 1990 through 2000, indicated by arrow.)

SOURCE: Same as Table 4-3.

186,000 larger than in 1974 (high assumption), or 173,000 smaller (low assumption). Thus, although there will be periods of growth and contraction, the size of the pool from which most college students are drawn can be expected to remain relatively constant for the next quarter of a century and perhaps for the quarter-century beyond.

Tables 4-2, 4-3, and 4-4 have broken the half-century into three separate parts, depending upon known or projected data;

FIGURE 4-2 *High school graduates and the 18-year-old population, 1950-2000 (in thousands)*

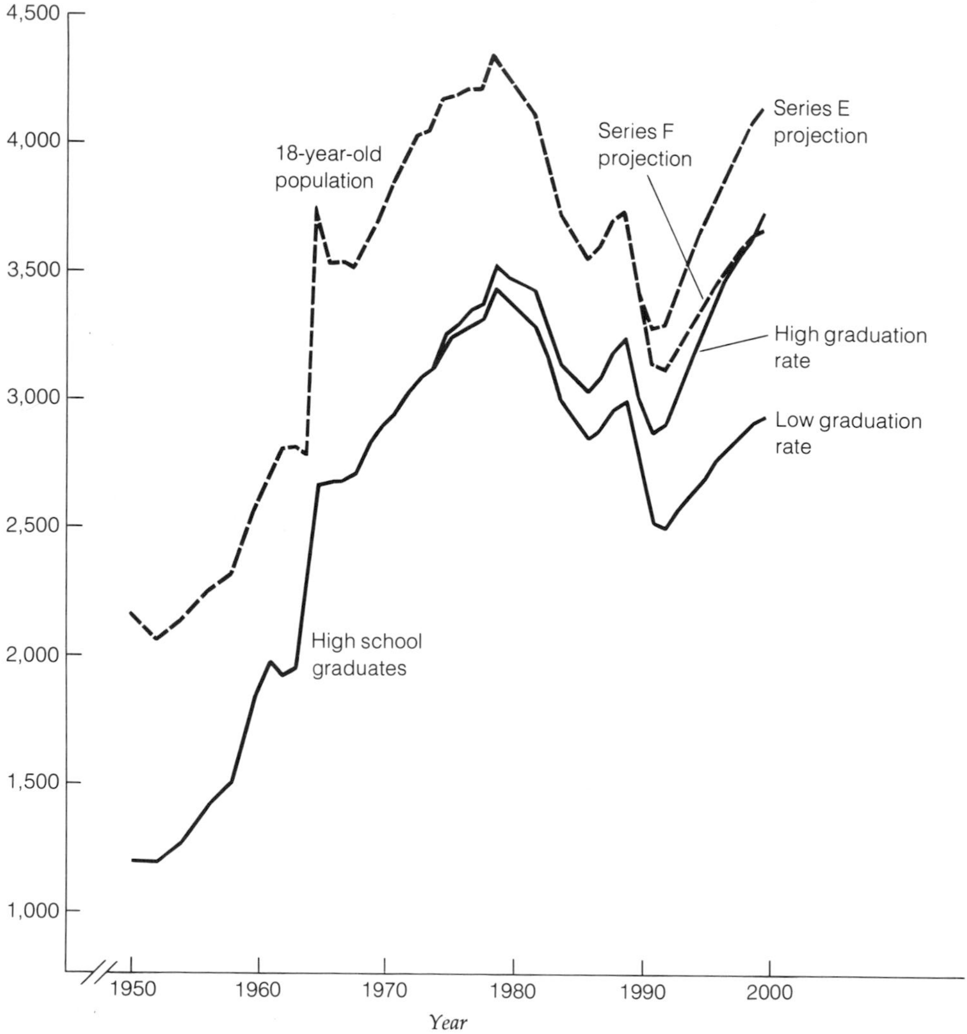

SOURCE: See Table 4-3.

Figure 4-2 plots the half-century series for the 18-year-old population and for high school graduates. Only the high and low graduation rate projections are shown, so Figure 4-2 indicates the range within which the likely actual path will fall. For each of the population series projections, the high and low graduation rate assumptions give figures for the year 2000 about 6 percent above or below the medium projected rate.

As indicated above, the most likely path, in the author's view, is Series F medium graduation rate.

PROJECTIONS OF COLLEGE ENTRANCE

As noted in Chapter 3, 73 percent of college freshmen are either 18 years old or within one year of that age, and we can assume that a slightly higher percentage of those entering college are not more than one (academic) year removed from high school graduation.[1] Thus, the comparison between college entrance and high school graduation should be useful for anyone attempting to project future college enrollments. Table 4-5 indicates first-time enrollments and the ratio of such enrollments to the 18-year-old population and to high school graduates. The ratios between college entrance and the age and graduate pools rose significantly during and immediately following the Korean War. During the 1955–1961 period, the college entrance rate rose in relation to high school graduates. Both ratios rose slightly in the 1962–1967 period, and then jumped dramatically for the several years when draft calls hung over the heads of young men turning 18. After 1970, when the draft lottery took effect, and particularly in 1972 and 1973, as draft calls diminished, both ratios declined again.

The data on college entrance for the last few years are puzzling in a number of respects. First, since 1967 a significant number of veterans have enrolled in college; how many would not be attending college if there were no GI benefits? Table 4-6 shows the number of veterans enrolled in institutions from the zero level in 1966, to the expected peak in 1973, but information indicating the proportion of first-time students on the GI Bill is not available. In Chapter 3, an estimated distribution of veterans was made which suggests that a little over 10 percent of

[1]In a recent NSF study, Lewis and Sulkin (1972, p. 21) estimate that in normal peacetime years, 93 percent of those who eventually attend college enter between the ages of 17 to 19.

TABLE 4-5 *Relationship between first-time college degree-credit enrollment and high school graduates and 18-year-old population, 1950–1973 (in thousands)*

Year	High school graduates (1)	18-year-old population (2)	First-time enrollment (3)	Ratio column (3)/ column (1) (4)	Ratio column (3)/ column (2) (5)
1950	1,200	2,164	512	.427	.237
1952	1,196	2,058	532	.445	.259
1954	1,276	2,135	625	.490	.293
1956	1,415	2,244	715	.505	.319
1958	1,506	2,307	772	.513	.335
1960	1,864	2,569	923	.495	.359
1961	1,971	2,832	1,018	.516	.359
1962	1,925	2,794	1,030	.535	.369
1963	1,950	2,802	1,046	.536	.373
1964	2,290	2,780	1,225	.535	.441
1965	2,665	3,743	1,442	.541	.385
1966	2,672	3,528	1,378	.516	.391
1967	2,679	3,527	1,439	.537	.408
1968	2,702	3,504	1,630	.603	.465
1969	2,829	3,606	1,749	.623	.485
1970	2,896	3,703	1,780	.615	.481
1971	2,943	3,847	1,766	.600	.459
1972	3,006	3,926	1,740	.579	.443
1973	3,037	4,030	1,757	.578	.436

SOURCES: Columns (1) and (2) from Table 4-2; column (3) from U.S. Office of Education (*Projections of Educational Statistics,* various years).

first-year male students were veterans in 1972. However, first-year and first-time entrants are not identical, the former being somewhat larger by virtue of part-time students who take more than a year to complete their first full academic year. The American Council on Education (ACE) freshman survey, on the other hand, indicated that only 3.1 percent of full-time male students were veterans in 1972, but veterans may have been underrepresented in the sample.[2] If—to use a hypothetical

[2]The survey questionnaires are voluntary, and older freshmen who have spent several years in the military may not have responded as frequently as did younger students just out of high school.

TABLE 4-6 ***Number of*** ***veterans*** ***receiving benefits*** ***enrolled in*** ***colleges and*** ***universities (in*** ***thousands)***	*Year*	*Number of* *veterans*	*Total males* *enrolled*	*Percentage of* *veterans*

Year	*Number of veterans*	*Total males enrolled*	*Percentage of veterans*
1967	339	3,822	8.9
1968	414	4,119	10.1
1969	529	4,419	12.0
1970	677	4,637	14.6
1971	917	4,717	19.4
1972	1,065	4,700	22.7
1973	1,200*	4,772	25.1

*Estimated.

SOURCES: Column (1) supplied by the Veterans Administration for the Carnegie Commission; column (2) from U.S. Office of Education (1975).

example—there were 50,000 veterans who entered college in 1973 who would not otherwise have attended, the ratio of first-time entrants to high school graduates in Table 4-5 for 1973 would normally have been .562 instead of .578. The difference could be fairly substantial in attempting to determine the long-term trend.

Another perplexing factor is that the 1968–1970 sharp rise in college entrance ratios, followed by a decline beginning in 1971, is most easily attributable to the impact of the draft. However, the ratios for women mirrored the men's ratios. Table 4-7 gives the experience of the last two decades for both sexes. The male first-time enrollment–high school graduate ratio has remained essentially constant, with the exception of the several years we have identified as exhibiting a significant draft effect. The female ratio, on the other hand, has been gradually moving upward, although it also indicates a marked jump in 1968. One might theorize that the draft had a large impact on male decisions to enter college, and that this in turn had a significant effect on the decisions of young women. The whole atmosphere of high schools may have temporarily been focused on college entry, and the fact that the 1968–1970 years were also the period when colleges were the scene of antiwar and antiestablishment protest may have made them seem more attractive places to be than they had been in the past. With the draft as a push on the young men, and the excitement of social action a pull on both men and women, perhaps it is not surprising that college entrance ratios for both sexes jumped up for those several years.

TABLE 4-7 *Relationship between first-time college degree-credit enrollment and high school graduates, by sex, 1950–1973 (in thousands)*

Year	Male			Female		
	High school graduates (1)	First-time enrollment (2)	Ratio column (2)/ column (1) (3)	High school graduates (4)	First-time enrollment (5)	Ratio column (5)/ column (4) (6)
1950	571	317	.555	629	195	.310
1952	569	321	.564	627	211	.336
1954	613	383	.625	664	242	.364
1956	680	442	.650	735	273	.371
1958	726	464	.639	780	308	.395
1960	898	540	.601	966	384	.398
1961	958	592	.618	1,013	426	.421
1962	941	598	.635	984	433	.440
1963	959	604	.630	991	442	.446
1964	1,123	702	.625	1,167	523	.448
1965*	1,314	829	.631	1,351	613	.454
1966*	1,326	787	.594	1,346	591	.439
1967	1,332	814	.611	1,348	625	.464
1968	1,341	925	.690	1,360	705	.518
1969	1,402	986	.703	1,427	763	.535
1970	1,433	984	.687	1,463	796	.544
1971	1,456	968	.665	1,487	798	.537
1972	1,490	929	.623	1,516	812	.536
1973	1,501	931	.620	1,536	826	.538

*First-time enrollments in 1965 and 1966 are estimates by the U.S. Office of Education. This may account for the unexpected drop in the college entrance ratios. See U.S. Office of Education (1975, Table 14, p. 32, fn. 2).
SOURCE: U.S. Office of Education (1975, pp. 32, 43).

It should also be remembered that Martin Luther King's assassination in the spring of 1968 had a significant impact upon the effort of colleges and universities to recruit students from ethnic minorities and probably also inspired many young black men and women to continue their education. This impact would have been first noticeable in 1968 and 1969 and may also account for a part of the increase in the college attendance ratios for both men and women.

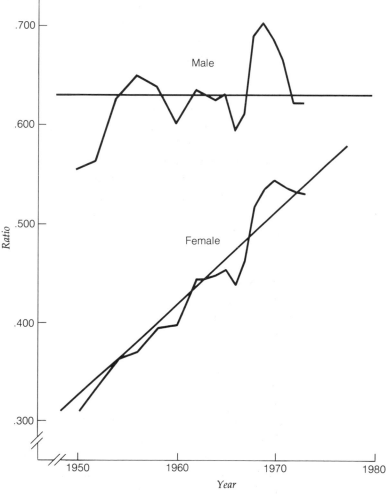

FIGURE 4-3 *Ratio of college entrants to high school graduates, by sex, 1950-1973*

SOURCE: Table 4-7.

Figure 4-3 plots the male and female ratios and overlays trend lines on the two series, discounting the 1968–1970 period. Clearly there is no apparent upward movement in the entrance rate for men; by contrast, the women's trend line rises at about .009 per year and would intersect the male line about 1983. Whether, as the female entrance rate approaches the male rate, it begins to plateau or to provide upward pressure on the male rate, is speculative.

A third factor that makes it difficult to interpret long-term trends is the relatively rapid growth in nondegree enrollment over the last 10 years. In the previous tables the focus has been on degree students, but by 1973 nondegree students constituted 11¼ percent of all enrollments, and nearly 20 percent of first-time enrollments.[3]

Over 90 percent of nondegree students are found in the two-year colleges, primarily in vocational and technical curricula. Nondegree enrollments have risen from one-fourth of two-year college enrollments in 1962 to one-third by 1972. When nondegree enrollments are included, the ratio of first-time students to high school graduates has remained about .70 for the last six years. Although no accurate age distribution data are available, it appears that the nondegree category includes a larger proportion of older (22 and above) students than does the degree-credit group.

The comparison between first-time enrollment and high school graduates is expressed as a ratio rather than a percentage, for entering students are not exclusively drawn from the same year's crop of high school graduates. However, the ratios in relatively stable periods provide a reasonably good indication of the proportion of the graduate cohort who eventually enter college. For example, in 1955 the college entrance ratio in relation to the 18-year-old population was .313, but only an estimated 20 percent of 18-year-olds actually entered college in that year. Census reports on educational attainment indicate that 27 percent of the age group had entered college by the time they reached 22, 30 percent had entered by age 27, and 31 percent by age 32 (Lewis & Sulkin, 1972, p. 19). Thus the ratios can be interpreted as approximate percentages of likely eventual attendees.

Turning to the question of projecting first-time enrollments for future years, it is helpful to use several alternative models in light of the lack of clarity about time trends evident in recent data. Five alternatives are offered.

[3]The staff at the National Center for Educational Statistics, which compiles the enrollment series, however, indicates that reporting of nondegree students has never been as reliable as that of degree-credit students. They believe that nondegree students have been underreported until quite recently, and thus the *apparently high* growth trend may be misleading.

Alternative A assumes that no further improvement in the degree-credit ratio takes place and that future increases in the proportion of the age group entering college take place in nondegree programs.

Alternative B is a low estimate that assumes that the ratio of total (degree and nondegree credit) enrollment to high school graduates has almost reached its zenith. From the 1973 level of .712 it is assumed that the ratio will rise to a maximum of .750, with non-degree-credit enrollments accounting for .140 and degree enrollments rising to .610 (about equal to the 1969–1970 draft period).

Alternative C is a medium projection that assumes a continuation of recent trends in the male and female college entrance rates respectively until the two are equal in 1983 and then that the ratio for degree-credit enrollment will rise at half the 1973–1983 annual increment for 10 years, dropping to one-quarter from 1994–2000.

FIGURE 4-4 *Ratio of first-time degree credit college students to high school graduates; actual, 1950-1973 and alternative projections 1974-2000*

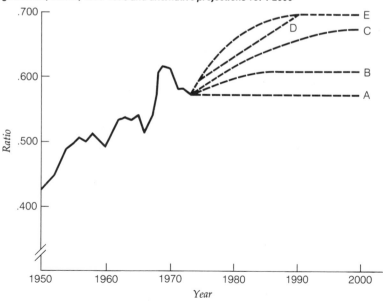

SOURCES: Tables 4-5 and 4-8.

TABLE 4-8 *Projected ratios of first-time college enrollment to high school graduates; five alternatives, 1973–2000*

Year	A	B	C	D	E
1973	.578	.578	.578	.578	.578
1974	↑	.583	.585	.598	.598
1975		.587	.592	.605	.610
1976		.591	.599	.611	.621
1977		.595	.606	.617	.632
1978		.598	.612	.624	.642
1979		.601	.618	.630	.651
1980		.604	.624	.636	.659
1981		.606	.629	.643	.666
1982		.608	.634	.649	.672
1983		.610	.639	.656	.678
1984		↑	.644	.662	.683
1985			.648	.668	.687
1986			.657	.675	.691
1987			.656	.681	.694
1988			.659	.687	.697
1989			.662	.694	.699
1990			.665	.700	.700
1991			.668	↑	↑
1992			.670		
1993			.672		
1994			.674		
1995			.675		
1996			.676		
1997			.677		
1998			.678		
1999			.679		
2000	.578	.610	.680	.700	.700

SOURCE: Projections by the author.

Alternative D is a linear projection of entrance rates based on the overall 1953–1973 trend, and assumes an annual increase in the degree-credit enrollment ratio of .00635 until 1990 then levels off at .70. (This would imply an overall ratio of about .85.)

Alternative E is a variant of D, assuming the same eventual stable ratio of .70, but reaching it asymptotically. Thus, the short-term increases are significantly greater than those in the 1980s.

Figure 4-4 plots these alternatives to the year 2000. A and E are probably outside boundary limits. C and D have identical slopes until 1983, although C begins from the 1973 actual ratio, and D returns to the 1950–1973 trend line. The author's intuition favors B and C, with a slight preference for C as a long-range forecast.

Table 4-8 gives the ratios for each of the five alternatives for 1973–2000. By 1990 D and E are 6.2 percent above alternative C, B is 7.4 percent below, and A is 11.1 percent below C. Looking back historically, the range between alternatives B and E would have encompassed all years except 1968–1970 if the projections had been applied from an earlier point on the trend line.

When the projected ratios are applied to high school graduates, the combined effect of variations in birthrates, high school graduation rates, and college entrance rates becomes evident. Table 4-9 shows the projected first-time enrollments from 1973 to 2000, and Figure 4-5 plots alternatives B, C and E as illustrative of the likely range within which actual enrollments will fall. It is apparent, under any of the assumptions, that increases are predictable over the 1973–1979 period, followed by a drop in 1979–1986, modest recovery in 1986–1989 followed by another drop in 1989–1992, and an upswing again beginning in 1993.

Table 4-10 highlights the upswing and downturn periods by showing the projected percentage changes from peak to trough to peak, and the overall change from 1973 to the end of the three decades. At the present time we are in the midst of a period where first-time enrollments are likely to increase by roughly 15 percent to 25 percent in the remainder of this decade, followed by several ups and downs that will leave the situation relatively unchanged on balance for the rest of the century. Under alternatives C and D, first-time enrollments in 2000 are likely to be the same as in 1979; under A or B they would be about 10 percent below 1979, and under E about 4 percent below 1979. Thus, under any one of these alternatives, any remaining net growth in the system is likely to take place over the 1974–1979 years.

TABLE 4-9 *Projected first-time college enrollment under five alternatives, 1973–2000 (in thousands)*

Year	A	B	C	D	E
1973	1,779	1,779	1,779	1,779	1,779
1974	1,794	1,809	1,815	1,856	1,856
1975	1,869	1,898	1,915	1,957	1,973
1976	1,890	1,933	1,959	1,998	2,031
1977	1,910	1,966	2,002	2,039	2,088
1978	1,924	1,990	2,037	2,077	2,137
1979	1,999	2,078	2,137	2,179	2,251
1980	1,969	2,058	2,126	2,167	2,245
1981	1,946	2,040	2,118	2,165	2,242
1982	1,926	2,033	2,113	2,163	2,240
1983	1,854	1,956	2,049	2,104	2,174
1984	1,761	1,858	1,961	2,016	2,080
1985	1,720	1,815	1,928	1,988	2,045
1986	1,691	1,784	1,907	1,974	2,021
1987	1,720	1,815	1,952	2,026	2,065
1988	1,770	1,868	2,019	2,104	2,135
1989	1,798	1,898	2,059	2,159	2,175
1990	1,661	1,753	1,911	2,011	2,011
1991	1,522	1,607	1,760	1,844	1,844
1992	1,509	1,593	1,749	1,828	1,828
1993	1,557	1,643	1,810	1,885	1,885
1994	1,601	1,690	1,867	1,939	1,939
1995	1,640	1,731	1,915	1,986	1,986
1996	1,684	1,778	1,970	2,040	2,040
1997	1,720	1,815	2,015	2,083	2,083
1998	1,752	1,850	2,056	2,122	2,122
1999	1,779	1,877	2,089	2,154	2,154
2000	1,800	1,900	2,118	2,180	2,180

SOURCE: Computed from medium projection in Table 4-3 and ratios in Table 4-8.

CONVERSION TO FULL-TIME-EQUIVALENT ENROLLMENT When projecting college attendance rates, it is preferable to consider total enrollments. Eventually, however, when turning to the demand for college teachers, total enrollments should be converted to full-time-equivalent (FTE) enrollments. Three stu-

FIGURE 4-5 *Projected first-time college enrollment under alternatives B, C, and E, 1973-2000 (in thousands)*

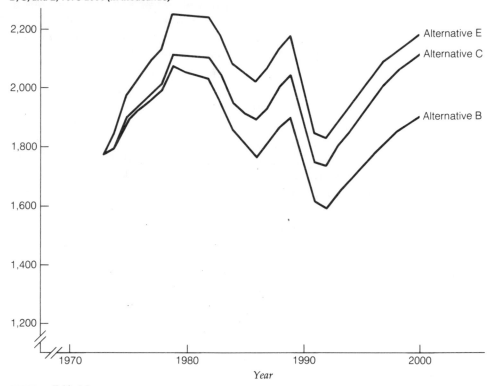

SOURCE: Table 4-9.

TABLE 4-10 *Percentage changes in projected first-time college enrollment, for selected years, 1973–2000*

Alternative	1973– 1979	1979– 1986	1986– 1989	1989– 1992	1992– 2000	1973– 1980	1973– .1990	1973– 2000
A	+12.4	−15.4	+6.3	−16.1	+19.3	+10.7	−6.6	+1.2
B	+16.8	−14.1	+6.4	−16.1	+19.3	+15.7	−1.5	+6.8
C	+20.1	−10.8	+8.0	−15.1	+21.1	+19.5	+7.4	+19.1
D	+22.5	−9.4	+9.4	−15.3	+19.3	+21.8	+13.0	+22.5
E	+26.5	−10.0	+7.6	−16.0	+19.3	+26.2	+13.0	+22.5

dents each enrolled one-third time make approximately the same demand on faculty resources as one full-time student. If the balance between full-time and part-time students continued unchanged over time, the difference between working with FTE and total enrollment would matter little in assessing enrollment changes, but the evidence is that these proportions are not constant.

Table 4-11 shows the proportion of first-time degree-credit students in two-year and four-year institutions who were engaged in full-time study from 1958 to 1972. Full-time students in the two-year colleges have decreased significantly since 1968. The sharp drop in 1972 and 1973 probably reflects both the end of the draft and the impact of the economic recession.

Figure 4-6 plots the data in Table 4-11 and also shows the projected percentages to 1982 as estimated by NCES. They anticipate a fairly constant 91 percent full-time enrollment for the four-year colleges, and 59 percent for the two-year colleges.

TABLE 4-11
Proportion of first-time degree-credit students in two-year and four-year institutions engaged in full-time study, 1958–1972

Year	Two-year institutions	Four-year institutions	Two-year and four-year institutions
1958	.651	.862	.814
1959	.643	.869	.819
1960	.650	.874	.821
1961	.652	.878	.825
1962	.650	.883	.823
1963	.654	.886	.826
1964	.658	.888	.828
1965	.656	.892	.827
1966	.656	.894	.827
1967	.653	.896	.821
1968	.653	.898	.815
1969	.639	.899	.803
1970	.631	.900	.801
1971	.627	.905	.799
1972	.593	.909	.787
1973	.578	.900	.775

SOURCE: U.S. Office of Education (*Projections of Educational Statistics,* various years).

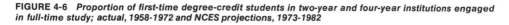

FIGURE 4-6 *Proportion of first-time degree-credit students in two-year and four-year institutions engaged in full-time study; actual, 1958-1972 and NCES projections, 1973-1982*

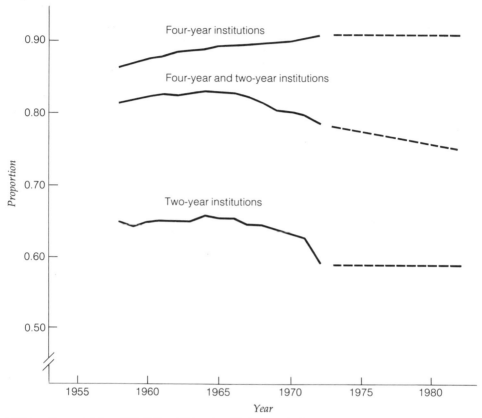

SOURCE: Computed from U.S. Office of Education (*Projections of Educational Statistics*, 1974 and earlier, Tables 14-16).

The overall percentage continues to fall due to the projected gradual change in the enrollment mix. The ratio of four-year to two-year first-time students, as estimated by NCES, moves from 2.96:1 in 1962, to 1.58:1 in 1972, and is projected to decline to 1.09:1 by 1982.

This observer is skeptical about the projected continued relative growth in two-year college enrollments. During a period of rapid growth it was logical to assume an expanding market share for the public community colleges. However, as enrollments begin to contract it seems unlikely that the two-year college will be almost immune from this trend. The 1973 NCES projections assume that first-time four-year college entrants by

1982 will have declined nearly 25 percent from their 1970 peak, while the two-year colleges are assumed to peak in 1978 and decline only about 2 percent by 1982. In many states the public universities and four-year colleges practice selective admission, and such institutions are likely to adjust their admission standards downward as the pool of potential students shrinks. Thus, it seems more probable that two-year and four-year institutions will share any contraction in the total number of degree-credit students—and it is even conceivable that the four-year institutions may slightly increase their share in a more competitive admissions market. Whatever the outcome, it seems probable that the higher education system will become even more accommodating to the part-time student and that the proportion of full-time students will modestly decline whether or not there is a continuing shift in the enrollment mix.

In Table 4-12, first-time FTE enrollments are projected assuming that the percentage of part-time students—21.33 percent in 1972—gradually rises to 25 percent by the end of the century. The NCES projections (1974) predict 24.5 percent by 1982; the projected increase in the part-time share is much more modest in Table 4-12. Conversion to an FTE basis is achieved, as in the NCES estimates, by counting part-time students as the equivalent of one-third of a full-time student.

Under each of the five alternatives, first-time FTE enrollment expands to 1979 (from 12 percent to 25 percent, depending upon the alternative), and then declines steadily to 1992. Under the most optimistic alternatives first-time enrollment then is about equal to 1973 again; under A or B it is 13 percent or 17 percent smaller than in 1973. In the rest of the 1990 decade first-time enrollment is projected to turn upward again.

The relationship between first-time FTE enrollment and total FTE undergraduate degree-credit enrollment has remained relatively stable over time. Enrollment in two-year colleges has expanded relative to four-year colleges, which would tend to depress the ratio, but a rising fraction of two-year college students have gained admission to upper-division programs in senior institutions. In addition, there has been a long-term trend in the four-year institutions toward a rising proportion of students engaged in full-time study, thus offsetting to some degree the relative growth of two-year college enrollments.

In the mid- and late 1960s the proportion of part-time students in both undergraduate sectors declined sharply, reflect-

TABLE 4-12 *Projected full-time equivalents of first-time college enrollment, under five alternatives, 1973–2000 (in thousands)*

Year	A	B	C	D	E
1973	1,525	1,525	1,525	1,525	1,525
1974	1,536	1,549	1,554	1,589	1,589
1975	1,598	1,623	1,637	1,674	1,687
1976	1,614	1,651	1,673	1,706	1,734
1977	1,629	1,677	1,708	1,739	1,781
1978	1,639	1,695	1,736	1,770	1,821
1979	1,701	1,768	1,819	1,854	1,916
1980	1,674	1,749	1,807	1,842	1,908
1981	1,652	1,732	1,798	1,838	1,903
1982	1,633	1,724	1,792	1,834	1,900
1983	1,570	1,657	1,736	1,782	1,841
1984	1,490	1,572	1,659	1,705	1,760
1985	1,453	1,535	1,629	1,680	1,728
1986	1,427	1,506	1,610	1,666	1,706
1987	1,450	1,530	1,646	1,708	1,741
1988	1,490	1,573	1,700	1,772	1,798
1989	1,512	1,596	1,732	1,816	1,829
1990	1,395	1,473	1,605	1,689	1,689
1991	1,277	1,348	1,477	1,547	1,547
1992	1,265	1,335	1,466	1,532	1,532
1993	1,303	1,375	1,515	1,578	1,578
1994	1,338	1,413	1,561	1,621	1,621
1995	1,369	1,445	1,599	1,658	1,658
1996	1,404	1,483	1,643	1,701	1,701
1997	1,433	1,512	1,678	1,735	1,735
1998	1,459	1,541	1,713	1,768	1,768
1999	1,482	1,564	1,740	1,794	1,794
2000	1,499	1,583	1,764	1,816	1,816

SOURCE: Conversion of data in Table 4-9 to full-time equivalents.

ing the sword of selective service hanging over the heads of many young men. For the 1970–1973 years, when the effect of the draft had largely disappeared, the percentage of students in four-year colleges engaged in part-time study was 21 percent, compared with 25 percent in the 1955–1962 years.

Table 4-13 shows the ratio of FTE enrollment to a weighted average of first-time FTE enrollment one to six years earlier. From 1960 to 1972 actual figures are reported; the ratio is projected beginning with 1973, stabilizing at 3.9 by 1980.

At first glance a ratio of 3.9:1 appears high for a system where the ratio of baccalaureate degrees to first-time FTE enrollment four years earlier is not more than .60. Bureau of Census data

	FTE undergraduate enrollment	Weighted average of FTE first-time enrollment	Column (1)/
Year	*(1)*	*(2)*	*column (2)*
Actual			
1960	2,535	714	3.550
1961	2,768	782	3.540
1962	2,972	831	3.576
1963	3,163	874	3.619
1964	3,493	945	3.696
1965	3,966	1,056	3.756
1966	4,256	1,129	3.770
1967	4,582	1,191	3.847
1968	4,977	1,273	3.910
1969	5,336	1,357	3.932
1970	5,586	1,445	3.866
1971	5,753	1,484	3.877
1972	5,764	1,493	3.861
Projected			
1973			3.85
1974			3.85
1975			3.85
1976			3.86
1977			3.87
1978			3.88
1979			3.89
1980			3.90
↓			↓
2000			3.90

TABLE 4-13 *Relationship between FTE undergraduate degree-credit enrollment and weighted average of FTE first-time enrollment*

SOURCE: Calculations by the author.

(Table 3-7) would suggest a ratio of 3:1 for both full-time and part-time students. However, Bureau of Census data gives "first-year" students, not "first-time" students, and thus a lower ratio would result.

If one imagined a stationary state where enrollment levels were unchanged over time and where every student remained in college until completion of the B.A., the minimal ratio of first-time to total undergraduates would be 4:1. In real life, however, at least three factors would contribute to a higher ratio. First, probably close to 10 percent of student registrations at the beginning of any term turn out to be failures, withdrawals, or incompletes—thus the ratio would be 4.4:1 even in the stationary-state model. Second, full-time is ordinarily defined as 12 credit hours when 15 or 16 is the standard load; thus, the total student FTE census might be 5 to 15 percent higher on the average than a standard four-year degree-completion program would imply. And, third, a small but significant proportion of students enter college at some point other than the fall term, and thus do not get counted as first-time students in the fall census. All these factors contribute to a higher apparent ratio of total to first-time enrollments. These modifying factors, however, are themselves relatively stable over time (with the possible exception of the third in a period when recently discharged veterans are entering college), and therefore the NCES-reported ratio of total to first-time enrollments seems to be a reasonable basis on which to project future enrollments.

Table 4-14 gives the five alternative projections of FTE undergraduate enrollments for the rest of the century. Figure 4-7 illustrates these alternative enrollment paths. For 1980, alternatives A and B are 6 percent and 2.6 percent, respectively, lower than the middle projection (C); alternatives D and E are 1.9 percent and 4.9 percent higher than C. As indicated earlier, the author feels at this time that C is the most likely enrollment path, that B and D are within a reasonably high probability range, and that A and E are rather unprobable extremes.

Before leaving undergraduate enrollments it may also be useful to speculate about the likely division of degree-credit students between the two-year and four-year colleges. This division is not as critically important as is the aggregate enrollment estimate in determining the likely demand for future college teachers, but the distribution between the sectors tells

TABLE 4-14 *Actual and projected FTE undergraduate degree-credit enrollment to 2000 under five alternatives (in thousands)*

Year	Series A	Series B	Series C	Series D	Series E
Actual					
1960			2,535		
1961			2,768		
1962			2,972		
1963			3,163		
1964			3,493		
1965			3,966		
1966			4,256		
1967			4,582		
1968			4,977		
1969			5,336		
1970			5,586		
1971			5,753		
1972			5,764		
Projected					
1973	5,852	5,852	5,852	5,852	5,852
1974	5,883	5,898	5,902	5,944	5,944
1975	5,971	6,014	6,037	6,110	6,125
1976	5,983	6,145	6,188	6,292	6,334
1977	6,177	6,289	6,358	6,478	6,564
1978	6,266	6,421	6,522	6,639	6,763
1979	6,387	6,582	6,718	6,850	7,018
1980	6,470	6,704	6,880	7,012	7,219
1981	6,478	6,743	6,950	7,090	7,316
1982	6,458	6,759	6,993	7,141	7,383
1983	6,338	6,657	6,919	7,079	7,316
1984	6,178	6,505	6,794	6,962	7,196
1985	5,987	6,318	6,642	6,809	7,032
1986	5,811	6,135	6,486	6,661	6,876
1987	5,729	6,053	6,439	6,646	6,821
1988	5,733	6,057	6,486	6,720	6,856
1989	5,772	6,088	6,560	6,829	6,938
1990	5,682	6,002	6,490	6,782	6,837

TABLE 4-14 *(continued)*

Year	Series A	Series B	Series C	Series D	Series E
1991	5,460	5,764	6,263	6,552	6,603
1992	5,269	5,561	6,068	6,357	6,380
1993	5,156	5,444	5,967	6,228	6,240
1994	5,335	5,452	5,987	6,248	6,252
1995	5,210	5,495	6,061	6,302	6,302
1996	5,277	5,573	6,162	6,396	6,400
1997	5,390	5,694	6,299	6,525	6,525
1998	5,507	5,815	6,451	6,669	6,669
1999	5,620	5,928	6,583	6,802	6,802
2000	5,710	6,029	6,696	6,919	6,919

SOURCE: Based on Tables 4-12 and 4-13.

FIGURE 4-7   *Projected FTE undergraduate degree-credit enrollment to 2000 under five alternatives (in thousands)*

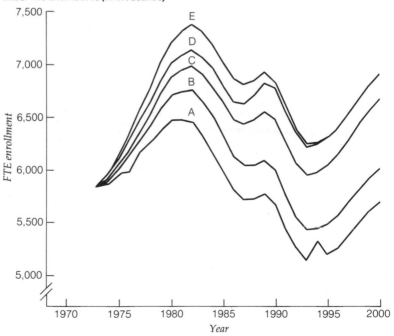

SOURCE: Table 4-14.

one something about the kinds of teachers who may be required. It is also likely that the errors will be greater in estimating enrollments for each of these subgroups than it will be for the aggregate, since there is another whole set of variables (for example, relative tuitions, upper-division transfer policies, changes in admissions selectivity) to contend with.

Table 4-15 shows the division between four-year and two-year institutions from 1960 to the present, and projects ahead using Series C aggregate enrollment estimates. The two-year colleges increased their enrollment share significantly in the 1964–1968 period, when total enrollment increased dramatically, but have made more modest inroads since 1968. Approximately two out of every five students entering college today matriculate at a two-year college, as opposed to one out of four a decade ago. Looking ahead 10 years, NCES projects a nearly 50-50 split for first-time enrollments, and assumes that the percentage of FTE total undergraduate enrollment in the two-year colleges will rise from 20.8 percent in 1972 to 27.8 percent in 1982. As indicated in the discussion of Table 4-11, this observer doubts that the two-year colleges will continue to increase their market share at the same rate that occurred in 1962–1972.

As indicated in the right-hand columns of Table 4-15, the two-year–four-year division assumed here shows a modest further increase for the junior college sector to 1980, then a leveling off at 22.5 percent. As argued above, it is anticipated in this projection that admissions selectivity in four-year colleges will adjust so as to minimize possible contraction in the 1980s, and an increasing rate of transfer to upper-division study in the senior institutions is also assumed.

The big enrollment growth in the two-year colleges was accompanied by extraordinary growth in the number and enrollment capacity of community colleges. To a considerable extent, supply created its own demand, and construction preceded enrollment demand. However, the construction of new facilities over the last year or two has been reduced to a trickle, and it seems likely that two-year enrollments will grow more slowly. Further complicating the picture is a rapid rise over the last several years in enrollment in non-degree-credit programs in two-year colleges—from 220,000 in 1963 to 1 million in 1973. In the face of this continued growth in nondegree programs, it

TABLE 4-15 *FTE enrollment of undergraduates in four-year and two-year institutions, actual and projected (based on Series C) (in thousands)*

Year	Total FTE undergraduates	FTE undergraduates in		Percent undergraduates in	
		Four-year institutions	Two-year institutions	Four-year institutions	Two-year institutions
Actual					
1962	2,972	2,564	408	86.3	13.7
1963	3,163	2,737	426	86.5	13.5
1964	3,493	2,992	501	85.7	14.3
1965	3,966	3,355	611	84.6	15.4
1966	4,256	3,566	690	83.8	16.2
1967	4,582	3,811	771	83.2	16.8
1968	4,977	4,055	922	81.5	18.5
1969	5,336	4,260	1,076	79.8	20.2
1970	5,586	4,459	1,127	79.8	20.2
1971	5,753	4,558	1,195	79.2	20.8
1972	5,764	4,564	1,200	79.2	20.8
Projected					
1973	5,852	4,611	1,241	78.8	21.2
1974	5,902	4,633	1,269	78.5	21.5
1975	6,037	4,721	1,316	78.2	21.8
1976	6,188	4,827	1,361	78.0	22.0
1977	6,358	4,947	1,411	77.8	22.2
1978	6,522	5,068	1,454	77.7	22.3
1979	6,718	5,213	1,505	77.6	22.4
1980	6,880	5,332	1,548	77.5	22.5
1981	6,950	5,396	1,564	↑	↑
1982	6,993	5,420	1,573		
1983	6,919	5,362	1,557		
1984	6,794	5,265	1,529		
1985	6,642	5,148	1,494		
1986	6,486	5,027	1,459		
1987	6,439	4,990	1,449		
1988	6,486	5,027	1,459		
1989	6,560	5,084	1,476		
1990	6,490	5,030	1,460		

TABLE 4-15 *(continued)*

Year	Total FTE undergraduates	FTE undergraduates in		Percent undergraduates in	
		Four-year institutions	*Two-year institutions*	*Four-year institutions*	*Two-year institutions*
1991	6,263	4,854	1,409		
1992	6,068	4,703	1,365		
1993	5,967	4,623	1,344		
1994	5,987	4,640	1,347		
1995	6,061	4,697	1,364		
1996	6,162	4,776	1,386		
1997	6,299	4,882	1,417		
1998	6,451	5,000	1,451		
1999	6,583	5,102	1,481	↓	↓
2000	6,696	5,189	1,507	77.5	22.5

SOURCES: Actual data from U.S. Office of Education (1974); projections are the author's.

seems even more likely that degree-credit enrollments will grow somewhat more slowly than in the past.

NCES projections for 1972 to 1982 anticipate a 25 percent expansion in FTE two-year college enrollments and a 1 percent growth for undergraduate and first-professional enrollment in senior institutions. [4] The projections in Table 4-15 are considerably more optimistic in terms of overall enrollment, and project 31 percent and 19 percent growth for the two-year and four-year colleges respectively between 1972 and 1982. The next several years need careful watching to see which of these two patterns develops.

The actual growth paths are not independent of pricing decisions in the various sectors. If tuition levels in public senior institutions rise along the lines suggested by the Carnegie Commission,[5] while community college tuitions remain at or close to zero, it could well happen that the two-year colleges will continue to increase their share of the market while enroll-

[4]U.S. Office of Education (1975, computed from Tables 8, 12, and 17).

[5]The Carnegie Commission on Higher Education (1973a) proposed a gradual increase in tuition from about 20 percent of educational cost to 33 percent by 1983.

ments in four-year institutions decline. However, if the price advantage of the two-year college now existing in most states is diminished over the decade, their market share might stabilize or even possibly decline. Whatever the eventual balance between two-year and four-year institutions, it seems likely that the private sector may be most severely hit by the contraction in the size of the college-age group after 1980.

5. Total Enrollment in Higher Education

Changes in undergraduate enrollment are the result of demographic changes on the one hand and the gradual shift in societal expectations on the other. Going to college has become the expectation of most youths and their parents over the last generation, and college education can be considered the educational analogue of a "consumers good" in the general economy. That is to say, undergraduate education is "purchased" primarily for the enrichment of life in its intellectual, social, and cultural context and only secondarily as "investment" in marketable job skills.

At the postbaccalaureate level, however, decisions to pursue advanced education are commonly job and career oriented; graduate and professional degree education are more nearly "investment goods" in the economic analogue.

Economic forces in the short run have only minimal effect on the level of undergraduate enrollment and are reflected largely in variations in the family's ability to meet college expenses. Thus, recessions in the general economy are reflected more in the choice of college (for example, substitution of low-cost local public education for higher-cost residential or private college) and in the choice of full-time or part-time status. Prospective job availability may significantly influence choice of major in college, but appears to have little impact on the decision of whether or not to attend college.[1]

At the graduate level, by contrast, market forces have a

---

[1]Stated differently, in a recession the family may have greater difficulty in meeting college costs, but this is partly offset by the fact that opportunity costs are lower. Forgone income is the major (although imputed) cost of college attendance, and if the alternative to college is thought to be unemployment, the opportunity cost becomes zero.

greater—although perhaps lagged—impact. Few persons would undertake the rigors of a Ph.D. program in seventeenth-century literature or particle physics, or go through medical school and internship, unless they intended to make their careers in such fields. (Legal training is one partial exception, although even those who do not intend to practice law per se ordinarily seek a J.D. or LL.B. as an avenue to preferred employment in government or industry.) Thus, the student attends graduate or professional school to attain expertise in a particular field, whereas in undergraduate college the baccalaureate degree is more often the goal, and the field of study is only a secondary (and often a mid-course) consideration.

When projecting enrollments, therefore, undergraduate study may most appropriately be handled by what is commonly called a fixed-coefficients model. In this framework, as indicated in Chapter 4, one can attempt to determine long-term trends in the relationship between high school graduation, college.entrance, and degree completion and to project into the future assuming that external forces or events do not significantly impinge on the behavior of students. (Fixed coefficients are not necessarily constant over time, but they are assumed to be independent rather than dependent variables.) Graduate enrollments, on the other hand, with their focus on career specialization, can be assumed to be much more responsive to current expectations concerning career opportunities.

Projections of graduate enrollment will be approached in this and succeeding chapters on two bases. In this chapter, a rough first approximation will be made in a manner similar to that used for undergraduate projections; in a later chapter, the fixed-coefficients assumption will be replaced by a variable-coefficients recursive-enrollment model in which market forces are assumed to influence student inputs. The coefficients used in this chapter are not completely divorced from market forces— that is, declining entrance and doctoral completion rates are assumed in the period when there are likely to be supply surpluses—but the coefficients are "fixed" by the outlook of the future as seen from 1974's vantage point.

GRADUATE ENROLLMENT The fastest-growing sector in higher education in the 1960s, except for the community colleges, was graduate education. Between 1960 and 1970, graduate enrollment grew by 153 percent. Since 1970, however, as the sellers' market advantage for students receiving advanced degrees has slackened, growth has been more moderate.

Enrollment and degree projections are difficult at the graduate level, for there are differing trends in various disciplines in response to different labor market conditions and changing degrees of intellectual excitement and apparent relevance. At the undergraduate level, fields such as engineering, psychology, nursing, or biology may increase or decrease their share of total enrollment over several years depending upon current fashions and job prospects—but total undergraduate enrollment is little affected. This is less true at the graduate level, where students decide upon graduate study primarily on the basis of whether they wish to become a professional in a particular field of study. There is a modest amount of mobility across fields, particularly in the sciences—a student may weigh alternative career paths in physics, engineering, or mathematics, for instance—but poor job prospects in literature do not divert many students into doctoral programs in anthropology or philosophy.

Despite the somewhat different set of motivating forces at the graduate level, the provisional attempt to project graduate enrollment in this chapter (modified in Chapter 7) will deal with aggregates as though the decision to pursue an advanced degree was primary and field was secondary. Alternatively, one could attempt to project enrollments field by field, but attempts by the author and others to do this and then aggregate fields have usually resulted in even greater errors. The relatively consistent trends in the relationship between college graduation, entrance to graduate study, and eventual degree completion also lend support to the approach as a first attempt to assess the likely magnitude of future graduate enrollments.

Table 5-1 shows the relationship between first-year graduate enrollments and baccalaureate degrees since 1960. Column (1) shows annual B.A.'s granted, while column (2) gives a weighted moving average of B.A.'s more appropriately related to first-year graduate study. In weighting baccalaureate degrees, 40 percent weights are given to B.A.'s in year $t - 1$ and $t - 2$, and 20 percent to $t - 4$. The latter weight is provided in recognition of the fact that small proportions of first-year students received their baccalaureate degrees from 3 to 10 or more

TABLE 5-1 *Comparison of baccalaureate degrees and first-year graduate enrollment (in thousands), 1960–1974*

Year	B.A.'s granted (1)	Weighted average of B.A.'s (2)	First-year graduate enrollment (3)	Ratio column (3)/column (2) (4)
1960–61	369	350	206	.589
1961–62	388	361	223	.618
1962–63	416	374	246	.658
1963–64	466	395	277	.701
1964–65	501	427	317	.742
1965–66	520	468	358	.765
1966–67	558	492	388	.789
1967–68	632	524	426	.813
1968–69	728	576	456	.792
1969–70	792	648	492	.759
1970–71	840	720	528	.733
1971–72	876	779	539	.692
1972–73	941*	832	558†	.671
1973–74	972*	884	585†	.662

SOURCE: U.S. Office of Education (1974, Tables 21 & B-7).

*Estimates by author, based on lagged relationship to first-time college entrants.

†Estimates based on reported percentage change indicated in surveys by Council of Graduate Schools.

years previously; the $t - 4$ weight is a proxy for these delayed entrants.

Column (4) in Table 5-1 shows the ratio of first-year graduate students to the weighted moving average of baccalaureate degrees. The ratio peaked in 1967–68 and declined to a 1973–74 level about equal to that of 1962–63. In the mid-1960s, several trends reinforced one another and boosted the proportion of college graduates who continued on to graduate school. The post-Sputnik expansion of graduate education, triggered by exciting developments on the scientific front and strongly assisted by rapidly expanding federal programs of student support, encouraged growth in doctoral programs. In addition, until about 1968 the relative shortage of Ph.D.'s to meet expanding teaching and research needs created a favorable doctoral labor market situation in which salaries rose steadily and job opportunities were relatively attractive. Added to this

TABLE 5-2 *Projected first-year graduate enrollment based on projected B.A.'s awarded (in thousands)*

Year	B.A.'s	Weighted average of B.A.'s	First year graduate enrollment weighted average of B.A.'s	Estimated first-year graduate enrollment
1972–73	941	884	0.671	558
1973–74	972	933	0.662	585
1974–75	968	951	0.660	616
1975–76	944	953	0.655	623
1976–77	943	949	0.650	619
1977–78	970	959	0.645	612
1978–79	1,005	979	0.640	614
1979–80	1,051	1,011	0.630	617
1980–81	1,074	1,044	0.620	627
1981–82	1,102	1,072	0.610	637
1982–83	1,138	1,106	0.600	643
1983–84	1,169	1,163	↑	664
1984–85	1,163	1,153		698
1985–86	1,167	1,159		692
1986–87	1,147	1,159		695
1987–88	1,104	1,134		695
1988–89	1,069	1,103		680
1989–90	1,053	1,078		662
1990–91	1,058	1,065		647
1991–92	1,087	1,072		639
1992–93	1,115	1,092		643
1993–94	1,085	1,092		655
1994–95	1,002	1,052		655
1995–96	957	1,007		631
1996–97	969	988		604
1997–98	1,000	988		593
1998–99	1,027	1,002	↓	593
1999–2000	1,054	1,027	0.600	601

SOURCE: Projections by the author.

was the incentive provided by selective service; until the summer of 1969 draft deferments were available for students enrolled in graduate school. The concerted action of those three forces pushed the graduate school entrance rate up to its peak of .813 in 1967–68.

After 1967 federal spending on research and development began to decline in real terms, the rate of overall enrollment expansion began to decrease and make academic job opportunities somewhat more competitive, and in 1968 (effective in the summer of 1969) draft deferments for graduate study were withdrawn (except for the health professions). The ratio of first-year graduate students to B.A.'s began, therefore, to decline beginning in 1968–69, and appeared to be still declining modestly in 1972 and 1973.

Table 5-2 gives a provisional projection of graduate first-year enrollments based on the interpretation of recent trends indicated in Table 5-1. It is assumed that the ratio of first-year graduate students to baccalaureate degrees declines by .005 annually until 1978, and then, as college enrollments level off and the presumed demand for new college teachers declines, decreases by .010 until it levels off at .600 in 1982. In a later chapter, market responses will be considered in more detail and projected graduate enrollments reviewed again, but at this stage Table 5-2 seems to provide a reasonable first approximation.

In Table 5-2 it appears that first-year graduate enrollments are likely to rise gradually to a peak in 1986–87 about 22 percent above 1973–74 levels. Thereafter, a gradual decline of about 12 percent is projected out to the late 1990s.

Total enrollment at the graduate level is closely correlated with first-year enrollment, as indicated in 1960–1973 portion of Table 5-3. The ratio has stayed close to 1.7:1 over the last 14 years, rising slightly between 1966 and 1968 when draft deferments apparently boosted the continuation rate, and dropping back to about 1.7 when deferments ended. As a first approximation to projecting total graduate enrollment, only a modest diminution in the ratio seems reasonable. Table 5-3 assumes a 1.68:1 ratio until 1981, then diminishing to 1.65:1 in the period when undergraduate enrollments are projected to decrease. Even in Chapter 7, when we allow for some feedback effect on enrollment in response to labor market pros-

TABLE 5-3 *Relationship between first-year graduate enrollment and total graduate enrollment: actual 1959–60 to 1971–72 and projected 1972–73 to 1990–91 (in thousands)*

Year	First-year enrollment (1)	Total enrollment (2)	Total FTE enrollment	Ratio column (2)/ column (1)
Actual				
1959–60	192	331		1.72
1960–61	206	356		1.73
1961–62	223	386		1.73
1962–63	246	422		1.72
1963–64	277	464		1.68
1964–65	317	540		1.70
1965–66	358	619		1.73
1966–67	388	682		1.76
1967–68	426	753		1.77
1968–69	456	797		1.75
1969–70	492	828		1.68
1970–71	528	900		1.71
1971–72	539	908		1.68
Projected				
1972–73	558	943	576	1.69
1973–74	585	988	603	1.69
1974–75	616	1,035	631	1.68
1975–76	623	1,047	639	↑
1976–77	619	1,040	634	
1977–78	612	1,028	627	
1978–79	614	1,032	630	
1979–80	617	1,036	632	↓
1980–81	627	1,053	642	1.68
1981–82	637	1,064	649	1.67
1982–83	643	1,067	651	1.66
1983–84	664	1,096	669	1.65
1984–85	698	1,152	703	↑
1985–86	692	1,142	697	
1986–87	695	1,147	700	
1987–88	695	1,147	700	
1988–89	680	1,122	684	
1989–90	662	1,092	666	↓
1990–91	647	1,068	651	1.65

SOURCE: Actual data from U.S. Office of Education (1974, Table B-7); projections by the author.

pects, the impact is presumed to be felt principally at the entry point rather than in attrition rates between entry and degree completion.

The projected total graduate enrollment series rises modestly from approximately 1 million in 1974 to 1.15 million in the mid-1980s, gradually declining again in the late 1980s. Experience suggests that the annual variations, influenced by student assistance, institutional policy, and job market prospects, will be greater than shown in Table 5-3; this table attempts to project the trend line based upon the observed relationship between the baccalaureate pool of potential graduate students and actual entrance over the last 10 to 15 years. Five to ten years ahead, actual experience should be fairly close to projected enrollments; the majority of Ph.D.'s to be granted in 1979 are already in graduate school, and the majority to be awarded in 1984 are already in undergraduate school. Beyond 10 years the estimates are subject to an increasing margin of error. However, distinguishing graduate from undergraduate enrollments makes projections of faculty needs somewhat more reliable since there are significant differences between student-faculty ratios at these different educational levels.

Table 5-2 indicated the overall relationship between B.A.'s and first-year graduate enrollment; however, there are significant differences in the series for men and women. At the high school graduation level, up to the 1920s the graduation rate (as a percentage of 18-year-olds) was about 50 percent higher for women. By 1960 the graduation rate for women was .706 and for men .641. By 1974 the differential had finally disappeared.

At the college graduation level, the situation has been the reverse. In the 1920s there were twice as many male graduates as there were female. By 1960, 62 percent of college graduates were male; by 1974 it was less than 55 percent.

Table 5-4 shows the weighted average of B.A.'s (as calculated in Table 5-1) and the division of first-year graduate enrollment by sex from 1955 through 1973. The graduate enrollment rate rose quite rapidly after 1957, and peaked in 1967–68 for both men and women. The percentage change was slightly greater for the women on the upswing, and the decline over the past six years has been less than for men. The period from 1963–64 through 1968–69, when the draft faced many male college graduates and when the Ph.D. job market was at its

TABLE 5-4 *Relationship between weighted average of bachelor's degrees and first-year graduate enrollment by sex, 1955–1973 (in thousands)*

Year	Weighted average of bachelor's degrees			First-year graduate enrollment			Graduate enrollment rate		
	Men	*Women*	*Total*	*Men*	*Women*	*Total*	*Men*	*Women*	*Total*
Actual									
1955	180	111	291	88	41	130	.49	.37	.45
1956	173	109	282	98	45	144	.57	.41	.51
1957	183	112	295	102	47	149	.56	.42	.51
1958	198	115	313	118	54	171	.60	.47	.55
1959	212	122	334	131	60	192	.62	.49	.57
1960	218	132	350	140	66	206	.64	.50	.59
1961	223	138	361	152	71	223	.68	.51	.62
1962	227	147	374	166	80	246	.73	.54	.66
1963	234	161	395	186	92	277	.79	.57	.70
1964	247	180	427	210	107	317	.85	.59	.74
1965	268	200	468	235	123	358	.88	.62	.76
1966	287	211	492	253	136	388	.88	.64	.79
1967	302	222	524	269	157	426	.89	.71	.81
1968	322	254	576	278	178	456	.86	.70	.79
1969	366	282	648	295	198	492	.81	.70	.76
1970	409	311	720	316	212	528	.77	.68	.73
1971	440	339	779	319*	220*	539*	.73	.65	.69
1972	466*	366*	832*	326*	232*	558*	.70	.63	.67
1973	487*	395*	884*	338*	247*	585*	.69	.62	.66
Projected									
1975	522	431	953	354	269	623	.68	.62	.66
1980	558	486	1,044	349	278	627	.63	.58	.62
1985	608	551	1,159	374	318	692	.62	.58	.60
1990	549	516	1,065	343	304	647	.62	.58	.60

SOURCES: 1955–1971 data calculated from U.S. Office of Education (*Projections of Educational Statistics,* various years); projections by the author.

*See notes to Table 5-1 for the derivation of these estimates.

best, was a high plateau for the male rate. The bottom four lines show the implicit assumptions involved in the projections in Table 5-2. It is expected that both rates will stabilize near a ratio of .60. The greatest spread between the male and female enrollment rates was in 1964, when .26 separated the rates. By

1973 the gap was only .07, and it is assumed to stabilize with the male rate .04 greater than the rate for females.

Women have come to be much more heavily represented in graduate enrollments since the mid-1960s, particularly in the last two or three years as affirmative action programs have diminished placement and salary differentials (see Cartter & Ruhter, 1975). By 1980, it is assumed that 45 percent of first-year graduate students will be women. It should be noted, however, that a larger proportion of women stop at the master's degree level, so there is still a fairly marked (although diminishing) difference in the rate of Ph.D. completion by sex.

In keeping with the development of provisional graduate enrollment estimates, it may be useful to also project the level of Ph.D. degrees that is likely to be associated with this enrollment path. Table 5-5 shows the relationship between first-year enrollments (lagged four to six years) and earned doctorates, by sex. The ratio of male doctorates to first-year male students inched up from slightly below 10 percent in 1960–61 to slightly over 11 percent in 1969–70, and then began to decline again. One presumes that the combined effect of the draft, job prospects, and availability of fellowship aid was responsible both for the rise and the decline in the ratio. The ratio for women, while only about one-third the level for men, climbed steadily from 1960 to 1970, and appears to have about leveled off. Improved job prospects for women doctorates probably buoyed this ratio even while it was falling for men (ibid.). From 1972–73 onward, doctorates are projected assuming the degree ratios shown in the right-hand columns. It is assumed that the male completion rate falls from 10.5 percent to 9.5 percent and that the rate for women stabilizes at 3.5 percent. One might assume a steady narrowing of the sex differential; however, a high proportion of women are attracted into fields where termination at the master's level is more common (for example, education and fine arts) and a larger proportion of women than of men graduate students aspire to teaching careers in institutions that do not ordinarily require the doctorate (for example, community colleges). The projected proportion of doctorates earned by women by 1980 (22.4 percent) is higher than at any time in the past.

Although projections of doctoral degrees in this first approximation for 1985 and 1990 are indicated in Table 5-5, before

TABLE 5-5 *Relationship of earned doctorates to first-year graduate enrollment four to six years previously, by sex*

Year	First-year graduate enrollments (in thousands)			Earned doctorates			Ratio of doctorates to average enrollment, lagged four to six years
	Men	*Women*	*Total*	*Men*	*Women*	*Total*	
1955–56	88	41	130	8,118	885	8,903	
1956–57	98	45	144	7,817	939	8,756	
1957–58	102	47	149	7,978	964	8,942	
1958–59	118	54	171	8,371	989	9,369	
1959–60	131	60	192	8,801	1,028	9,829	
1960–61	140	66	206	9,463	1,112	10,575	.099 .025 .075
1961–62	152	71	223	10,377	1,245	11,622	.098 .026 .075
1962–63	166	80	246	11,448	1,374	12,822	.098 .026 .075
1963–64	186	92	277	12,955	1,535	14,490	.100 .026 .076
1964–65	210	107	317	14,692	1,775	16,467	.104 .027 .080
1965–66	235	123	358	16,121	2,117	18,237	.106 .129 .081
1966–67	253	136	388	18,163	2,454	20,617	.108 .030 .083
1967–68	269	157	426	20,183	2,906	23,089	.108 .031 .082
1968–69	278	178	456	22,752	3,436	26,188	.108 .032 .083
1969–70	295	198	492	25,890	3,976	29,866	.111 .033 .084
1970–71	316	212	528	27,530	4,577	32,107	.109 .033 .082
1971–72	319	319	539	28,112	5,258	33,370	.105 .033 .079
1972–73	326	232	558	28,910	6,040	34,950	.103 .034 .076
1973–74	338	247	585	29,925	6,665	36,590	.101 .034 .074
1974–75	348	266	614	30,000	7,030	38,030	.100 .034 .073
1975–76	352	274	626	31,710	7,745	39,455	.099 .035 .072
1976–77	357	279	636	32,115	8,155	40,270	.098 .035 .072
1977–78	361	286	647	32,720	8,690	41,410	.097 .035 .071
1978–79	364	291	655	33,215	9,180	42,395	.096 .035 .070
1979–80	366	297	663	33,470	9,555	43,025	.095 .035 .069
1980–81	367	301	668	33,885	9,790	43,675	.095 .035 .069
1985–86			715			45,810	.068
1990–91			674			48,415	.068

SOURCES: 1955–1972 data from U.S. Office of Education (1974, Tables 21 & B-7); projections by the author.

attempting to analyze feedback effects these should be interpreted only as trend projections. The only point worth noting is that present trends, if interpreted correctly, suggest that the growth rate in doctorates awarded would appreciably slow down from the 76 percent increase between 1965 and 1970, to 23 percent between 1970 and 1975, to 11 percent and 5 percent increases in the succeeding five-year periods. In Chapter 7 market responses will be integrated in an attempt to refine doctoral degree projections.

FIRST-PROFESSIONAL DEGREE ENROLLMENT

Until 1967 first-professional degree enrollment data were lumped together with undergraduate enrollments, but beginning with fall 1967 NCES has reported separately both first-year and total first-professional enrollment. From this limited 1967–1971 enrollment data and from information on degrees, one can reasonably well reconstruct earlier enrollment patterns. A high percentage of entrants into the professional fields complete the degree and thus one can work backward from reported annual degrees to estimate enrollments in years prior to 1967. For the several documented years, the ratio of medical and dental degrees to first-year students four years earlier is .94; in the case of law, the ratio of degrees to first-year students three years earlier is .75.

In Table 5-6 the information in column (1) is known through 1972. In columns (2) through (6) the data is as reported by NCES for 1967 through 1971, imputed from degree data for 1960–1966, and projected from 1972 onward assuming that FTE first-professional enrollment remains constant at its 1968–1972 average of 25 percent of average baccalaureates awarded three and four years earlier.[2] Degree projections after 1972 are based on projected first-year enrollments three and four years earlier.

Table 5-6 must be treated as a very rough approximation based on inadequate data. However, for the remainder of the 1970s the degree and enrollment projections appear reasonable, and, given the diminishing shortages in health manpower

---

[2]This implies, on the average, that first-professional students represent 7.14 percent of their corresponding undergraduate graduation class. Approximately 65 percent of first-professional students are engaged in a three-year course of advanced study (i.e., law, theology), and 35 percent are in four-year programs (i.e., medicine, dentistry). We have used 3.5 years (instead of 3.35) as the average in determining the ratio of professional enrollment to lagged baccalaureates.

TABLE 5-6 *Estimated first-professional degree enrollment and reported degrees to 1973, and projected to 1990 (in thousands)*

Year	First-professional degrees (1)	First-year enrollment (2)	Total enrollment (3)	Full-time enrollment (4)	Part-time enrollment (5)	Total FTE enrollment (6)
1960	26.2	33	96	86	10	91
1961	26.5	34	98	88	10	93
1962	27.1	36	102	92	10	97
1963	27.7	38	109	98	11	104
1964	28.8	40	115	103	12	109
1965	30.8	42	123	111	12	117
1966	32.5	43	128	115	13	122
1967	34.8	47	138	125	10	130
1968	36.0	47	152	126	12	132
1969	35.7	56	152	138	14	145
1970	37.9	63	170	155	15	163
1971	45.0	70	191	173	18	182
1972	50.2	72	207	187	20	197
1973	55.8	74	219	199	20	209
1974	60.5	77	232	210	22	221
1975	61.3	78	244	221	23	233
1976	63.4	77	253	229	24	241
1977	65.1	76	251	228	23	240
1978	65.1	77	249	226	23	238
1979	64.3	79	249	226	23	238
1980	64.3	83	255	231	24	243
1981	65.9	86	264	239	25	252
1982	68.0	89	275	249	26	262
1983	71.0	92	282	256	26	269
1984	73.5	94	289	262	27	276
1985	76.0	95	298	270	28	284
1986	78.1	96	304	276	28	290
1987	79.4	96	306	277	29	292
1988	80.2	92	305	276	29	291
1989	80.6	88	300	272	28	286
1990	79.0	87	290	263	27	277

SOURCES: 1960–1972 degrees (column 1) and 1967–1971 enrollment data (columns 2–5) from U.S. Office of Education (1974, Tables 19 & B-7); earlier enrollment estimates and projections by the author.

fields and some indications of surplus in law, it seems appropriate to anticipate a declining rate of growth after 1974 and a leveling off in the 1980s. With such limited historical time series, and the assumed responsiveness of professional enrollments to market forces, there is little point in carrying the projection beyond 1990.

Column (6) in Table 5-6 indicates estimated FTE enrollment, assuming that the 1967 to 1971 years are representative over time in terms of the division between full-time and part-time study.

COLLEGE GRADUATES ENTERING POSTBACCA-LAUREATE STUDY
In the case of graduate and first-professional degree study, first-year students were reported in Tables 5-1 and 5-6. It should be noted, however, that first-year graduate students include all registered graduate students who have not completed a full year of study—thus the number is considerably greater than the number of *first-time entrants* to graduate study. The Council of Graduate Schools (CGS) in its survey conducted jointly with the Educational Testing Service, reports 138,083 first-time students in 1971–72. Comparing total graduate enrollment and master's degrees awarded with reported NCES figures, the CGS survey appears to include about 65 percent of all graduate students in the country. Thus, for 1971–72 we can estimate that about 215,000 of the 539,000 first-year students were first-time entrants to graduate study. The ratios in Tables 5-1 and 5-2, therefore, should be multiplied by approximately .4 to estimate the percentage of B.A.'s who go on to graduate school. In the case of first-professional enrollments, on the other hand, reported first-year enrollments are apparently only about 10 percent greater than the number of first-time entrants. This reflects the virtually lock-step curriculum in the first year or two of medicine, dentistry, and legal studies and the high proportion of full-time students in professional schools.

Table 5-7 estimates the percentage of baccalaureate-degree students who enter graduate or post-B.A. professional-degree studies. (The latter category consists of about 50 percent law students, 35 percent in the medical professions, and 15 percent in other professional fields—such as theology.) Although these estimates are approximations, assuming a fixed relationship over time between first-time professional enrollments and

TABLE 5-7 *Ratios of estimated first-time students in professional and graduate schools in relation to weighted average of B.A.'s one to five years earlier (in thousands)*

Year	Weighted average of B.A.'s (1)	First-time professional enrollment (2)	First-time graduate enrollment (3)	Column (2)/ column (1)	Column (3)/ column (1)	[Column (2) + column (3)]/ column (1)
1955	291	26	55	.09	.19	.28
1956	282	27	62	.10	.22	.32
1957	295	27	65	.09	.22	.31
1958	313	27	71	.09	.23	.32
1959	334	28	75	.08	.22	.30
1960	350	28	81	.08	.23	.31
1961	361	29	89	.08	.25	.33
1962	374	31	98	.08	.26	.34
1963	395	32	111	.08	.28	.36
1964	427	34	130	.08	.30	.38
1965	468	36	147	.08	.31	.39
1966	492	37	152	.08	.31	.39
1967	524	40	175	.08	.33	.41
1968	576	40	188	.07	.33	.40
1969	648	48	203	.07	.31	.38
1970	720	54	216	.08	.30	.38
1971	779	60	215	.08	.28	.35
1972	832	61	223†	.07	.27	.34
1973	883*	63	233†	.07	.26	.33

*Preliminary data.

†Increases based on ETS-CGS surveys.

SOURCE: Estimates by the author, based on assumed ratios of first-time to first-year enrollments (see Tables 5-1 & 5-6).

degrees four years later, as well as a fixed relationship between first-time graduate students and first-year graduate enrollment, they seem consistent with general observations of the higher educational scene.

In the post-Sputnik years graduate entrance rates increased rapidly from an estimated 20 percent of baccalaureates to 33 percent by 1967. Beginning in 1969, as draft deferments in nonhealth fields were discontinued, and as job prospects for Ph.D.'s appeared somewhat less attractive in many fields, the percentage began to decline again. By contrast, first-professional degree enrollments expanded more slowly than did the baccalaureate pool between 1956 and 1969, but reversed this trend in 1970 and 1971 as both law and medical studies became relatively more attractive. A decline in the ratio occurred again in 1972 and 1973, reflecting the leveling off of law school enrollments. By the end of the 1980s the first-year enrollments in Tables 5-2 and 5-6 imply a combined first-time entrance rate of .33 into graduate and advanced professional studies, a return to the level of 1961.

COMBINED ENROLLMENT PROJECTIONS The projections for pre- and postbaccalaureate enrollment can now be combined to project total degree-credit enrollments to 1990. Table 5-8 brings the FTE projections together, and in column (5) gives a projection for all degree-credit enrollment. It should be recalled that the undergraduate projections are based on the median alternative high school graduation rates and college entrance rates that, from a vantage point of 1974, seem the most reasonable assumptions to the author. Table 5-9, however, indicates the variation in FTE enrollment projections that would result from substituting alternative rates. The author's earlier (1970) projections were based on assumptions that are close to the high graduation rate from high school and Series D college entrance rates. This combination would produce FTE enrollment projections 4.4 percent and 8.4 percent higher than in Table 5-8 for 1980 and 1990, respectively. If Series A and E are eliminated as extreme and rather unlikely growth paths, then the combinations of the two rates suggest a range of approximately ± 6 percent for 1980 and ± 8.5 percent for 1990.

While the range of likely error may seem relatively small in percentage terms, ± 8.5 percent means ± 630,530 students for 1990. As the next chapter will illustrate, that variation implies a difference of from 30,000 to 40,000 in total faculty required, a not insubstantial number in such a highly specialized job market.

Column (6) in Table 5-8 gives the NCES estimate of non-degree-credit enrollment to 1972, and its projection to 1982 in FTE terms (assuming, in this case, that four part-time students equal one FTE student). Ninety-two percent of nondegree enrollment is in two-year colleges, principally of a technical or vocational nature.

TABLE 5-8 *Actual and projected FTE enrollments, 1960–1990 (in thousands)*

Year	Undergraduate Four-year (1)	Undergraduate Two-year (2)	First-professional (3)	Graduate (4)	Total degree-credit (5)	Nondegree (6)	Total enrollment (7)
Actual							
1960			91				
1961			93				
1962	2,564	408	97	259	3,328	129	3,457
1963	2,737	426	104	280	3,547	154	3,701
1964	2,992	501	109	327	3,929	188	4,117
1965	3,355	611	117	377	4,460	228	4,688
1966	3,566	690	122	427	4,805	275	5,080
1967	3,811	771	130	462	5,174	303	5,477
1968	4,055	922	132	494	5,603	351	5,954
1969	4,260	1,076	145	519	6,000	314	6,314
1970	4,459	1,127	163	553	6,302	410	6,712
1971	4,558	1,195	182	561	6,496	509	7,005
1972	4,564	1,200	197	576	6,537	557	7,094
Projected							
1973	4,611	1,241	209	603	6,664	593	7,257
1974	4,633	1,269	221	631	6,754	629	7,383
1975	4,721	1,316	233	639	6,909	675	7,584
1976	4,827	1,361	241	634	7,063	713	7,776
1977	4,947	1,411	240	627	7,225	745	7,970
1978	5,068	1,454	238	630	7,390	779	8,169
1979	5,213	1,505	238	632	7,588	807	8,395
1980	5,332	1,548	243	642	7,765	826	8,591
1981	5,396	1,564	252	649	7,861	851	8,612
1982	5,420	1,573	262	651	7,906	865	8,761
1983	5,362	1,557	269	669	7,857	856	8,713
1984	5,265	1,529	276	703	7,773	841	8,614
1985	5,148	1,494	284	697	7,623	822	8,445
1986	5,027	1,459	290	700	7,476	802	8,278
1987	4,990	1,449	292	700	7,431	797	8,228
1988	5,027	1,459	291	684	7,461	802	8,263
1989	5,084	1,476	286	666	7,512	812	8,324
1990	5,030	1,460	277	651	7,418	803	8,221

SOURCES: Based on Tables 4-15, 5-3, and 5-6.

TABLE 5-9	*Alternative assumptions*	*1975*	*1980*	*1985*	*1990*

TABLE 5-9
***Variation in FTE
enrollment
projections
resulting from
alternative
assumptions (in
percentages)***

Alternative assumptions	*1975*	*1980*	*1985*	*1990*
High school graduation rates				
High		+1.5	+2.8	+4.0
Low		−0.4	−1.7	−3.6
College entrance rates				
Series A	−0.3	−2.3	−7.6	−11.0
Series B		−0.5	−2.5	−5.2
Series D	+1.0	+2.9	+3.1	+4.2
Series E	+1.1	+4.3	+6.6	+6.9

SOURCES: Calculated from Tables 4-3, 4-9, and 5-8.

Nondegree students are shown separately for two reasons. First, the kind of instructional staff required is commonly quite different from that required for associate degree programs and only infrequently includes Ph.D.-level personnel. And second, NCES staff who assemble the information are themselves somewhat distrustful of the validity and comparability of enrollment data. Reported enrollments have increased dramatically over the last several years, probably reflecting significant numbers of veterans enrolled in vocational programs, but also possibly because of changes in reporting practice. NCES projections are accepted uncritically in the absence of any other information, although, from 1982 onward, it is assumed that nondegree enrollments change in step with changes in two-year college degree-credit enrollment.[3]

Nondegree students are included in Table 5-8 to give an overall picture of space and resource requirements, but they will be excluded in assessing faculty needs in Chapter 6 on the assumption that most instructional personnel are more nearly the equivalent of secondary level.

COMPARISON OF ENROLLMENT PROJECTIONS Figure 5-1 presents the data in Table 5-8, giving the author's "best guess" based on observed trends up to fall 1973. Graduate and professional enrollments are carried ahead only to 1990 in this first approximation and will be modified in

---

[3]As noted in Chapter 4, projected nondegree enrollments may be subject to a wider margin of error than degree enrollments. They have been heavily affected by the enrollment of veterans in the post-Vietnam period, and many observers believe that the next revolution in higher education may be the implementation of lifelong recurrent education as a citizen's right.

Chapter 7 dealing with market feedback effects. Undergraduate enrollments, on the other hand, based on Alternative Series C assumptions (see Table 4-15), are carried out to the close of the century.

Figure 5-1 clearly reflects several quite different periods:

FIGURE 5-1 *Actual and projected FTE enrollment*

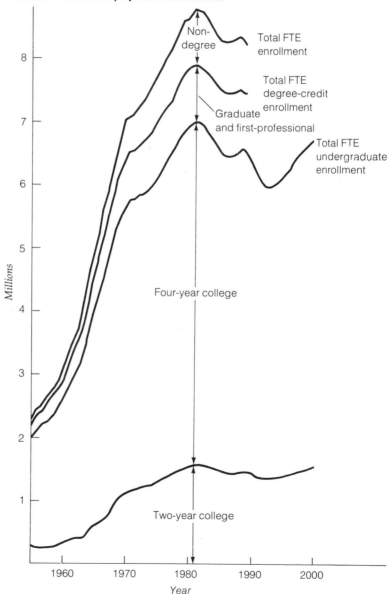

SOURCE: Table 5-8.

(1) rapid growth, particularly in 1964–1969, (2) a more moderate growth rate from 1970 to 1982, (3) contraction in 1983–1993 almost symmetrical to the growth pattern of the 1970s, and (4) partial recovery after 1993. The general pattern of these enrollment curves, at least up to the mid-1980s, was clear 10 years ago. It was the anticipated sharp decline in the growth rate after 1969 that first alerted this researcher to a potential doctoral manpower imbalance in the 1970s and 1980s, for the demand for new college faculty members is largely a function of the rate of growth in total enrollments. The extent of the likely enrollment contraction in the 1980s and 1990s, on the other hand, has only become clear over the last several years as the birthrate has continued to drop. Even the projected upturn in enrollment after 1993 depends upon as yet unborn children, but Series F projections by the Bureau of Census seem relatively conservative and are unlikely to overestimate the college-age population in the 1990s.

Figure 5-2 shows successive FTE degree-credit enrollment projections made by the U.S. Office of Education and NCES. Clearly, until the 1973 edition of *Projections of Educational Statistics* (published in May 1974), NCES did not foresee a slowing down in enrollment growth rates, and—as indicated in earlier chapters—the artificial limitation to only a 10-year time horizon did not alert readers to an impending major change in growth trends. Contrasting the pictures provided by Figures 5-1 and 5-2, the former, even if the projections should turn out to be mistaken by several percentage points, at least provides a warning signal that overexpansion is an imminent danger. To know that 1993 undergraduate enrollments are likely to be approximately the same level as 1973 suggests quite different strategies for coping with the intervening years than might be deduced from the 10-year time horizon in Figure 5-2.

For several of its reports the Carnegie Commission has projected enrollments ahead to the end of the century.[4] Gus Haggstrom developed a sophisticated statistical projections model for the Commission that was frequently revised as new demographic and enrollment data became available. The Commission used Haggstrom's 1970 Projection C as the basis of several of its early policy studies, but, by 1973, when the Commission

---

[4]See particularly *Carnegie Commission on Higher Education* (1971).

FIGURE 5-2 *U.S. Office of Education-NCES FTE degree-credit enrollment projections*

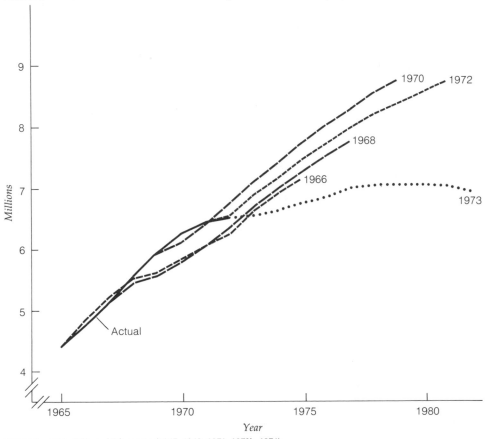

SOURCES: U.S. Office of Education (1967, 1969, 1971, 1973*b*, 1974).

prepared its final report, changes in birth and college attendance rates warranted a substantial revision.

Table 5-10 shows the Carnegie Commission's 1971 and revised 1973 projections for pre- and postbaccalaureate enrollments and compares these with the median enrollment projections developed in this and the preceding chapters. It should be noted that the estimates are for total enrollment, including nondegree students, according to the Carnegie Commission manner of reporting. The last lines, however, also show the projections developed here in FTE degree-credit terms.

The anticipated changes in total enrollment up to 1990 are very close in comparison with the 1973 Commission estimates. In the 1970s the projections developed here are slightly more

TABLE 5-10 *Comparison of enrollment projections, 1970–2000 (in thousands)*

	1970	1980	1990	2000	*Percentage change* 1970– 1980	1980– 1990	1990– 2000
CCHE (1971)							
Total enrollment	8,649	13,015	12,654	16,559	50.5	−2.8	30.9
Prebaccalaureate	7,443	11,082	10,587	14,123	48.9	−4.5	33.4
Postbaccalaureate	1,206	1,933	2,068	2,436	60.3	7.0	17.8
CCHE (1973)							
Total enrollment	8,649	11,446	10,555	13,209	33.3	−7.8	25.1
Prebaccalaureate	7,443	9,720	8,882	11,221	30.6	−8.6	26.3
Postbaccalaureate	1,206	1,726	1,673	1,988	43.1	−3.1	18.8
AMC (1974)							
Total enrollment	8,581	11,346	10,773		32.2	−5.1	
Prebaccalaureate	7,502	10,020	9,394	9,770	33.6	−6.2	4.0
Postbaccalaureate	1,079	1,326	1,379		22.9	4.0	
FTE degree-credit enrollment	6,302	7,765	7,418		23.2	−4.5	
Prebaccalaureate	5,586	6,880	6,490	6,696	23.2	−5.7	3.2
Postbaccalaureate	716	885	928		23.6	4.9	

SOURCES: Carnegie Commission on Higher Education (1971, Projection C; 1973*b*, Technical Note A). The author's projections are derived from Tables 4-15 and 5-8.

optimistic at the undergraduate level and less optimistic at the graduate level. For the 1980s, the Carnegie Commission projects an actual decline in postbaccalaureate enrollment, whereas here a modest increase is anticipated. (However, see market-response projections in Chapter 7.) The lower set of 1974 projections is in FTE degree-credit terms, which show a considerably more modest growth pattern. Since the demand for doctoral-level faculty is closely related to this latter magnitude, this set of comparisons is more relevant to our concern here than the gross headcount.

There is, however, a substantial difference between the two projection sources in the anticipated change between 1990 and 2000. Half of the difference in the prebaccalaureate projection for the year 2000 is due to the Carnegie Commission's choice of the Census Series E population projection and our choice of Series F. If we had used Series E, the prebaccalaureate total for

2000 would have been 10.75 million instead of 9.77, and the percentage increase over the 1990s decade 14 percent instead of 4 percent. For the latest reported year (1973) the actual birthrate fell between the two series, but was closer to Series F than to E. (See Chapter 3.)

In the 1973 edition of *Projections of Educational Statistics*, NCES, for the first time, has given alternative high and low enrollment projections. In Figure 5-3 these are plotted to 1982–83 (solid lines), and contrasted with our Series B, C, and D (broken lines). It is evident that the range of alternatives pro-

FIGURE 5-3 *Comparison of Series B, C, and D total degree-credit enrollment projections with NCES high- and low-enrollment projections*

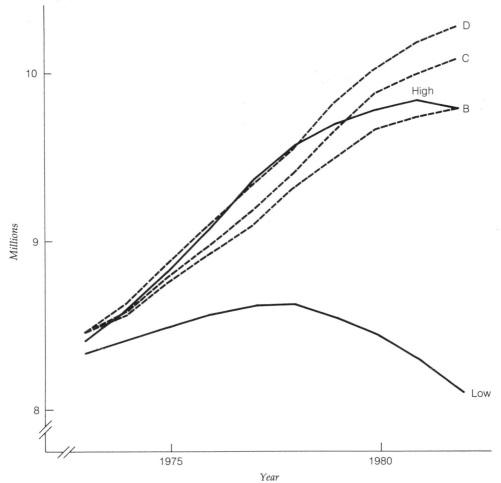

SOURCES: U.S. Office of Education (1974, Tables B-5 & B-6); and Table 4-15.

jected in this and the preceding chapter cluster around the NCES high estimate. Even Series A, which assumed frozen college entrance rates from 1972 on, is well above the medium NCES projection. Table 5-11 shows the ratio of total enrollment to the weighted composite college-age group for 1972, 1977, and 1982 for each of the projections, and it is apparent that NCES, except in its high alternative, is projecting a continuing decline over the next 10 years in the proportion of youth who attend college. A dip in 1977 is understandable, since the post-Vietnam, post-draft, enrollment effect will still be working its way through the system. That is to say, high college entrance rates for 1968–1970 were still reflected in total enrollment figures by 1972, and 1977 can be expected to more nearly reflect long-term trends. A continuing decline, however, between 1977 and 1982 of .024 or .053 reflected in NCES medium and low projections reflects a rather pessimistic view of the future. A careful review of NCES projections indicates that their critical estimate is the high school graduation rate, where they project a drop from 77.15 percent of 18-year-olds in 1973–74 to only 71.84 percent in 1981–82. While a modest downward adjustment of two or three percentage points was to be expected after the end of the draft, the NCES anticipated drop in the high school graduation rate in the late 1970s seems unprecedented and unlikely.

When comparing the enrollment series in this chapter with other projections, it would be somewhat unfair not to also look back on one's own earlier projections. The earlier estimates

		1972		
	Alternative projection	*(actual)*	*1977*	*1982*
TABLE 5-11 *Ratios of alternative total enrollment projections to college-age population: 1972, 1977, and 1982*	Series A		.550	.552
	Series B		.558	.574
	Series C	.577	.563	.592
	Series D		.572	.596
	Series E		.579	.619
	NCES Low		.537	.484
	NCES Medium	.577	.559	.535
	NCES High		.583	.585

by the author fall into two groups: (1) projections made in 1964–1966[5] and (2) projections made in 1969–1972.[6] The former were based on Census Series B population projections and the latter on Series D. Interestingly, up to the present time the earlier enrollment projections have turned out to be much more accurate, and out to 1980 are within 3 percent of the projected total in Table 5-8, above. By contrast, this author, along with most others estimating future enrollments from the vantage point of four or five years ago, was much too optimistic in outlook. For example, the 1970 estimates for *Science* (Cartter, 1971) exceeded the actual FTE count by 2.8 percent in 1973, are 11 percent greater than the Table 5-8 estimate for 1980, and 5.5 percent greater for 1990. The 1990 difference is principally accounted for by recent declines in the birthrate, but the 1980 difference is fully attributable to more optimistic expectations about college entrance and retention rates as seen from 1970.

Many observers thought this author's projections of five or ten years ago were much too pessimistic in terms of the implications for the demand for college teachers. Current trends now make those earlier estimates seem relatively rosy. The combination of lower birthrates and disappointing college participation rates of the last five years now casts a somewhat gloomier pall over the outlook for the coming decade or two.

[5]See, for example, Cartter (1965*a*; 1966*b*; and 1966*c*).
[6]See Cartter (1969; 1971; 1974).

6. Estimating the Demand for Faculty

The enrollment projections in Chapter 5 provide the basis for estimating the demand for new college teachers. At this stage "demand" is interpreted merely as a quantity—the number of additional teachers required to handle additional enrollment based on an assumed fixed relationship between these increments. (In Chapter 7 demand will be interpreted in a more nearly economic sense, where the coefficients themselves are variable depending upon price.)

Table 6-1 shows actual (1963–1972) and projected (1973–1990) FTE enrollment increments, derived from Table 5-8. The rapid expansion of higher education in the 1964–1969 period is seen in the magnitude of increments, ranging between one-third and one-half million students annually. Similarly, the present job placement difficulties that many new Ph.D.'s are finding today are indicated by the considerably smaller enrollment increments beginning in 1971. Modest improvement is anticipated again in the 1975–1980 years, followed by an expected sharp decline in increments finally turning negative in 1983.

Graduate and first-professional degree enrollments show a slight decline in the late 1970s and again in the late 1980s, reflecting a lagged adjustment to changes in undergraduate enrollment. Undergraduate enrollment increments, based on Series C projections, become negative for 1983–1987 and again in the early 1990s.

Figures 6-1 and 6-2 illustrate the annual change in enrollments from 1957 to 1990 based on Tables 6-1 and 5-8. From 1961 through 1970, annual increments were in excess of 200,000. The average annual percentage increase was 8 percent. In the 1971–1980 decade, by contrast, the average increment is likely to be 140,000, or an average annual growth rate of approximately 2

99

TABLE 6-1 ***Actual and*** ***projected FTE*** ***enrollment*** ***increments,*** ***1963–1990 (in*** ***thousands)***	

Year	Increment
Actual	
1963	+244
1964	+416
1965	+571
1966	+392
1967	+397
1968	+477
1969	+360
1970	+398
1971	+293
1972	+ 89
Projected	
1973	+163
1974	+126
1975	+201
1976	+192
1977	+194
1978	+199
1979	+226
1980	+196
1981	+ 21
1982	+149
1983	− 48
1984	− 99
1985	−169
1986	−167
1987	− 50
1988	+ 35
1989	+ 61
1990	−103

SOURCE: Derived from Table 5-8.

FIGURE 6-1 *Annual percentage changes in actual and projected degree-credit enrollment 1957-1990*

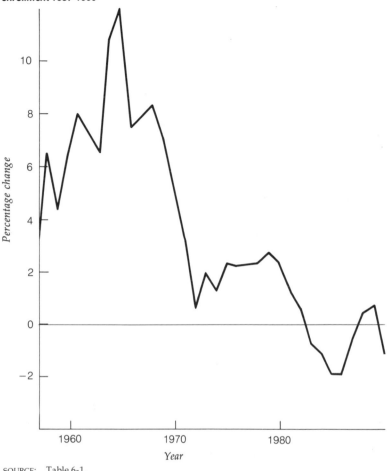

SOURCE: Table 6-1.

percent. In the 1980s, if Series C enrollment projections are correct, there will be an average annual contraction of about 35,000 annually.

Clearly, the current decade promises to be quite different from the 1960s, which experienced sustained rapid growth of higher education. The year 1972 was a low point for the 1970s, if actual enrollments are anything like the projected picture under any of the five alternatives shown in Chapters 4 and 5. The period from 1973 through 1979 is one of modest recovery, approximately duplicating the experience of the late 1950s. The periods of likely contraction are 1980 through 1986 and 1990

FIGURE 6-2　*FTE enrollment increments, actual and projected, 1957-1990*

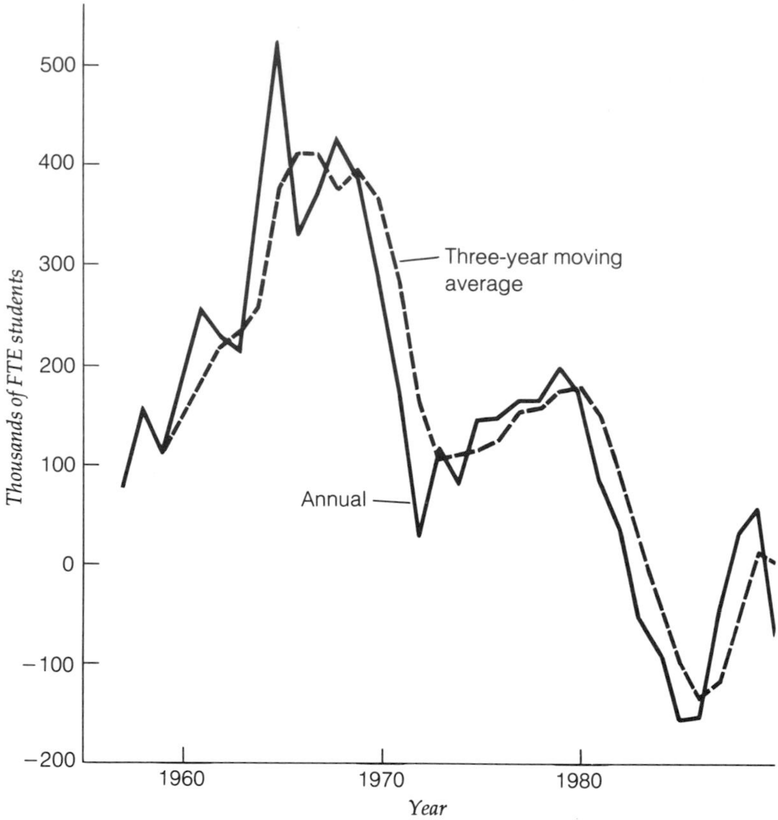

SOURCE:　Based on Table 5-8.

through 1993. By the end of the century, total degree-credit enrollments are likely only to return to their late-1970s level.

THE RELATIONSHIP BETWEEN FTE ENROLLMENT AND FTE FACULTY INCREMENTS

Significant shifts in enrollment in a college or university ordinarily are accompanied by adjustments in the number of instructional staff. So, too, for the universe of higher education the size of teaching faculty varies with the magnitude of the total enrollment. For any single year, one can measure the ratio of total students to total faculty, and between any two points in time one can measure the relationship between increments of enrollment and increments of instructional staff. The average and marginal student-faculty ratios give one an insight into the educational organization of higher education and how its institutions adapt to changing student demand.

Table 6-2 shows these ratios for the last 15 years in full-time equivalents. The average student-faculty ratio has increased from 14.14 students per faculty member to 15.06. Rather interestingly, the average ratio has moved counter to what might have been anticipated from a casual knowledge of the history of the last 15 years. The average ratio drifted upward (that is, incremental ratios exceeded the average ratio) in 1958 through 1963 when enrollment grew relatively modestly. Between 1963 and 1968, however, when rapid enrollment growth might have been expected to outstrip the ability of institutions to expand their instructional staffs, the teaching faculty expanded more rapidly than did enrollment. From 1969 through 1972, when growth diminished, the reverse occurred.

TABLE 6-2 *Average and incremental FTE student-faculty ratios, 1958–1972*

Year	FTE enrollment (in thousands)		FTE faculty (in thousands)		Average student-faculty ratio	Incremental student-faculty ratio
	Total	Actual increments	Total	Actual increments		
1958	2,658	161	188	6	14.14	26.83
1959	2,775	117	194	6	14.30	19.50
1960	2,943	168	204	10	14.43	16.80
1961	3,198	255	214	10	14.94	25.50
1962	3,457	259	228	14	15.16	18.50
1963	3,701	244	242	14	15.29	17.43
1964	4,117	416	274	32	15.03	12.91
1965	4,688	571	317	53	14.79	10.77
1966	5,080	392	351	34	14.47	11.53
1967	5,477	397	378	27	14.49	14.70
1968	5,954	477	413	35	14.39	13.63
1969	6,314	360	431	18	14.65	20.00
1970	6,712	398	452	21	14.85	18.95
1971	7,005	293	466	14	15.03	20.93
1972	7,094	89	471	5	15.06	17.80
1958–1972		4,436		283		15.67
Average of annual ratios						17.72

SOURCES: Computed from enrollment and faculty data, U.S. Office of Education (*Projections of Educational Statistics*, Tables 12 & 33, various years).

By five-year periods, which successively represent slow growth, rapid growth, and moderate growth, the incremental student-faculty ratios were:

1957–1962	20.87
1963–1967	13.47
1967–1972	17.39

If one averages the annual incremental ratios for the 15 years, the average is 17.72. However, if one takes the 15 years as a single period, the incremental ratio is 15.67.

The variability of the incremental student-faculty ratio suggests that a number of factors other than the general expansion of enrollment were at work during the 15 years. Changes in overall faculty productivity, varying degrees of financial constraint imposed by external events (for example, the Vietnam War and the recession), and shifts in the enrollment "mix" among graduate and undergraduate, two-year and four-year college, public and private, undoubtedly account for much of the variation over the 15 years.

As a first-step in analyzing the changing student-faculty ratios it is useful to determine how much of the long-term variation is due to the changing enrollment mix by category of institution, for qualitatively it is one thing to have a rising average student-faculty ratio because of higher incremental ratios for all types of institutions, and it is quite another thing for the overall ratio to rise just because an increasing proportion of students are attending public two-year colleges rather than universities or four-year institutions.

Table 6-3 provides a relatively simple test to see to what extent the changing enrollment mix has affected the overall student-staff ratio. In 1968, the last year for which NCES detailed instructional staff data is available by sector, there were 61,125 FTE instructors teaching in two-year colleges and 304,872 in four-year institutions. Using FTE enrollment data from Table 5-8, the student-staff ratios were 20.4:1 in the two-year college sector (including FTE nondegree students) and 15.4:1 for the four-year institutions. If we assume that the ratio is approximately 10:1 for graduate and first-professional degree

TABLE 6-3 FTE enrollment increments, and predicted additions to teaching faculties, compared with reported actual additions (in thousands)

	Enrollment increments				Faculty increments				
Year	Four-year under-graduate (1)	Two-year under-graduate (2)	Graduate and first-professional (3)	Total (4)	Four-year under-graduate (5)	Two-year under-graduate (6)	Graduate and first-professional (7)	Total predicted (8)	Actual (9)
1963	173	43	28	244	10.6	2.1	2.8	15.5	14
1964	255	109	52	416	15.6	5.3	5.2	26.1	32
1965	363	150	58	571	22.3	7.4	5.8	35.5	53
1966	211	126	55	392	12.9	6.2	5.5	24.6	34
1967	245	109	43	397	15.0	5.3	4.3	24.6	27
1968	244	199	34	477	15.0	9.8	3.4	28.2	35
1969	205	117	38	360	12.6	5.7	3.8	22.1	18
1970	199	147	52	398	12.2	7.2	5.2	24.6	21
1971	99	167	27	293	6.1	8.2	2.7	17.0	14
1972	6	53	30	89	0.4	2.6	3.0	6.0	5
					122.7	59.8	41.7	224.2	253

SOURCE: Enrollment increments from Table 5-8; faculty increments extrapolated from 1968 base year as reported in U.S. Office of Education (1972).

programs,[1] this would imply a 16.3:1 ratio for undergraduates in four-year institutions.

In Table 6-3 it is assumed that these ratios remain constant at their 1968 level for the 1962–1972 period. Enrollment increments are shown in the first four columns, and predicted faculty increments in the next four. Columns (8) and (9) contrast actual reported faculty increments with the predicted numbers if each sector had responded to enrollment changes consistently with its 1968 student-staff ratio. Incremental student-staff ratios, even under these conditions, vary from 14.8:1 (1972) to 16.9:1 (1968).

Over the period of a decade, the predicted value of the overall average student-staff ratio would rise by .23, an increase of 1.5 percent. The actual ratio declined from 15.16:1 to 15.06:1, a decline of .7 percent. The change in the enrollment mix between 1962 and 1972, therefore, had very little effect upon the number of new college teachers required to meet expanding enrollments. Increases in enrollment in more highly teacher-intensive sectors (graduate and first-professional) very nearly offset the more rapid expansion at the undergraduate level of two-year college enrollments. As we shall see in a later section, of much greater importance than its effect on student-staff ratios are the different kinds of faculty required when the enrollment mix is changing.

Of particular interest in Table 6-2 is the seeming contradiction of the number of students per faculty member falling in the 1964–1968 years, the very period when undergraduate enrollments were increasing so dramatically and new college teachers seemed to be in such short supply. One might conclude that the colleges and universities exacerbated the faculty shortage in the mid-1960s, just as the higher incremental student-faculty ratios beginning in 1969 have worsened the oversupply of doctorates in many fields. Two factors may account for this seemingly contrary behavior. First, we might expect the reverse behavior when *unanticipated* enrollment changes occur—but

---

[1] If one assumes that the student-staff ratio is about 3.5:1 in medicine, 10:1 in dentistry, 12:1 in theology, and 15:1 in law, the first-professional degree ratio would be 10:1. In graduate education, it is often assumed that the ratio is about 12:1 at the master's degree level and 8:1 or less at the doctoral level. Thus, 10:1 as an overall ratio for postbaccalaureate study seems reasonable.

the great expansion of 1964–1968 had been clearly foreseen, and by 1970 most institutions had begun to worry about the likely slowdown in enrollment growth. If, when facing known changes in enrollment, institutions alter their hiring and faculty retention policy a year or two in advance, then the annual incremental ratios reflect this anticipatory effect. It should be recalled that much of the enrollment growth in the 1960s occurred in new institutions where advance hiring is a necessary practice.

Second, and perhaps more importantly, adjustments at the margin do not take place in complete isolation. Slight variations in the size of classes or in teaching loads for the other 95 percent of the faculty who are not new in a given year are reflected in incremental student-faculty ratios. For example, imagine a year when enrollment increases from 4,500,000 to 4,650,000, and where the customary average student-faculty ratio is 15:1. Ordinarily, the faculty would expand by 10,000 to 310,000. However, if in that same year the overall efficiency of the entire faculty (as measured by the student-faculty ratio) increased or decreased by 1 percent, the number of new faculty required would be lower or higher than usual by some 31 percent, and the apparent incremental student-faculty ratio would be 11.4:1 or 21.7:1. Thus minor shifts in the proportions in which total students and faculty are combined may have large effects on incremental ratios. In the mid-1960s, when faculty were scarce and enrollments escalating, there was some erosion of average student-faculty ratios that probably reflected the fact that existing faculties were in a good bargaining position when deliberating outside offers and could often insist on somewhat lighter teaching loads as the price of remaining in their current position. By contrast, when the academic labor market has the characteristics of a buyers' market, as it did about 15 years ago and does again today, one can expect a gradual increase again in the number of students per faculty member. Thus, whatever the long-run trend in class size and teaching loads dictated by educational standards and organization, changing market forces can be expected to push incremental student-faculty ratios frequently above or below that trend line. To a degree, therefore, market forces in the short-run act to exaggerate faculty shortages or surpluses.

An estimated 600,000 persons served on college and university instructional staffs in 1972–73, double the number serving in 1961. Only 384,000, however, were regular full-time faculty. Table 6-4 shows the FTE numbers as reported by NCES, and indicates the percentage breakdown for each year. Despite the popular mythology that a rising proportion of the teaching is performed by graduate students and part-time staff, the reverse appears to be the case. Full-time faculty, instructor and above, now represent 81.4 percent of the FTE instructional staff, up five percentage points over the last decade. Somewhat surprisingly, the greatest relative increase in full-time staff occurred during the rapid expansion of enrollment between 1964 and 1968.

Part-time faculty consistently declined, and now represent only about 7 percent of the FTE total. Junior instructional staff— largely graduate teaching assistants, but probably including some persons on postdoctoral appointments—remained relatively constant as a share of the total.

It can be argued that, of the several categories of instructional staff, only full-time faculty are important in analyzing the academic labor market and assessing the quality of faculty. Junior instructional staff are chiefly graduate students at the institution where they are seeking a degree. In one sense they represent a kind of captive reserve labor supply—they can easily be laid off or displaced depending on the vagaries of undergraduate enrollment, and their salary rates are set more by fellowship standards than by going wage rates. Most instructors in this group have not yet entered the market in the sense of seeking and weighing alternative offers. In 1972–73 the total number of such staff was 107,000 (53,000 FTE), representing about 11 percent of the graduate student population. They tend to be heavily concentrated in universities, and are often of high caliber as teachers. Indeed, most of them will be full-time faculty in another year or two.

Part-time faculty of professional rank numbered 109,000 in 1972–73 (34,000 FTE). A significant fraction of this number are career professionals in such fields as medicine, dentistry, law, public administration, management, and the like, and frequently are distinguished practitioners who make a significant contribution to professional education that would be lost if an institution insisted upon only full-time service. Not atypical of a large urban university is the New York University pattern of

TABLE 6-4 Composition of FTE faculty (in thousands)

Year	Total FTE faculty (1)	Full-time instructor or above (2)	Part-time instructor or above (3)	Full-time junior instructor (4)	Part-time junior instructor (5)	Percent full-time instructor or above (2)/(1)	Percent part-time instructor or above (3)/(1)	Percent full-time junior instructor (4)/(1)	Percent part-time junior instructor (5)/(1)
1960	202	154	27	8	13	76.2	13.4	4.0	6.4
1961	214	163	29	9	14	76.2	13.5	4.2	6.5
1962	228	173	30	10	15	75.9	13.2	4.4	6.6
1963	242	184	32	10	16	76.0	13.2	4.1	6.6
1964	274	212	31	12	19	77.3	11.3	4.4	6.9
1965	317	248	31	15	23	78.2	9.8	4.7	7.3
1966	351	278	29	17	27	79.2	8.3	4.8	7.7
1967	378	299	32	14	33	79.1	8.5	3.7	8.7
1968	413	331	33	16	33	80.1	8.0	3.9	8.0
1969	431	349	33	15	34	81.0	7.7	3.5	7.9
1970	452	368	33	15	36	81.4	7.3	3.3	8.0
1971	466	379	34	16	37	81.3	7.3	3.4	7.9
1972	472	384	34	16	37	81.4	7.2	3.4	7.8

SOURCE: Calculated from U.S. Office of Education (1974, Table 32).

several years ago, where the college of medicine had 327 full-time faculty and 1,015 part-time; dentistry 46 full-time and 271 part-time; law 51 full-time and 65 part-time. For institutions in urban centers, there is an almost inexhaustible supply of well-qualified personnel available; thus a fairly high proportion of part-time staff does not necessarily mean that quality of instruction is being sacrificed, although part-time teachers seldom carry their share of departmental nonteaching duties.

The remaining numbers of part-time faculty include faculty wives, teachers at other colleges who occasionally moonlight, and some less-qualified staff who may be pressed into service to meet unexpected enrollment increases. Since part-time instructors rarely share in the general departmental administrative, advisement, and committee work, most institutions attempt to keep the numbers of part-time personnel reasonably low.

If the great bulk of part-time and junior instructional staff are either apprentice college teachers or individuals who could qualify for full-time positions provided they preferred regular academic employment and if there is a considerably larger supply of such persons than can be utilized, they may be thought of as a kind of shadow labor supply, available when needed, but having little impact upon the determination of salaries.[2]

Shortages or surpluses of available faculty affect the market principally at the entry point where former graduate students seek full-time employment on instructional (or research) staffs. The quality of faculty hired varies from year to year as hiring standards rise or fall depending largely on market conditions in the various disciplines. Over time, one can most appropriately measure quality differences (insofar as quality can be inferred from highest-degree attainment) by comparing the highest-degree distribution of the full-time faculty. Thus, for the purposes at hand in this study, the most relevant consideration is the relationship between FTE enrollment and the number of full-time teachers of the rank of instructor or above.

---

[2]In several institutions, such as the City University of New York, part-time faculty are organized and bargain collectively on matters of salary and working conditions. This is relatively rare, however, and has usually tended to encourage an institution to rely more heavily upon full-time instructional staff.

RELATIONSHIP
OF FULL-TIME
FACULTY TO
DEGREE-CREDIT
STUDENT
ENROLLMENT
If one is concerned primarily with the full-time faculty, and ultimately with doctoral faculty, then the most important relationship is between degree-credit enrollment and full-time instructional staff. Nondegree students represent less than 8 percent of total FTE enrollment at the present time, 92 percent of nondegree students are found in community colleges, and doctorate level faculty are only rarely engaged in nondegree teaching programs.[3]

Table 6-5 shows the average and incremental student-faculty ratios for full-time faculty from 1958 through 1972. With the exception of several unusual years—for example, 1959 and 1972—the picture is similar to that shown in Table 6-2. If one breaks the 15 years into three periods, the incremental ratios for 1957–1962 are 29.1:1, 14.7:1 for 1962–1967, and 16.0:1 for 1967–1972. Accordingly, the average ratio rose to a peak of 19.3:1 in 1963, declined to 16.9:1 in 1968, and has hung about 17:1 for the last few years. The surprisingly low incremental ratio for 1972 is based upon preliminary NCES estimates, and may be subject to revision. For the past five years, the latest NCES faculty estimates have been revised the following year by an average of 12,000 full-time teachers.[4]

Although revisions of NCES preliminary data are to be expected in subsequent reports, recently there have been significant revisions in the historical faculty series going back over the last decade. Such changes not only make it difficult for one to determine the real historical trend in average and incremental student-staff ratios, but also raise doubts about the reliability of the faculty data in the first place. Up to 1968, the NCES 10-

[3]It is estimated that about 18,000 FTE faculty are engaged in non-degree-credit instruction, only about half of them on a full-time basis. Given the low representation of doctorates on community college faculties, and the even lower presumed participation in nondegree programs, it seems likely that only about 500 doctorate holders are full-time teachers in this area, and that only 40 to 50 new doctoral staff members are added each year. Thus, the nondegree sector apparently accounts for only about 1/10 of 1 percent of jobs for new Ph.D.'s each year and can be ignored for statistical purposes. However, if there were a real revolution in recurrent education along some of the lines proposed by the Carnegie Commission (1973c) and the Commission on Non-Traditional Study (1973), this exclusion might have to be reconsidered 10 or 15 years from now.

[4]Since this was written the 1974 edition of the U.S Office of Education's *Educational Statistics* (1975) has appeared. The 1972 increment remains unchanged at 5,000 and the increment for 1973 is reported at 12,000.

TABLE 6-5 *FTE degree-credit enrollment and full-time faculty, instructor and above (in thousands)*

Year	Enrollment Total	Enrollment Annual increment	Faculty Total	Faculty Annual increment	Average student-faculty ratio	Incremental student-faculty ratio
1958	2,552	155	147	6	17.36	25.83
1959	2,665	133	149	2	17.89	56.50
1960	2,835	170	154	5	18.41	34.00
1961	3,092	257	163	9	18.97	28.56
1962	3,328	236	173	10	19.24	23.60
1963	3,547	219	184	11	19.28	19.91
1964	3,929	382	212	28	18.53	13.64
1965	4,460	531	248	36	17.98	14.75
1966	4,805	335	278	30	17.28	11.17
1967	5,174	379	299	21	17.30	18.05
1968	5,603	429	331	32	16.93	13.41
1969	6,000	397	349	18	17.19	22.06
1970	6,302	302	368	19	17.13	15.89
1971	6,496	194	379	11	17.14	17.64
1972	6,537	41	384	5	17.02	8.20
1958–1972		4,140				17.04
Average of annual incremental ratios						21.55

SOURCE: Computed from U.S. Office of Education (*Projections of Educational Statistics,* Tables 12 & 33, various years).

year historical data on full-time faculty were consistent from year to year. Except for revisions in the most recent year figures one year later, no earlier figures were revised by more than 1,000 between 1964 and 1968. In 1969, however, the most recent five years were revised upward; in 1970, the most recent three years were again scaled upward; and in 1971, substantial changes were made which increased significantly the 1965–1970 count and decreased the 1960–1964 numbers by up to 10 percent. These revisions have dramatically changed the picture of faculty expansion; if we are to accept the 1971 revisions, the incremental growth of faculty between 1960 and 1969 is 27 percent greater than it appeared to be five years ago.

Table 6-6 shows the number of full-time faculty for 1960 to 1972 as reported in successive volumes of *Projections of Educational Statistics* over the last 10 years. In 1971, according to NCES, the figures for earlier years were adjusted to reflect actual headcount rather than number of positions filled. Reading NCES table footnotes and methodological explanations in the text and appendixes gives a plausible explanation for the downward adjustments for 1964 and earlier, but does not explain the significant upward adjustment of headcount for 1966 through 1969. One reviews the data in Table 6-6 with an uneasy feeling about the reliability of this critically important information. Judging by quoted information sources, the series is based on published data collected for fall 1961, 1963, 1966, 1967, and 1968, plus unpublished data from a survey of employees in higher education in fall 1970 (U.S. Office of Education, 1974, Table 32, p. 71). As late as the 1970 edition of *Projections*, however, it was indicated that data for 1966 through 1969 were estimates, and 1960, 1962, 1964, and 1965 were "interpolated." (In the 1973 edition 1969 is also indicated as an interpolation.)

The 1971 NCES revisions have significantly rewritten the history of the 1960s, dropping the apparent 1960–1968 incremental student-staff ratio from 21.46:1 to 15.55:1—nearly a one-third reduction! For the next several years, as total enrollments increase by about 150,000 annually, this variation makes a difference of about 2,600 doctorates a year—a not insignificant number.

In the case of part-time faculty, instructor and above, the 1971 revisions left the estimates for 1963 and earlier unchanged, but reduced the 1964–1970 figures by about one-third. In the case of junior instructional staff, FTE estimates for the early 1960s were revised upward by about 50 percent, and for the late 1960s by more than 75 percent. None of these adjustments readily appear to follow from the explanation that the series data shifted from positions to number of persons.

Given the seeming uncertainty over the number and type of faculty teaching in the nation's colleges and universities, it seems surprising that no exhaustive surveys have been undertaken since the two major studies conducted by the Office of Education in 1962 and 1963 (Dunham, Wright, & Chandler, 1966; Rogers, 1967). In the one, extremely useful information was gathered concerning the characteristics of teachers in four-

TABLE 6-6 Changing NCES reporting of full-time instructors and above (in thousands)

Year for which data are reported	Edition of Projections of Educational Statistics									
	1964	1965	1966	1967	1968	1969	1970	1971	1972	1973
1960	172	170	170	170	169	169	169	154		
1961	179	179	179	179	177	177	177	162	163	
1962	191	192	192	192	190	190	190	173	173	173
1963	200	205	205	205	202	202	202	184	184	184
1964		221	221	221	220	222	222	212	212	212
1965			245	245	243	247	247	248	248	248
1966				262	255	264	264	278	278	278
1967					271	281	296	299	299	299
1968						298	315	332	331	331
1969							328	356	350	349
1970								375	372	368
1971									384	379
1972										384

year institutions and their mobility patterns; the other provided a detailed look at the staffing requirements in higher
educational institutions and attempted to assess future needs.
In addition, NCES published biennial surveys of teaching and
research staff up through 1968, but no published reports have
appeared since that time. The only recent information available
appears in a few tables in the annual *Digest* and *Projections*
volumes (as summarized in Table 6-6). Considering the wide
concern with the shortage of qualified personnel in the 1964–
1969 period, and the partial reversal of doctoral market conditions in 1970–1973, one would have thought that improved
knowledge of the academic labor market and its characteristics
would have been a high priority issue for the U.S. Office of
Education. Instead, this is the area where the data are the most
inadequate, and where changes in definition and methods of
estimation have been most unsettling.

**PROJECTING
FUTURE
FACULTY NEEDS**
As the preceding discussion suggests, faculty staffing trends
over the last 10 to 15 years are not known with a high degree of
confidence. Until 1971, based on NCES data, one would have
concluded that the overall student-faculty ratio was rising and
that the average incremental ratio for full-time faculty was
approximately 20:1.[5] The fact that the incremental ratio apparently exceeded the average ratio was attributed to the more
rapid rate of enrollment growth in the two-year colleges, some
academic economies of scale, and emerging budgetary constraints in higher education.

Since the 1971 revision of the historical data, which lowered
the full-time and FTE faculty count for the pre-1965 years and
raised the estimated numbers by about 10 percent for the most
recent years, the picture appears quite different. Apparently,
the average student-faculty ratio fell sharply between 1963 and
1968, and incremental ratios since then have hovered around
17:0. The fact that the impressions of what was taking place in
the academic labor market held by most observers and participants are somewhat counter to these data does not necessarily
mean that the data are incorrect. As noted in Chapter 2, most

[5]The author's faculty projections in *Higher Education and The Labor Market*
(Cartter, 1974) were based on the 1960–1970 period, and concluded from NCES
1970 data that the incremental ratio was 20:1 and the average ratio in 1970 was
18.2:1. See Table 8-2 in that volume.

observers in the early 1960s thought that the proportion of college teachers with the doctorate was falling sharply when in fact it turned out that it had been rising. Fact and folklore frequently run counter to one another.

Thus, in projecting likely future faculty requirements, it seems appropriate at this stage, where fixed coefficients are being posited, to use several alternative student-faculty ratios. For the median assumption 17:1 seems reasonable, since it approximates the current average ratio and the average incremental ratio of the last several years.[6]

For the low student-faculty ratio assumption 15:1 will be used. It approximates the average experience of 1963–1967. Individual years may drop below this level, but it seems unlikely that the incremental ratio would intentionally drop below this level for any sustained period given the likely balance of enrollment growth in two-year and four-year institutions. One qualification should be added, however. It is obvious that when expected enrollment increments do not materialize, the incremental student-faculty ratio will temporarily decline; a similar unintentional but longer-term imbalance may occur when enrollments are contracting rather than expanding. Because a high proportion of college professors are tenured, the situation is not symmetrical between expansion and contraction. Institutions can expand staff instantaneously, but orderly contraction is a difficult and slow process. Thus, when enrollments are shrinking, as seems likely in the 1980s for most institutions, and is true even today for some institutions, incremental student-faculty ratios are likely to fall.

For the high estimate in projecting faculty, a 20:1 ratio between FTE enrollment change and increments of full-time faculty will be used. The incremental ratio has been above 20:1 in 6 of the last 15 years, but this seems a reasonable upper limit for any sustained period of time for the universe of higher education. The current budgetary attitude in many state legislatures and the increasing concern for more effective use of

[6]For the 1967–1971 years the incremental ratio averaged 17.4:1, as shown in Table 6-5. The 1972 incremental ratio appeared much lower, but the reported faculty figures for that year are an NCES preliminary estimate. As Table 6-6 clearly indicates, if one reads it diagonally, the most recent year estimates are commonly substantially revised a year later and thus are not a reliable indicator of trends.

institutional resources in both public and private institutions make a 20:1 ratio seem plausible for the near future.

Table 6-7 shows the projected annual increments in FTE degree-credit enrollments and the associated growth of full-time faculty under three alternative student-faculty ratios. The projected growth rate is reasonably stable during the 1970s, but becomes negative for most of the 1980s. In 1990, under each of the alternative ratios, the size of the total full-time faculty would be approximately equal to its size in 1978. As will be recalled from the projections of undergraduate enrollment in Chapter 5, demographic factors suggest a decline to 1993, only returning at the end of the century to its 1979 level. Thus, unless

TABLE 6-7 *Full-time faculty increments under three student-faculty ratio assumptions, 1973–1990 (in thousands)*

Year	Degree-credit FTE enrollment increment	Faculty increments with student-faculty ratios of:			Total size of full-time faculty under incremental student-faculty ratios of:		
		15:1	17:1	20:1	15:1	17:1	20:1
1973	127	8.5	7.5	6.4	343	392	390
1974	90	6.0	5.3	4.5	399	397	395
1975	155	10.3	9.1	7.8	409	406	403
1976	154	10.3	9.1	7.7	419	416	410
1977	162	10.8	9.5	8.1	430	426	419
1978	165	11.0	9.7	8.3	441	435	427
1979	198	13.2	11.6	9.9	454	447	437
1980	177	11.8	10.4	8.9	466	457	446
1981	96	6.4	5.6	4.8	472	463	450
1982	45	3.0	2.6	2.3	475	465	453
1983	−49	−3.3	−2.9	−2.5	472	463	450
1984	−84	−5.6	−4.9	−4.2	466	458	445
1985	−150	−10.0	−8.8	−7.5	456	449	439
1986	−147	−9.8	−8.6	−7.4	447	440	431
1987	−45	−3.0	−2.6	−2.3	444	438	429
1988	30	2.0	1.8	1.5	446	439	430
1989	51	3.4	3.0	2.6	449	442	433
1990	−94	−6.3	−5.5	−4.7	443	437	428

SOURCE: Enrollment increments computed from Table 5-8.

the pattern of college attendance or instruction changes markedly in unforeseen ways, the only remaining net growth in the higher educational system in this century appears to be between now and 1979—hence, the popularity of the terms "steady-state" or "stationary state" to describe the likely long-term status of higher education over the last quarter of this century.

The projected picture for the next decade or two is markedly different from the experience of the last 15 years. Table 6-8 indicates, by five-year periods, the absolute and percentage growth in full-time faculty past, present, and projected. The total number of full-time faculty grew by 214,000 between 1960 and 1970, is expected to grow by 79,000 to 98,000 in the 1970–1980 decade, and would shrink by from 18,000 to 23,000 in the 1980s, depending upon the appropriate student-faculty ratio. Higher education has moved from a decade where 10 percent annual growth in faculty and enrollment was common, to a current decade where 2 to 2½ percent is the standard, and a prospective decade where modest contraction may be typical.

THE REPLACEMENT DEMAND FOR FACULTY The demand for new faculty personnel depends partly on the need for teachers to handle enrollment increments and partly on the need to replace those departing from teaching. Replacements fall into four categories, only two of which will be treated in detail in this chapter.

TABLE 6-8 *Full-time faculty increments by five-year period, number (in thousands) and percent change*

	1960–1965	1965–1970	1970–1975	1975–1980	1980–1985	1985–1990
Low ratio (15:1)						
Number			41	57	−10	−13
Percent change			11	14	−2	−3
Medium ratio (17:1)	Actual					
Number	94	120	39	51	−8	−12
Percent change	61%	48%	11	13	−2	−3
High ratio (20:1)						
Number			36	43	−8	−10
Percent change			10	11	−2	−2

SOURCE: Table 6-7.

First, some college teachers leave one institution, where they must be replaced, and take a teaching position at another institution. Such movements from one campus to another create a job vacancy in one institution but simultaneously fill a vacancy at another institution. It has been estimated that such job changes within higher education, in the mid-1960s, included about 8 percent of the teaching labor force annually (Cartter, 1974, p. 288). Such changes, however, have a zero impact upon total employment in higher education, and therefore may be ignored as a component of aggregate demand for new faculty.

Second, each year a number of persons engaged in full-time college teaching leave the academic setting to take jobs in government, industry, or nonprofit agencies. Several studies in the 1960s, however, indicated that while there is a significant gross outflow each year, the net flow of senior personnel (defined as those who have been employed full-time for a year or more since completion of graduate studies) is approximately zero. For the 1953–1963 decade Cartter (1966c, pp. 28–29) found that there was a net annual outflow of 0.11 percent, although the gross flows in each direction were in the neighborhood of 3 percent. A 1965 study by NSF staff (Bolt, Koltun, and Levine, 1965), based on National Register data, indicated a net inflow of 0.1 percent annually for scientists and engineers. In Chapter 9 changes in the balance of these flows will be examined in more detail; for the first-approximation projections in this chapter a zero net flow will be assumed.

Third, a number of faculty retire each year at the end of their teaching careers and must be replaced. If there were a normal stationary-state distribution of faculty with teachers commonly entering at age 30 and retiring at age 65, with no net departures in between, the annual retirement rate would be about 1.85 percent of the teaching force. In fact, the current age distribution is skewed so that the average age of college teachers in 1970 was about 39 rather than 45 under stationary-state conditions. The actual retirement rate in 1970 is estimated to have been 0.93 percent, or about 3,400 teachers (see Cartter, 1972). Because of the rapid growth of college faculties in the 1960s and early 1970s, the projected retirement rate will continue to decline until the early 1980s when it is expected to reach 0.65 percent. After that time, as the median age begins to rise, the retirement rate will rise again to about 0.92 percent in 1990 under current retirement practices.

The fourth factor contributing to the replacement demand is mortality. For 1970 the estimated mortality rate, given the age distribution of faculty members, was .68 percent. Under a stationary-state age distribution, it would be approximately .94 percent, but the relatively youthful age of faculty in the 1970s will depress the mortality rate to about .62 percent before it begins to rise again in the 1980s. In 1970 it is estimated that approximately 2,500 college professors died while still actively employed as teachers.

For the purposes of projecting faculty requirements to 1990 within the limits of a fixed-coefficients model, the first two factors above are ignored as representing no net drain on the system, but the latter two factors must be incorporated as creating significant replacement needs. Table 6-9 indicates the estimated annual replacement needs caused by death and retirement from 1973 to 1990.

During the 1970s, declining death and retirement rates are offset by increasing total faculty numbers, resulting in a fairly constant replacement need. In the early 1980s, however, death and retirement rates rise sufficiently to offset the modest decline in total faculty. By the end of the century (not shown in Table 6-9), the combined death and retirement rate should rise above 2.5 percent (assuming continuation of current policies), reflecting the disproportionate share of faculty who entered teaching in the 1960s. Replacement needs at that time are likely to rise to about 12,000 annually.

COMBINED TEACHER REPLACEMENT AND GROWTH NEEDS Combining the replacement and growth needs projected in the preceding section, Table 6-10 provides projections of new junior-faculty hires[7] under three student-faculty ratio assumptions. For the remainder of the 1970s, total hiring to serve degree-credit students is expected to remain reasonably steady at between 10 and 16 thousand under the low estimate, or between approximately 12 and 19 thousand under the high estimate.

After 1980, however, the expected contraction in total degree-

---

[7]As noted on p. 119, movements of senior faculty into and out of academic employment are assumed to cancel out. This assumption is relaxed in Chapter 9.

TABLE 6-9 *Estimated replacement needs due to deaths and retirement, 1970–1990*

Year	Estimated annual rates (in percentages)			Total faculty (in thousands)†	Annual replacement needs (in thousands)‡
	Death	Retirement	Combined*		
1970	.68	.93	1.61	368	5.79
1971			1.56	379	5.92
1972			1.50	384	5.91
1973			1.45	392	5.76
1974			1.40	397	5.68
1975	.62	.74	1.36	406	5.56
1976			1.34	416	5.52
1977			1.32	426	5.57
1978			1.30	435	5.62
1979			1.29	447	5.66
1980	.62	.66	1.28	457	5.77
1981			1.28	463	5.85
1982			1.29	465	5.93
1983			1.31	463	6.00
1984			1.34	458	6.07
1985	.75	.62	1.37	449	6.14
1986			1.42	440	6.15
1987			1.50	438	6.25
1988			1.62	439	6.57
1989			1.74	442	7.11
1990	.95	.92	1.87	437	7.69

*Combined rates interpolated between quinquennial years.

†Based on medium alternative student-faculty ratio (17:1). See Table 6-7.

‡Replacement needs in year t are computed from faculty population and death and retirement rates in year $t - 1$.

SOURCE: Computed from projected age-distribution data by the author.

credit enrollment reduces new hiring to less than 10,000 per year, and might actually be negative in 1985 and 1986. (Total new hiring would become negative if there were involuntary separations greater than the number of new hires—for example, contraction of staff by terminating positions held by experienced teachers.) While demographic factors provide an expected modest upturn in hiring in 1988 and 1989, no significant net improvement is expected before the mid-1990s.

	Student-faculty ratio		
Year	15:1	17:1	20:1
1973	14.4	13.4	12.3
1974	11.7	11.0	10.2
1975	15.9	14.7	13.4
1976	15.9	14.7	13.3
1977	16.4	15.1	13.7
1978	16.6	15.3	13.9
1979	18.9	17.3	15.6
1980	17.6	16.2	14.7
1981	12.3	11.5	10.7
1982	8.9	8.5	8.2
1983	2.7	3.1	3.5
1984	0.5	1.2	1.9
1985	−3.9	−2.7	−1.4
1986	−3.6	−2.4	−1.2
1987	3.3	3.7	4.0
1988	8.6	8.4	8.1
1989	10.5	10.1	9.5
1990	1.4	2.2	3.0

SOURCE: Tables 6-7 and 6-9.

The extent of the projected change in labor market demand conditions is most clearly seen by comparing the experience of the last decade and a half with expected future conditions. Table 6-11 compares quinquenniums since 1955. The level of hiring in the 1960s was more than double the rate in the late 1950s, and approximately twice the rate that is expected throughout the 1970s. By the 1980s, however, unless there are major changes in the demand for education, it appears that hiring will be at about one-sixth the rate of the 1960s. Although it has not been considered appropriate to project postbaccalaureate enrollments beyond 1990 with a fixed-coefficients model (indeed, it is probably unwise to place much reliance on such projections of graduate enrollment beyond 1980), if one were to do so, the quinquennial new hiring for replacement and growth would be approximately 18,000 for 1991–1995 and 85,000 for 1996–2000. Thus the 15-year period between 1980 and 1995

	Replacement	Growth	
Period	*needs*	*needs**	*Total*
1955–1960	14.7	37.7	52.4
1961–1965	17.6	94.0	111.6
1966–1970	25.9	120.0	145.9
1971–1975	28.8	37.9	66.7
1976–1980	28.1	40.3	68.4
1981–1985	30.0	−8.4	21.6
1986–1990	33.8	−11.9	21.9

TABLE 6-11 *Actual and projected numbers of new junior faculty required to meet replacement and growth needs, 1955–1990 (in thousands)*

*Assuming median 17:1 student-faculty ratio for 1973–1990.

SOURCES: Projections based on Tables 6-7 and 6-9; 1955–1973 growth needs calculated from U.S. Office of Education (*Projections of Educational Statistics,* various years); replacement needs estimated by the author.

would apparently see only as much total new hiring as occurred in 1971–1975, a period currently viewed as "lean." Put in an even worse light, the cumulative academic demand for new personnel from 1980 to 1995 *if all other parameters remain unchanged* (for example, retirement, relative salaries, tenure, etc.), is projected to be about equal to the total demand for only 1965 and 1966, the two peak years of the past.

It would be a mistake to conclude this chapter with Table 6-11 without a reminder of the limitations of these first approximations. At each step of the way in Chapters 3 through 6, several alternative assumptions have been examined for birthrates, high school graduation, college entrance, completion of the baccalaureate, entrance to graduate school, doctoral-degree completion, and student-faculty ratios. In each successive step, one projection has been built on a prior one, so that by the nature of the process the margin of error becomes greater as one proceeds up the educational ladder and through time. Looking ahead only as far as 1990, the degree-credit enrollment projections are probably correct within a margin of 10 to 15 percent. In addition, the reasonable variation in incremental student-faculty ratios one might expect is about ± 15 percent. However, these variations only affect growth needs, which are estimated in Table 6-11 to total less than 60,000 between 1971 and 1990. When these ranges of possible error are cumulated, the total faculty estimate for 1990 can be said to be subject to a

± 25,000 error. That figure sounds substantial, but with a median projection of 437,000 full-time faculty in 1990 it represents only a 6 percent range. Between now and 1990 that represents only about a 1,500 average annual difference in hiring.

In fact, if there are not radical changes in the financing of higher education and its organizational and instructional patterns, errors at one level are likely to be partially offset by compensating variations at another level. More importantly, the preceding analysis should be useful in pointing up likely directions of change and orders of magnitude.

However, radical changes may indeed occur over the next 10 to 20 years; the very picture of trends sketched here may contribute to such changes. Also, our experience since World War II only comprehends growth (at varying rates); we do not know for certain how symmetrical the adjustments will be in periods of expansion and contraction. As the experience of the last several years indicates, even when aggregate enrollment for the nation is still rising modestly, some institutions and some state systems are experiencing contraction, although it is too soon to conclusively judge the response in faculty hiring.

In succeeding chapters, attempts will be made to make some key coefficients flexible and responsive to market forces so that the model will be closer to the real world and its processes of adjustment.

7. Fixed-Coefficient and Market-Response Models

More than 80 percent of the new faculty required to meet enrollment growth and as replacements for deaths and retirements are principally engaged in prebaccalaureate instruction. Enrollments in these areas, it has been previously argued, are only minimally market responsive.[1] Variations in growth trends have been employed, indicating a range of possible enrollments with different probabilities of occurrence. In this chapter, however, it will be simplest to work with a median series of projections which seem most probable.

Approximately 15 percent of college and university teachers are principally engaged in doctoral education (excluding professional degrees); in this area market forces are assumed to have a considerable impact upon enrollments. In graduate education there is likely to be a significant enrollment response to changing job opportunities, which in turn has a feedback effect on faculty demand for the training of graduate students.

In Chapter 7, the first section compares the faculty needs implicit in previously projected enrollment patterns (based on fixed coefficients) with the availability of doctorates resulting

---

[1]The argument has been made that while enrollment in any particular area of study—for example, chemistry, engineering, prelaw—may be sensitive to job prospects and long-term career outlook, students are relatively unlikely to drop out of higher education if the employment prospects in their first-choice field change for the worse. Thus, while there may be a relatively high degree of substitution across fields of study, total enrollment is presumed to be relatively insensitive to changes in employment prospects in one or a few fields. This is not to argue that the demand for undergraduate education is completely inelastic (that is, insensitive to all economic forces); that is another issue related to the overall health of the economy. For the purpose of projecting academic labor market conditions we assume here that the general health of the economy remains constant and the academic labor market responds primarily to the changing growth pattern of undergraduate (and induced graduate) enrollments.

from those projections. In the second section, the assumption of fixed coefficients is relaxed and the enrollment and degree consequences of assumed market-response patterns are explored. In Chapter 8 a further step will be taken in the direction of real-life dynamics by dropping the assumptions of constant student-faculty ratios, retirement policies, and net flow of senior doctorates between academic and other employment sectors.

THE BALANCE BETWEEN TEACHERS REQUIRED AND AVAILABLE PH.D.'S Over the last two decades, about half of all new Ph.D.'s have entered college teaching. The data are not precise, partly because a significant number of new college and university staff members have split assignments for teaching, research, and administration and partly because National Research Council reporting depends upon the new Ph.D.'s indication of plans at the time the degree is received—which usually is several months before entering into those work duties. Prior to 1967, the only comparable data are from the biennial surveys conducted by the National Education Association (NEA) between 1955 through 1965. Those survey data were supplied by the graduate departments which granted the doctorates.

Table 7-1 reviews the available data and indicates the relative stability of the proportion of new doctorates entering academic employment. The percentage of new doctorates employed by colleges and universities has ranged between 57 and 64 percent, but no clear long-term trend is visible. Apparently, during the period of rapid growth in both enrollment and university research and development activities between 1958 and 1968, the percentage employed in higher education moved up several points, decreasing again in 1973 to the 1954–55 level. The NEA series for employment as college teachers shows a modest but steady upward movement between the mid-1950s and mid-1960s.

Beginning in 1967, the office of the National Research Council (NRC) maintaining the Doctorate Records File has reported the employment and work activity of new doctorate holders. The data are not precisely comparable with those in the NEA series for several reasons. First, NRC categorizes employing institutions as "educational institutions" rather than colleges and universities. According to special tabulations NRC ran for this study (reported in Chapter 9), about 1.5 percent of teachers

	Percentage employed by	Percentage teaching as
Year	*college or university*	*primary work activity*
1954	57.4	45.1
1955	57.1	45.2
1956	59.7	47.0
1957	60.4	46.4
1958	62.1	47.7
1959	61.8	47.4
1960	63.9	49.0
1961	62.9	48.5
1962	62.7	49.5
1963	62.9	52.7
1967	61.9	51.9
1968	63.0	52.9
1969	58.4	54.4
1970	59.0	55.4
1971	59.3	56.8
1972	59.4	56.9
1973	57.2	55.3

TABLE 7-1 Percentage of new Ph.D.'s employed in higher education

SOURCES: Data for 1954–1963 from National Education Association *(Teacher Supply and Demand in Universities, Colleges, and Junior Colleges,* various years); data for 1967–1973 from National Research Council *(Summary Report,* various years).

reporting employment in "educational institutions" were in primary and secondary schools in 1968 rather than in higher education, and this proportion had risen to 3½ percent by 1973. Figures for 1967–1973 in column (1) of Table 7-1 are also probably overstated by several percentage points by virtue of new doctorate holders (particularly E.D.'s) entering administration in precollegiate institutions. In column (2) a further complication arises because those for whom teaching was the reported primary work activity were not limited to persons employed by educational institutions. A small number of persons employed by government or industry also perform teaching functions. One further problem arises in that some persons who indicated that they were engaged in postdoctoral study [and, under NRC definitions were excluded from the employed category in column (1)] apparently also indicated teaching as their primary work activity. Thus, it appears that the 1967–1973 figures in column (1) of Table 7-1 would have to be reduced by four or five percentage points to be comparable with the 1954–1963 data.

Within each series, the data are presumed to be consistent from year to year, and it seems reasonable to conclude from the NRC data that the percentage of new doctorates employed by educational institutions declined about five or six percentage points between 1967 and 1973 (from an estimated 60 percent to about 54 percent for colleges and universities) and that the percentage entering college teaching increased about two or three percentage points in the equivalent period (from an estimated 48 percent in 1967 to about 50 percent in 1973).

Significant variations exist from field to field—41.6 percent of science doctorates in 1973 reported teaching as their primary job activity, as compared with 61.7 percent of nonscientists (National Research Council, 1973, pp. 10, 11); however, the data support the generalization that approximately half of new doctorate holders enter college teaching.

From the other side of the academic labor market, the observation can also be made that nearly half of those who enter the college teaching profession have a doctorate (or obtain it shortly after entering). The biennial NEA surveys from 1955 through 1965 indicated that the ratio of new doctorate recipients in college teaching to total new college teachers hired averaged .445 (Cartter, 1965*b*, Table 4, p. 274). Similarly, an Office of Education survey in spring 1963 found that 50.6 percent of all full-time faculty in four-year institutions had the doctorate.[2]

If, over a decade or two, approximately half of new doctorate recipients entered teaching and about half of new college teachers had the doctorate, it is possible to get an approximate measure of the adequacy of supply of new teachers with the doctorate by comparing total doctorates awarded with total new hires of college teachers. Figure 7-1 shows this relationship from 1948 to 1973, and projects the number of new teachers needed to 1990 based on Table 6-10 and the number of doctorates likely to be awarded to 1980 based on Table 5-5. (In Chapter 5 this latter series was indicated as a first approximation, based on moderately declining coefficients applied to baccalaureate-degree totals.)

---

[2]See Dunham, Wright, and Chandler (1966). The percentage would have been about 44 percent if the two-year colleges had been included.

FIGURE 7-1 *Comparison of junior faculty openings with earned doctorates awarded, actual 1948-1973, projected 1974-1990*

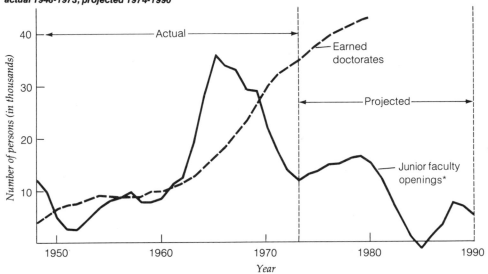

*Three-year moving average.
SOURCES: Earned doctorate data from Table 5-5; faculty openings for 1973–1990 from Table 6-10; earlier estimates by the author based on U.S. Office of Education reports of faculty in higher education.

If we interpret an approximate equality of doctorates awarded and new hires as a rough equilibrium (set by traditional job aspirations of new doctorates and traditional college hiring standards), then periods of relative under- or oversupply can be identified. From 1950 to 1955 the number of new job openings was probably insufficient to employ the number of doctorates seeking academic employment. From 1962 through 1968 there appeared to be significant shortages of doctoral manpower to meet teaching needs. 1970 and beyond are years when the market imbalance is on the side of oversupply once again. This reading of the curves in Figure 7-1 fits well with the general observations of participants in the academic labor market for the last 25 years. The common observations have been that faculty salaries lagged far behind comparable rates in the early and mid-1950s, that good teaching jobs were hard to come by, and many institutions in the early 1950s tightened up on tenure regulations. Beginning about 1957, real faculty salaries began to increase more rapidly than other occupations ("Surviving the Seventies," 1973, p. 191). By 1963 doctorates were becoming scarce, and during most of the 1960s, there was some deterioration in hiring standards. Starting in 1970 the real increment in faculty salaries dropped to zero (ibid; see also Table 8-1), and in almost every discipline there was increasing concern with "overproduction."

Figure 7-1 shows a three-year moving average of estimated number of junior faculty hired, or required, after 1973 (with constant student-faculty ratios). The average smooths out the irregular year-to-year movements and more nearly reflects the decision base for institutions that respond partly to last year's actual experience, the current year's anticipated enrollment, and next year's projected needs.

Viewing Figure 7-1, it appears that the number of doctorates awarded responded after World War II to the shortage of faculty, rising steadily from 1948 to 1954. The sharp drop in hiring between 1948 and 1952 is reflected several years later in the leveling off of Ph.D.'s in 1954—approximately the six-year lag one would anticipate. The number of new hires increased rapidly from 1960 to 1965, and the number of doctorates awarded experienced an increasing growth rate between 1962 and 1970. The appearance of Sputnik in 1957 and the rapid expansion of federal graduate fellowship programs in the late 1950s appear to have reduced the response lag in the early 1960s.

The number of college teaching openings declined again after 1965, although it was 1970 before the total number of new hires fell below the number of earned doctorates awarded. In some science fields, first-time graduate enrollments began to decline in the late 1960s; physics peaked in 1965 and had dropped about one-third by 1972. Overall, first-time graduate enroll-ments increased 7.9 percent in 1969, 6.8 percent in 1970, but only 0.7 percent in 1971 (National Board on Graduate Education, 1973).

Beyond 1973, the fixed-coefficients model produces contin-ued growth in Ph.D.'s at a level far exceeding the projected number of academic openings. By implication, this would mean that a rapidly increasing share of doctorate holders would enter nonacademic occupations; we would also expect academic hiring standards to rise. The American Council on Education surveys of college faculty in 1968 and 1972 showed 26 percent of new hires directly from graduate schools had the doctorate in the former year, as contrasted with 53 percent in the latter survey.[3] This dramatic increase fits well with the expectation one would have from traditional labor market analysis. If one adds to this the number of college teachers already in service who ordinarily complete the doctorate each year, which in the 1960s was a number equal to about 22 percent of new teachers hired (Cartter, 1965b, p. 274), it appears that in today's academic labor market, the annual number of doctorates added to college faculties as a proportion of new teachers hired is approximately 75 percent.

Looking ahead to the remaining years of the 1970s, however, it seems likely that only 10,000 to 12,000 doctorates will be employed as college teachers. This would represent only about 30 percent of all doctorates awarded—considerably less than the traditional proportion of about 50 percent for the last decade or two. Beginning about 1980, the gap would become much larger unless there were a corresponding downward adjustment in the number of doctorates awarded.

The picture provided by Figure 7-1 leads one to believe that market forces will modify the projected output of Ph.D.'s; the fixed-coefficients model may have been reasonably well suited to a period of reasonably steady growth, but it seems unlikely to be suited to a situation where an imbalance between doctoral supply and demand emerges.

MARKET RESPONSES AND GRADUATE ENROLLMENTS Up to this point, the academic labor market has been treated as though the number of new job openings were purely a technical derivative of the level of enrollment, and the number of doctorates awarded were dependent on demographic factors and relatively fixed school- and college-participation rates. True, on the demand side of the market we have seen that some cyclical variation is to be expected in student-faculty ratios and have projected a range of likely future ratios; it has also been noted that there is a considerable degree of substitution between doctorates and nondoctorates, so that changes in the availability of doctorate holders show up more noticeably in short-run variations in hiring standards than in total numbers hired. On the supply side, it has also been indicated that graduate school entrance rates rose rapidly until 1968 during the period of rapid enrollment growth, declined steadily over the next six years,

[3]See pp. 156–167 for a review of these findings.

and are projected to decline still further during the 1970s. Similarly, the ratio of doctorates awarded to first-year enrollment four to six years previously peaked in 1970, and the initial degree projections in Chapter 5 assumed a continued decline through the early 1980s. Thus, some long-term trends have been built into the projections that reflect the change in market conditions, although the coefficients have not been assumed to be flexible and reversible depending upon current conditions.

In building a more dynamic market-response model, one would expect to find entrance to graduate school correlated with the current or projected state of the job market for persons with advanced degrees. Freeman, analyzing undergraduate enrollments in engineering, found that the number of baccalaureate graduates was reasonably predictable from knowledge of starting salaries four years previously (Freeman, 1971). Similarly, Freeman and Breneman (1974) have illustrated how first-year graduate enrollments in many academically oriented disciplines have declined since 1970 (with some exceptions, such as biology), while enrollments in most applied and professional fields have continued to increase significantly. This would seem to reflect the current outlook for job opportunities in academic and nonacademic sectors.

Several limiting factors make it extremely difficult to test various hypotheses concerning the determinants of graduate school entrance. First, data on first-year enrollment for advanced degrees are available only after 1960, so one can only go back for a 12- (certain) to 14- (estimated) year period. For professional degrees, first-year enrollment data have been available only since 1969. Second, NCES data are collected for first-year, rather than first-time, enrollment at the graduate level. As was indicated in Chapter 5, first-year figures are more than double first-time estimates, indicating that a high proportion of students defined as first-year have been in graduate school for several years on a part-time basis. Thus, the enrollment response at the graduate school entry-point will be blurred and somewhat lagged, and there is no way of telling whether the mix of full-time and part-time entering students has varied. Third, only a small fraction (about 10 percent) of graduate school entrants eventually complete the doctorate, and the first-year enrollment data is dominated by those who seek or receive only a terminal master's degree.[4] Fourth, labor market data are not readily available in a form that would be useful for correlating enrollment with economic indices. Salary data for new graduates are available only in bits and pieces from several professional societies;[5] unemployment is a relatively rare experience for persons trained at the doctoral level, but significant information on underemployment is not generally available; national data are available for broad first-job breakdowns by sector and by work activity, but they are insufficiently detailed to provide more than very rough indicators.[6]

Given the current state of enrollment and market information, what can be gleaned from existing data that would shed light on the market-responsive mechanism? The closest fit in searching for a model that would predict 1955–1973 first-year graduate enrollments has been found to be a formula including the following elements:

- A constant trend, independent of market conditions, whereby the ratio of first-year students to B.A.'s rises by .01 annually, beginning at .33 in 1955[7]

- A factor reflecting research and development demand for scientists, where one graduate enrollment would result for each $335,000 of current research and development spending

---

[4]In those graduate schools where only Ph.D. students are catered to, about 50 percent of entrants actually get the doctorate. If this proportion were applied to all schools, it would suggest that 75 to 80 percent of all first-year students only seek the master's degree. If the labor market demand for master's and doctor's differs considerably—as it has at times in such fields as engineering, mathematics, and education where the doctorate is essentially a college teaching degree—then first-year enrollments would not be very responsive to changing demand conditions for Ph.D.'s.

[5]The new *Doctoral Scientists and Engineers in the United States* (National Academy of Sciences, 1974) has information on the salaries of 1972 doctorate holders compared with earlier cohorts. This is the first in a series of reports replacing the National Register of Scientific and Technical Personnel and should eventually be a useful source of information.

[6]The American Institute of Physics, over the years, has done the best job in surveying enrollments, first-job placements, and academic mobility. Salary information has traditionally been best collected and reported by the industrially oriented disciplines—for example, engineering and chemistry.

[7]The baccalaureate series used was the weighted average of recent B.A.'s utilized in Chapter 5. See Table 5-1.

- A factor reflecting the number of junior academic positions opening each year, where 2.75 first-year students would be enrolled for every current opening (based on a three-year moving average)

Table 7-2 shows these components, and Figure 7-2 compares predicted first-year graduate enrollments with actual enrollments for 1955–1973. The fit is remarkably good except for the 1967–1970 years when the draft had its greatest impact providing a strong incentive for continuous full-time enrollment. For

TABLE 7-2 *Predicted and actual first-year graduate enrollments, 1954–1973 (in thousands)*

Year	Predicted components based on:			Predicted first-year enrollment*	Actual first-year enrollment	Actual less predicted
	B.A.'s awarded	R & D expenditure	Academic openings			
1955	90	19	22	131	134*	− 3
1956	99	25	24	148	151*	− 3
1957	112	30	27	169	160*	+ 9
1958	121	32	22	175	173*	+ 2
1959	129	37	22	188	184*	+ 4
1960	133	41	23	197	197	0
1961	141	43	31	215	217	− 2
1962	150	47	34	231	240	− 9
1963	162	52	53	267	271	− 4
1964	179	57	78	314	318	− 4
1965	201	61	98	360	359	+ 1
1966	216	67	93	376	371	+ 5
1967	236	71	91	398	428	−30
1968	265	75	80	420	458	−38
1969	305	78	79	462	494	−32
1970	346	79	60	485	528	−43
1971	382	82	48	512	525	−13
1972	416	83	38	537	543†	− 6
1973	451	85	33	569	569†	0

*First-year graduate enrollments were not reported by the U.S. Office of Education prior to 1959. However, as Table 5-3 indicated, the ratio of first-year to total graduate enrollment has remained relatively stable over the years for which data are available, and the estimates shown here with an asterisk are 55.5 percent of total graduate enrollment.

†Preliminary. See Table 5-1.

SOURCES: Computations by the author, based on Table 5-1, Figure 7-1, U.S. Office of Education (1975, Table B-7), and National Science Foundation (1972).

FIGURE 7-2 *Actual and predicted first-year graduate enrollments, 1955-1973*

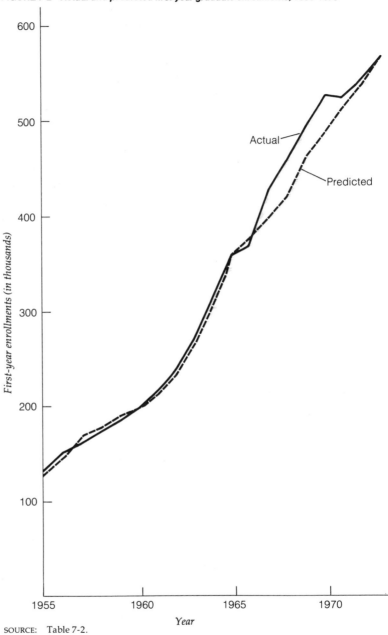

the entire period , the average annual difference between predicted and actual enrollments was less than 3 percent; but for the 15 years omitting 1967–1970 the average difference was only 1.6 percent. The data suggest that the military draft boosted first-year enrollments by about 8 percent in the 1967–1970 years. Apart from that brief period, the difference between predicted and actual enrollments was greater than 2.5 percent in only two years.

The predictive formula suggests that the predominant influences on first-year graduate enrollments over the last 15 years were non–market oriented. The trend factor based upon baccalaureate degrees accounted for nearly 70 percent of the predicted enrollments in the mid-1950s, dropped to about 55 percent in 1965, and rose again to nearly 80 percent by 1973. This would seem to indicate either that there is a high "consumption component" in the demand for postbaccalaureate education (as contrasted with the more common view that the demand for graduate education is essentially for investment in human capital) or that the continuously rising population-based component reflects a credential inflation where, in the modern world, every student generation needs a little more education and training than the preceding generation. (This latter could represent a qualitative deterioration in education as measured in standard time units, but this seems less likely.)

The rising advanced-degree aspirations of young people is probably attributable to a variety of factors. Beginning with Sputnik there was a resurgence in interest in scientific and technical training encouraged by federal programs of support for graduate education. In the early and mid-1960s, the enthusiasms of many young people were caught up by the increased public attention devoted to social and economic ills—such as poverty, urban decay, and problems of underdeveloped nations —and the social sciences were the most rapidly growing fields. In the late 1960s the impact of the Vietnam War was at its highest; it encouraged many college graduates who might not have done so without selective service hanging over them to test out advanced study and also generated an attitude among young people that encouraged professionalism as a means of assuring somewhat greater personal freedom in their work careers. (It is well known that a disproportionately large share of those who were most active in campus disruption went on to graduate school with the aim of becoming college professors.) Just as the war issues began to subside, public pressures for greater equality of opportunity, both for ethnic minorities and for women, began to have an impact on graduate enrollments. Thus, since 1970 there has been no appreciable increase in the number of white males entering graduate school; almost all of the increase is attributable to increased proportions of women and ethnic minorities.

Therefore, in reviewing the seemingly steady increase in the proportion of B.A.'s going on to graduate school since the late 1950s, it may be more appropriate to see this baccalaureate degree trend factor not as a constant, but as the result of a series of external shocks. This point of view would make it less surprising if this apparently nonmarket factor stabilized in the future rather than continued to rise.

Turning to the market-oriented factors that contributed to the predicted enrollments shown in Table 7-2, one finds that they are not quite what one would have anticipated. The research and development component, one would have speculated, should be related to increments of expenditure rather than to totals, since new Ph.D.'s represent the key manpower resource available to fill new positions. And, even if total, rather than incremental, expenditures was the key independent variable, it would seem more sensible to measure it in constant dollars (which would more nearly reflect number of positions) than in current dollars. However, the data suggest that total expenditure in current dollars is more closely related to the behavior of first-year graduate students than the year-to-year change in spending.

In the academic sector, on the other hand, the best fit is obtained for this factor in relation to new junior positions opening up rather than the total number of teaching positions. However, one would have speculated that the balance of new positions in relation to the number of new doctorates seeking academic employment would have been more appropriate— but a variety of such measures tested were all found to be much less reliable predictors than the total number of new openings.

In the aggregate, entering graduate students do not seem to be very sensitive to current employment imbalances—it is almost as though they were saying: if there are a large enough number of jobs out there, I will be willing to take my chances regardless of how many other job seekers there are. Freeman's data for several selected fields (Freeman, 1971, Ch. 9), and even the casual observer's review of enrollment patterns in some of the scientific and technical fields, seem to belie this conclusion for individual disciplines. This would suggest that there is a high degree of substitutability among fields and that, while students may be induced into or deflected away from a particular field of study, they are less easily discouraged from undertaking some form of graduate study. But it may also reflect a different kind of supply response in certain fields where doctorate holders and persons without doctorates do the same kind of work, but where the doctorate credential provides somewhat greater job security. In most fields a poor job market (and poor job prospects) would tend to discourage students from embarking on an advanced-degree program. In other fields—notably in education—poor job prospects often seem to encourage students to seek one more degree to improve their marketability. For the last several years, for example, when there has been a widely publicized oversupply of certified classroom teachers for the public schools, first-time entrants to graduate education programs have risen significantly. In 1972, first-time students in education were up 8.8 percent, while in the physical sciences first-time students were down 8.6 percent. In 1973, education entrants jumped 17.8 percent, while the number of new students in physical science increased 5.5 percent. The supply response in education can only be explained by the fact that opportunity costs were low and the anticipated benefit of an added degree credential seemed high to many thousands of students who were committed to a precollegiate teaching career. For that commitment, unlike physics or chemistry, there is no substitute field.

While the model described above appears capable of explaining behavior over the last 15 years, can it be assumed to be equally useful in predicting future enrollments? To answer this question, it is necessary first of all to see what the implications would be for the next 15 or 20 years if the forces that now prevail were still present. Column (1) of Table 7-3 shows extrapolated first-year enrollments in graduate school if the same set of factors could be presumed.

This extrapolation model produces an average annual growth rate of 3.4 percent until 1990, with first-year enrollment peaking at about 960,000. Because the B.A. component represents such a large fraction of the total, and also because in the model research and development expenditures are assumed to grow at a constant 5 percent rate over the period, the projected growth is almost constant throughout the period, with variations principally caused by changes in the size of the baccalaureate population. In fact, research and development expenditures will not grow at a constant rate, as the experience of the last eight to ten years has proved. The major decisions affecting research and development behavior are made by the federal government, based largely on factors that are nonmarket in nature, and thus one can only guess what the long-term trend may be.

The extrapolation model, even with its modest market feedback factor, is unsatisfactory for any long period of time . It may explain reasonably well behavior over the last 15 years, and perhaps for the next several years, but one cannot safely postulate a steadily rising graduate school entrance rate largely independent of other market and nonmarket constraints.

In searching for more appropriate long-term models, three alternatives combining the three component parts in somewhat different fashion are presented in Table 7-3. The two components that seem least likely to apply unchanged to future years are the baccalaureate and research and development factors. In model I, therefore, it is assumed that the baccalaureate coefficient remains constant (instead of continuously rising) at its 1972–73 level of .52. In addition, it is assumed that demand derived from research and development increases from its 1972–73 level at 2.5 percent per year. (This is what one might anticipate as the long-term growth rate of real research and development expenditures over the next decade or two, and gets away from the problem of using current dollars in a period where the long-term inflation rates may vary.) Model I produces continuing growth in projected first-year graduate enrollments to 1987, although, beginning in 1975, the rate of growth drops to about half of the rate for the preceding decade.

Models II and III in Table 7-3 are similar to model I, but recast the weight among the baccalaureate, research and development, and teaching factors so that respectively they are, for 1972–73, 50/25/25/ for model II and 33/33/33/ for model III.[8]

Columns (2), (3), and (4) show projected first-year enroll-

---

[8]For models II and III, the percentages of baccalaureates assumed to be first-year graduate students independent of market forces are 32.57 and 21.75, respectively; research and development expenditure per entering student is $47,180 and $63,025; each junior teaching position is assumed to generate 10.5 and 14 first-year students.

TABLE 7-3 *First-year graduate enrollments under alternative projection models (enrollments in thousands)*

	Alternative models				First-year students/B.A.'s			
	Extrapolation model	I	II	III	Extrapolation model	I	II	III
1973	569	567	565	560	.64	.64	.64	.63
1974	625	597	590	582	.67	.64	.63	.62
1975	653	615	612	609	.69	.65	.64	.64
1976	668	620	618	617	.70	.65	.65	.65
1977	682	637	630	634	.72	.67	.66	.67
1978	706	638	646	651	.74	.67	.67	.68
1979	729	650	636	634	.75	.66	.65	.65
1980	755	664	619	605	.75	.66	.61	.60
1981	779	675	590	558	.75	.65	.57	.53
1982	805	687	569	525	.75	.64	.53	.49
1983	833	700	545	485	.75	.63	.49	.44
1984	883	730	548	478	.76	.63	.47	.41
1985	902	740	559	493	.78	.64	.49	.43
1986	931	758	604	553	.80	.65	.52	.48
1987	963	777	653	618	.83	.67	.56	.53
1988	965	772	646	613	.85	.68	.57	.54
1989	959	760	616	571	.87	.69	.56	.52
1990	951	764	596	560	.88	.71	.55	.52

SOURCE: Computations by the author.

ments under each of the models, and columns (5) through (7) show the resulting ratios of the first-year graduate students to the weighted average of B.A.'s awarded. While the models are speculative and, ideally, should relate to first-time students (NCES only reports first-year enrollment at the graduate level), they provide a range of estimates that seem reasonable. Both models II and III provide a wavelike movement, peaking in 1978–79, reaching a trough in 1983–1985, peaking again in 1987, and declining once again by 1990. All three models produce much less expansion in the 1970s than a pure extrapolation of the 1960–1972 experience would suggest [in column (1) of Table 7-3], but the three stay quite close together through 1979–80. Beginning in 1980, the anticipated drop in new hires begins to have a noticeable effect on first-year enrollment projections under models II and III. Model III, which gives greater weight to the effect of the academic demand for new Ph.D.'s, exhibits the most extreme cyclical effect. Under model II, the contraction in the early 1980s brings projected enrollment back to its 1972 level; under model III, enrollment dips almost to its 1968 level.

If the author were to hazard a guess about the future pattern of first-year graduate enrollments, he would take models I and III as likely outer boundaries, and predict that actual entrance rates and enrollments would come closest to model II. One limitation of each of the models is that student behavior is assumed to depend upon current and past market experience, rather than upon anticipated future conditions. The experience of the late 1960s and early 1970s seems to support this position, as graduate enrollments continue to expand moderately in many fields of study even in the face of discouraging predictions about future market conditions. Only in the physical sciences have students apparently weighed the prospective as well as the retrospective outlook. However, if the poor academic job market projected for the early 1980s actually materializes, this may have the effect of making students more sensitive to manpower projections. At present, most students seem to discount the future heavily; the implicit discount rate may fall if experience bears out the predictions.

It should be noted, however, that for many disciplines the job market for baccalaureate degree holders in the last several years has not been extremely good—thus the sacrifice of immediate earnings occasioned by pursuing an advanced degree has also declined. To the extent that students make a rational (even if quite rough) calculation of anticipated rates of return over cost in deciding whether or not to enter graduate school, a drop in perceived opportunity costs (that is, what could have been earned in the immediate future if one did not go to graduate school) might more than offset any projected decline in estimated future earnings with an advanced degree. The continued high rate of growth in first-time enrollments in education is a case in point; given the poor immediate job prospects with only a B.A. many students have chosen to seek a higher degree in the interests of job preference or job security.

Market conditions also appear to influence the Ph.D. completion rate of graduate students once they are enrolled in graduate school. As Table 5-4 indicated, the completion rate peaked in 1969–70 at .085 and had fallen to .075 by 1972–73. The initial projection of doctoral degrees in Table 5-4 assumed that this rate would continue to fall until it reached .067 in 1980. However, it seems reasonable to assume that job market conditions influence the decision of students to continue beyond the master's degree and that the completion ratio is another important market-response variable.

Various hypotheses were tested in an attempt to explain behavior of the doctoral completion rate in the 1960–1973 period—a period that is complicated by the effects of the draft. The closest approximation that could be found was to assume that under normal equilibrium conditions the completion rate would be approximately .076, and that departures from that rate were dependent upon the short-term cumulative excess or deficiency of Ph.D.'s to fill academic openings.

The resulting model for predicting completion rates took the difference between number of Ph.D.'s awarded in any year and the total number of junior faculty openings (see pp. 129–130), and cumulated the excess or deficiency over a five-year period, assuming that year t counted as 100 percent; year $t - 1$ as 80 percent; $t - 2$, 60 percent; $t - 3$, 40 percent; and $t - 4$, 20 percent. This is analogous to an inventory model, assuming an obsolescence write-off of 20 percent per year. This is to say, excess Ph.D.'s in any one year are assumed to have some discounted impact upon the market in the immediately following years. After a five-year period, Ph.D.'s who either were initially placed in inferior jobs or who did not find any suitable academic openings are assumed to no longer constitute supply pressure upon the market.

The cumulated excess or shortage of doctorates, so calculated, was then divided by the number of doctorates awarded in any given year to provide a measure of the relative stimulant or depressant effect on the job market. This ratio of excess or deficiency varied from −.71 (excess) in 1960, to 2.62 (shortage) in 1966, to −3.28 in 1987. The best fit was found by multiplying this ratio by a factor of .004 and adding or subtracting the result from the assumed equilibrium value of .076. The predicted completion rate was then applied to the following year's doctorate estimate based on average first-year enrollments four to six years earlier.

TABLE 7-4 *Actual and projected doctorates awarded and doctoral completion ratios, 1960 to 1990: model II (in thousands)*

Year	Number of doctorates (1)	Number of junior faculty openings (2)	5-year discounted excess (−) or shortage (+) (3)	Ratio column (3)/ column (1) (4)	Doctoral completion rates Predicted (5)	Doctoral completion rates Actual (6)
1960	9.8	8.1	−7.0	−0.71	.0728	.0713
1961	10.6	12.2	−1.7	−0.16	.0732	.0713
1962	11.6	13.4	0.3	0.03	.0754	.0720
1963	12.8	14.7	2.7	0.21	.0761	.0743
1964	14.5	32.0	20.4	1.41	.0768	.0785
1965	16.5	40.6	40.3	2.44	.0816	.0826
1966	18.2	35.0	47.7	2.62	.0858	.0837
1967	20.6	26.2	40.9	1.99	.0865	.0850
1968	23.1	37.6	42.2	1.83	.0840	.0836
1969	26.2	23.8	24.1	0.92	.0833	.0829
1970	29.9	24.9	7.4	0.25	.0797	.0855
1971	32.1	16.9	−13.7	−0.43	.0770	.0832
1972	33.4	10.9	−35.7	−1.07	.0747	.0797
1973	34.4	13.3	−50.7	−1.47	.0717	.0748
1974	34.6	11.0	−61.1	−1.76	.0701	
1975	35.6	14.7	−64.5	−1.81	.0690	
1976	36.6	14.7	−65.7	−1.79	.0688	
1977	37.4	15.1	−66.0	−1.76	.0688	
1978	39.1	15.3	−67.9	−1.74	.0690	
1979	40.6	17.3	−68.7	−1.69	.0690	
1980	42.0	16.1	−72.7	−1.73	.0692	
1981	42.8	10.8	−80.7	−1.89	.0691	
1982	43.2	8.5	−89.9	−2.08	.0684	
1983	43.1	3.1	−102.0	−2.37	.0677	
1984	42.1	1.2	−111.7	−2.65	.0665	
1985	40.2	−2.7	−119.9	−2.98	.0654	
1986	38.0	−2.4	−122.2	−3.22	.0641	
1987	34.8	3.7	−114.3	−3.28	.0631	
1988	34.8	8.4	−100.9	−2.90	.0629	
1989	35.5	10.1	−89.9	−2.53	.0644	
1990	37.6	2.2	−91.5	−2.43	.0659	

SOURCES: Column (1) 1960–1973 data from U.S. Office of Education (1974, Table 21); column (2) from Table 6-10; column (6) calculated from Table 5-5. All other figures generated by the model.

Table 7-4 shows the predicted and actual values for the completion rate in columns (5) and (6) from 1960 through 1972. The predicted rate reasonably well matches the movement of the actual rate through 1969, but drops more sharply in 1970–1972. This latter departure is assumed to be the temporary effects of selective service regulations, which encouraged students in the late 1960s to remain in graduate school through doctoral completion. By 1973, this effect is expected to be dissipated. Between 1975 and 1981 the predicted completion rate stabilizes at about .069, as the ratio of the five-year discounted excess or shortage of doctorates in relation to available teaching positions levels off at approximately −1.75. Beginning in 1982, however, academic positions are projected to become scarcer, and the predicted completion rate declines to .0629 in 1988. Thereafter, a modest improvement appears likely, and doctorates awarded are projected to rise again above the 40,000 level. For the doctoral projections in column (1), predicted first-year enrollments in market model II (Table 7-3) have been used as a basis for estimating degrees. Column (3) of Table 7-4 shows the discounted cumulative impact of prior market imbalances, and column (4) expresses this as a ratio to current doctorates awarded.

Figure 7-3 shows the predicted first-year enrollments in graduate school and the resulting doctoral degree estimates for this market supply model, and contrasts these projections with the preliminary fixed-coefficients estimates derived in Chapter 5 (Table 5-5). As can be seen, the market model runs somewhat counter to the fixed-coefficients model. The latter is largely demographic-based and chiefly reflects varying levels of B.A. output. By contrast, the market model predicts a continued growth in the first-year enrollments out to 1979 during the period of projected modest, but constant, excess of doctorates over junior teaching positions. In the early 1980s, as the fixed-coefficients enrollment projection rises, the market model declines sharply. The upper curves in Figure 7-3, representing projected doctorates awarded, more or less mirror the enrollment curves with a four- to five-year lag; thus, beyond 1992 (not illustrated) both doctorate projections would decline.

The market-response supply model illustrated above is highly speculative, based on inadequate data and too few observations to sustain a high degree of confidence in its pro-

FIGURE 7-3

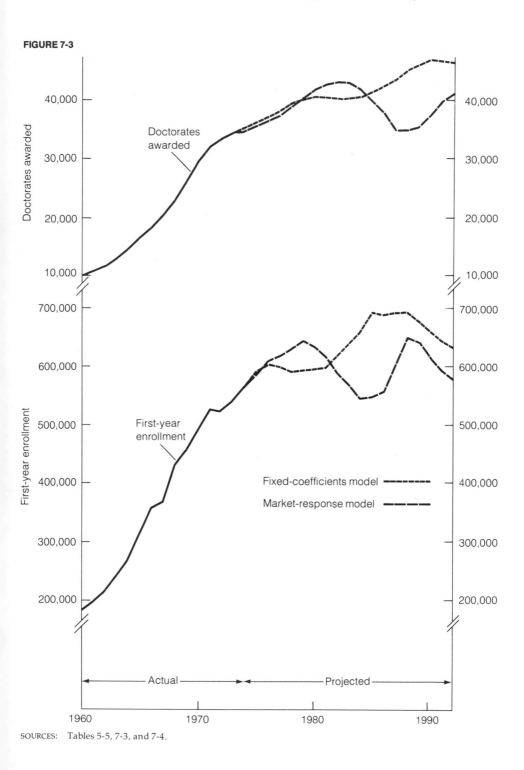

SOURCES: Tables 5-5, 7-3, and 7-4.

jections. In addition, it is limited only to quantity variables rather than price variables. The balance between projected supplies and projected new positions is assumed to affect the graduate school entrance and doctorate completion rates principally through its effect upon the outlook of students as to job availability and career advancement opportunities. Typically, market responses are influenced by pecuniary calculations of current and discounted expected future earnings. In the short run, it can be argued, academic salaries are relatively inflexible; however, over longer periods of time, significant variations in starting salaries (and related benefits and work conditions) can be observed. During the doctorate shortage in the 1960s, salary differentials between assistant and full professor ranks widened; during a period of excess supply one can anticipate a compression of differentials once again. Similarly, as noted in Chapter 5, teaching loads were reduced in the shortage period, when faculty were in a strong bargaining position, and there are indications that work loads are beginning to rise again today. In addition, if academic salaries in general lag behind returns to doctorate holders in nonacademic employment sectors over the next decade or two, this can be expected to contribute to a net outflow of senior personnel from colleges and universities.[9] For most of the 1960s the net flow of senior personnel was close to zero; however, a deterioration in relative salaries can be expected to increase the numbers leaving higher education and to depress the numbers seeking entry to higher education. If a gap even as small as 1 percent of the total teaching faculty were to open (in the mid-1960s there was an approximate 3 percent gross flow in each direction, resulting in an approximate zero net flow) it would add about 4,000 to the number of junior positions to be filled annually. This phenomenon will be analyzed in some detail in the next chapter.

The market-response model in Table 7-4 is also limited in that it concentrates on supply adjustments but assumes that demand factors are independently determined by institutions depending upon their enrollment level. Two qualifications should be recognized on the demand side. First, even in the short run, price (salary) has some effect upon the number of faculty who will be hired in any year. The demand for new

[9]See Chapter 8 for a more detailed discussion of this point.

teachers is not perfectly price inelastic. Freeman suggests an elasticity coefficient of .3 for scientists and engineers—that is, that a 1 percent decline in salaries will increase the number of new scientists hired by .3 percent (Cain, Freeman, & Hansen, 1973, p. 29). Presumably the long-run demand for faculty would be somewhat more price-elastic, given time for institutional adjustments. Thus, in a typical year in the 1970s the number of junior faculty hired might be 500 or 600 greater than indicated in Table 7-4 if beginning salaries were to fall by 10 percent.

A second qualification on the demand side is that graduate education itself is part of a feedback network. The estimated demand for new hires in Table 7-4 was based on the fixed-coefficients enrollment model of earlier chapters; however, the market model described above not only involves variations in the levels of graduate enrollment and doctoral output, but also implies further variation in the number of faculty required to teach graduate students. One further refinement should therefore be introduced—a recognition that greater variability in the estimated first-year enrollment of graduate students in response to market forces will, in turn, produce greater variation than suggested in Table 7-4 in the number of new faculty hired each year. For example, if the anticipated supply response is such that in a given year 20,000 fewer graduate students are likely to be enrolled than the initial enrollment projection in Table 5-8 indicated, then in that year there will be 2,000 fewer new faculty employed if the graduate student-faculty ratio is 10:1.

As a last step, therefore, a market response in the demand for new faculty must also be incorporated into the model. To accomplish this the first-year graduate enrollment series in model II (Table 7-4) was converted to an FTE estimate of total graduate enrollment and substituted for the enrollment projections in Table 5-8. Incremental enrollments were then recalculated. Since this change in projected enrollments is attributed entirely to variations in graduate education, a 10:1 student-faculty ratio has been applied to the difference, and new estimates of annual junior faculty openings were derived.

Table 7-5 presents the revised projections comparable with those in Table 7-4, but including the demand as well as supply market response. Figure 7-4 compares the two models—what was referred to as model II in Table 7-4 and what might be

TABLE 7-5 *Projected doctorates awarded and doctoral completion ratios, 1970–1990: model IIA (in thousands)*

Year	Number of doctorates (1)	Number of junior faculty openings (2)	Five-year discounted excess (−) or shortage (+) (3)	Ratio column (3)/ column (1) (4)	Predicted doctoral completion rate (5)
1970	29.9*	24.9*	7.4	.25	.0832*
1971	32.1*	16.9*	− 13.7	− .43	.0797*
1972	33.4*	10.9*	− 35.7	−1.07	.0748*
1973	34.4*	13.7*	− 50.3	−1.51	.0717
1974	34.5	11.4	− 51.3	−1.49	.0700
1975	36.1	17.3	− 56.8	−1.57	.0700
1976	37.1	17.8	− 59.5	−1.60	.0697
1977	38.0	18.9	− 59.2	−1.56	.0696
1978	39.6	17.0	− 61.6	−1.56	.0698
1979	41.3	16.0	− 66.3	−1.61	.0698
1980	42.8	9.9	− 78.2	−1.83	.0696
1981	44.2	2.7	− 95.9	−2.17	.0687
1982	44.8	3.1	−109.3	−2.44	.0673
1983	44.8	1.8	−119.5	−2.67	.0662
1984	44.3	1.3	−125.6	−2.84	.0653
1985	42.8	−1.9	−129.9	−3.04	.0646
1986	39.8	−0.7	−127.6	−3.21	.0638
1987	36.4	6.5	−114.9	−3.16	.0632
1988	34.5	9.8	− 99.4	−2.88	.0634
1989	34.9	9.7	− 88.0	−2.52	.0645
1990	36.4	1.2	− 90.8	−2.50	.0659

*Actual

SOURCE: Calculations by the author, based on variation of model II (Table 7-4) described in text.

called model IIA in Table 7-5. Model IIA exhibits a somewhat more exaggerated movement in the projected number of junior faculty openings, reflecting the additional faculty needed in 1974–1978 to handle additional market-induced graduate enrollments, and the smaller number of new faculty required in 1979–1984 when graduate enrollments may decline more sharply due to market factors. The projected doctorate curves remain fairly close together, but the variations are somewhat more marked in the case of model IIA.

Figure 7-4 does point up once again, however, the likely magnitude of the placement problem in the early 1980s. While the mid-1970s represents a period of relative abundance of doctorate holders in relation to anticipated openings for college teachers, the 1970s are an approximate negative image of the 1960s. Thus, in the 1960s there was some modest deterioration

FIGURE 7-4 *Market-response model projections of doctorates awarded and junior-faculty openings*

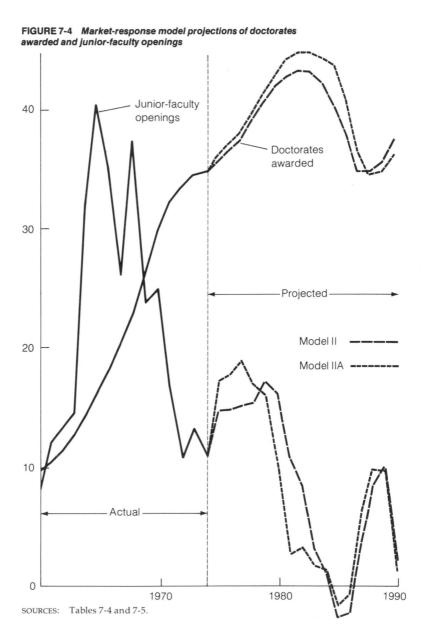

SOURCES: Tables 7-4 and 7-5.

in the preparation level of new college teachers, and a smaller percentage possessed the doctorate than had been true early in the decade. In the 1970s the situation is reversed, and significant faculty enrichment is now taking place. But the ratio of Ph.D.'s to faculty openings is expected to remain relatively stable during the 1970s, and the excess of doctorates, as indicated in Tables 7-4 and 7-5, remains relatively constant. In the early 1980s, however, the gap between doctorates and academic openings jumps from approximately 20,000 annually to nearly 40,000, and the estimated excess of doctorates doubles. In the late 1980s, as doctorates begin to contract in the market-response models, and academic hiring picks up briefly from 1987 to 1989, the gap narrows, but only to open up again in the early 1990s. (1993 is likely to be another enrollment trough, as Table 5-8 indicated.)

The market models illustrated here are speculative, but are probably a significant improvement over fixed-coefficients projections. While the latter can accommodate changes in market conditions that are anticipated at the time the projections are made, there is a tendency to freeze the coefficients beyond the short-range future because the uncertainties rise the further ahead one looks. More importantly, the construction of a market model forces one to seek causal relationships and to test out various hypotheses on the experience of the recent past; and, if the projections turn out to be poor, one can learn from the experience in attempting to devise a better model for the future.

The models illustrated here are based largely upon the experience between 1960 and 1973, and the components provide a reasonably good explanation of variations in first-year enrollments and degree completion rates in that short period of time. Data deficiencies (for example, the absence of good first-time graduate enrollment data, and inadequate information on the number of faculty openings filled by new doctorates) restrict one's ability to correlate changes in the variables, and the abnormalities of the 1966–1972 period due to the Vietnam War make the 1960–1973 years less than ideal as a base for constructing a market-response model. Beyond 1973 the models incorporate one intuitive judgment of the author that is not supported by the experience of the preceding decade—an assumption that gave heavier weights to the market-factor components (that is, to anticipated research and development expenditure levels and to the projected number of junior faculty openings).

While the models seemingly abstract from price considerations, the projected imbalances between number of doctorates available and job openings in research and development and academic sectors themselves are partially a proxy for price adjustments. Thus, in periods when the five-year discounted excess or deficiency of doctorates (Tables 7-4 and 7-5) is high in relation to doctoral output, the mechanism by which the market tends to reestablish an equilibrium is likely to be price adjustment as well as occupational diversion. Observing Figure 7-4 would lead one to expect that the 1961–1968 period was one in which relative salary improvement would have been the norm in academic employment; by contrast, in 1971–1980 one would anticipate some erosion of faculty salaries in relation to alternative employment, and in the 1980s a more substantial adjustment. However, about three-fourths of college teachers today are in public institutions where, because of intragovernmental relationships and the rise of collective bargaining, salaries may become more inflexible than in the past. To the extent that salaries are prevented from acting as a mechanism for achieving a market equilibrium, then strict limitations upon hiring will perform the market function by diverting an increasing share of doctorates to nonacademic employment. These alternative employment paths may appear less rewarding to an individual even if the actual pecuniary return is as high or even higher. Price adjustments may also be hidden from the observer by gradual adjustments in the work load; and increased teaching load at the same nominal salary is a price adjustment for labor inputs as seen from the employer's point of view.

In the models presented here, attention has been concentrated on the point of entry to the academic labor market. In the next chapter, the focus will be broadened to look at the total flow of faculty up through the age and seniority ranks, among institutions, and between academic and nonacademic employment. Given the mobility of doctorate manpower, the inflow from the graduate schools to the corpus of the teaching faculty is only one among many streams, albeit an important one where changing market conditions are most visible.

8. The Changing Composition of College and University Faculties

In the preceding chapters, attention has been focused primarily upon the point of entry into the academic labor market. College teaching faculties have been treated, to put it simply, as though they lost personnel only by death and retirement and their stock was replenished only by hiring new teachers directly from the graduate schools. Although the movement of new doctorates from the graduate schools to teaching positions is perhaps the most critical vantage point from which to view changes in market conditions, this manpower flow is actually overshadowed by other movements within the academic manpower pool.

Two other types of personnel change must be taken into consideration. First, a considerable number of faculty members change institutions in any given year. In the mid-1960s this number has been estimated to have been the equivalent of about 8 percent annually for teachers with the doctorate (Cartter, 1974, p. 288). Thus, about 1 out of every 12 faculty members with the doctorate shifted institutions each year during the period of most rapid enrollment growth. Second, a significant number of college teachers each year leave higher education for jobs in other employment sectors, and a number of persons with similar credentials enter higher education from government, industry, or other nonacademic employment. In the mid-1960s, the author's estimate is that this gross flow of senior personnel was approximately 3 percent each year, with the net flow being close to zero (ibid.; Cartter, 1966c). With total full-time faculty expanding by more than 10 percent in the mid-1960s, it is estimated that slightly over 20 percent of full-time teachers were newly employed by their college or university each year, and only about one-third of this number were new doctorates coming directly from the graduate schools.

Movements from one institution to another, and between nonacademic and academic employment sectors, are also responsive to changing market conditions. Changes in relative salary and career opportunity are as influential on the senior person with college teaching qualifications as they are on the junior person just completing graduate school. Thus, a realistic view of the operation of the academic labor market must take all these flows into consideration.

Academic institutions are not perfectly analogous to business firms in the profit sector of the economy, but they are not unlike profit-making enterprises in the way in which their maximizing behavior expresses itself in the demand for college teachers. Within the constraint of feasible expenditure levels, colleges and universities ordinarily attempt to make the most effective possible use of available resources to ensure institutional survival and to enhance their educational reputations. The most important factor in the reputation of an institution is the quality of its faculty, and thus institutional maximizing behavior is most clearly seen in its efforts to renew and to strengthen faculty quality.

Traditional labor market analysis would lead us to expect several phenomena as market conditions change. In a period of high demand and limited qualified labor supply in any employment sector, one would anticipate, first of all, that wages and salaries would rise relative to other employment sectors. Obversely, in periods of plentiful supply, relative salaries would be expected to fall. In addition, given the prestige-maximizing behavior of colleges and universities, during periods when demand for teaching faculty is high relative to the available supply of new entrants, we would expect the bidding for highly qualified senior professors to intensify. This competition would exhibit itself in an increase in relative salaries for established teachers (that is, a widening of the salary differentials between higher and lower ranks) and an increase in the interinstitutional mobility rate (and vice versa in periods of declining demand).

Another labor market phenomenon common to all employment sectors is the variation in hiring standards associated with changing market conditions. In a tight labor market, employers will ordinarily lower entrance standards for employment as an alternative to raising the general level of salaries.[1] As Brown (1967, p. 17) has noted, "quality deterioration is expeditious in that it is relatively inconspicuous." In a period of plentiful supply, on the other hand, employers will only hire the most highly qualified applicants. In higher education, the most obvious evidence is the proportion of the faculty (or newly employed faculty) who have the doctorate.

There is a corresponding supply response that reinforces variations in hiring standards. When good jobs are difficult to find, potential teachers attempt to improve their attractiveness in the eyes of employers. The most obvious economic manifestation of this phenomenon is the increased willingness of those seeking a career in college teaching to invest more in human capital in the form of additional schooling, advanced degrees, postdoctoral experience, or work experience. Thus, although a declining demand for college teachers may result in a decreasing number of persons eventually preparing for a teaching career, those who do persist are likely to invest more in themselves as a means of differentiating themselves in the eyes of potential employers. One of the clearest examples of this today is the decline in the number of persons seeking teaching certification at the undergraduate level (a decrease in the supply of new public school teachers) at the same time that the number of entering graduate students in education is still increasing more rapidly than other fields (an enrichment of supply qualifications). A parallel is also found in many science fields where the number of new doctorates seeking postdoctoral experience has risen significantly since the late 1960s. Under the reverse market conditions that existed in the late 1940s and the mid-1960s, when standards were relatively low for entering college teaching, a high proportion of young people entered teaching with only master's degree credentials or were content to remain ABDs (all-but-dissertation students).

Another phenomenon common to most labor markets is the tendency of senior individuals to move into or out of an employment sector depending upon relative salaries and career advancement opportunities. In recent years only about half of all Ph.D.'s, and probably not more than 10 percent of all mas-

---

[1]For a more detailed discussion, see Cartter (1959, pp. 52–58).

ter's degree holders, have been employed in college teaching. Thus there is a reasonably plentiful supply of men and women in the labor force who have the customary degree credentials for entering college teaching. In every year there are some college teachers who leave academic employment for positions in government, industry, nonprofit or service employment. Others are drawn back to college teaching from foundations, government agencies, research institutes, banks, and the like. Intersector or interoccupational mobility is sensitive to changing market forces, and variations in these flows of senior personnel can moderate or reinforce changes in demand for new entrants emerging from the graduate schools.

In this chapter, these phenomena are explored to provide the basis for reasonable assumptions in building a model of faculty flow. There are various points where institutional policy can influence the evolving age and rank composition of college faculties—for example, retirement, promotion, and tenure practices—and the interaction of market forces and institutional response can best be illustrated by such a model.

Despite the vast quantities of data collected about higher education, there is a paucity of information about career selection, advancement, and institutional and occupational mobility of doctorates. As noted in Chapter 6, even the historical data on college and university faculty members have been frequently revised by the U.S. Office of Education. And, despite the dramatic changes in the job market for college teachers, no recent detailed study of college faculty experience and characteristics has been undertaken by the U.S. Office of Education since the spring of 1963.

The only source of reasonably accurate information is the two faculty surveys conducted by the American Council on Education (ACE) in 1968–69 and 1972–73.[2] These surveys are used in this chapter as the basis for estimating the faculty age distribution and the source of new faculty appointments.

The survey data, as reported in the ACE publications, are for total faculty (full-time and part-time). As argued in Chapter 6, the present study concentrates on full-time faculty appoint-

[2]The former was jointly sponsored by the Carnegie Commission and ACE under Martin Trow's supervision. The 1972–73 survey was conducted by Alan Bayer at ACE. For comparable presentation of the findings, see Bayer (1970; 1973).

ments because the author believes that long-term analysis of the academic labor market can best be measured by examining changes in full-time employment and characteristics of full-time faculty. We were fortunate in obtaining the data tapes for the two surveys[3] and were thus able to extract information that applied only to full-time faculty and then reweight the sample to represent the universe of higher education.

Using the ACE survey data and the detailed report of the Office of Education's 1962–63 survey for basic information on the age distribution of faculty members entering and leaving college teaching, a model of faculty flow has been created which is useful in simulating the growth and characteristics of faculty under a number of different policy and market-response conditions.

MOBILITY AND SALARY LEVELS Academic salaries are not as flexible as are those in business and industry for persons of comparable training and background. Tenure regulations limit the ability of institutions to lay off or replace the majority of their faculty; most institutions have publicly announced salary schedules, often with intrarank steps clearly delineated; academic salary scales are usually established from three to six months prior to the opening of the school year and are set for a year at a time. Despite these rigidities, real salary levels would be expected to vary—even if somewhat sluggishly—in response to imbalances between the number of job openings and the available supply of qualified college teachers. Unlike price determination in a purely competitive market, the salary level cannot be expected to vary sufficiently to "clear the market" in the short run; however, variations in the level of relative salaries can be expected to influence the decision of doctorate holders to enter or continue in college teaching.

Table 8-1 shows changes in average academic salaries over the last 10 years relative to the average wage or salary of all workers (column 1), relative to per capita income (column 2), and in real (constant) dollars (column 3). Academic salaries apparently moved favorably in comparison with each of these

[3]The author is indebted to Alexander W. Astin and the Cooperative Institutional Research Program at UCLA for making this data source available for further analysis.

TABLE 8-1   *Changes in relative faculty salaries, 1963–1973*

Year	Faculty salary relative to weekly earnings of all workers (percentage change) (1)	Faculty salary relative to total per capita income (percentage change) (2)	Percentage change in real purchasing power faculty salary (3)	Cumulative index of faculty, shortage or surplus (4)
1963	4.1	1.7	7.4	0.2
1964	1.1	1.1	5.0	1.4
1965	0.4	(2.0)	2.5	2.4
1966	3.1	(1.4)	2.5	2.6
1967	2.1	(0.6)	2.5	2.0
1968	(1.3)	(2.4)	0.8	1.8
1969	1.5	(1.3)	0.8	0.9
1970	0.2	(0.7)	0.4	0.3
1971	(3.0)	(2.8)	(0.7)	(0.4)
1972	(4.3)	(3.9)	(1.4)	(1.1)
1973	1.3	(3.7)	(1.7)	(1.5)

NOTE: For columns 1, 2, and 3, parentheses denote a negative number. For the cumulative index of faculty, figures in parentheses are surpluses, other figures are shortages.

SOURCES: American Association of University Professors (1974 and various preceding years); *Federal Reserve Bulletin* (1974).

indices until the mid-1960s. Professors began to lose ground in 1966 compared with the movement of per capita income, and, in 1968, in comparison with other wages and salaries. Since 1971 the purchasing power of the average professor's salary has absolutely declined. Column 4 of Table 8-1 repeats the index of cumulative doctoral shortage (+) or excess (−) from Table 7-4. The similarity with column 3 is quite striking, suggesting that real academic salaries have responded closely to over- or under-supply conditions in the academic market place.

Despite this similarity, traditional wage theory does not suggest that real salary levels would steadily decline during a continuing period of cumulative excess doctorates, but rather that relative salary levels would lag sufficiently behind salaries in alternative employment sectors to encourage a net outward flow of doctorates from higher education. Until 1986, when, as Table 7-4 indicates, the cumulative excess of doctorates is likely to increase, relative salaries (although not necessarily real salaries) will probably decline. Little relative improvement can be anticipated in professorial salaries until the number of faculty openings increases again in the late 1990s.

Salary differentials between junior and senior ranks can also be expected to respond to changing market conditions. In a period of relative affluence, academic institutions attempt to maximize their prestige by hiring prominent or visible promising professors at middle and upper ranks from other institutions. This competition tends to raise salaries at upper ranks more rapidly than at junior levels. This tendency is reinforced during a period of rapid employment growth in an industry or occupation. Also, as Stigler (1970, p. 264) has noted, "experienced practitioners will earn more, relative to neophytes, in a growing than in a stable occupation because their numbers will be relatively smaller in a growing occupation."

The 1960s was a period of rapid occupational growth for college professors. By 1972, 42.2 percent of full-time college teachers were 40 years of age or younger, while only 15.9 percent were between 55 and 70 (see Table 8-6). In a stationary-state situation, it has been estimated that these percentages would be 37 and 24, respectively (Cartter, 1972, p. 84). Because of the rapid growth rate over the last 15 years, the age distribution of college teachers is skewed toward the lower end of the spectrum, with the median age today about eight years younger than it would be under a stationary condition (ibid.).

Table 8-2 shows the ratio of average full professors' salaries to the average of assistant professors' and instructors' from 1964 to 1973. From 1964 to 1968, the rank-salary differential widened concurrently with a rapid expansion of the size of faculties and a general improvement of academic salaries relative to other incomes. Since 1968, there has been a slight decline in the rank-salary differential as market conditions have reversed.

In all likelihood the true-salary differential by age and seniority cohorts has moved in even more extreme fashion. During the middle and late 1960s when qualified senior faculty were in great demand and mobility rates were high, the rate of promotion speeded up. Thus faculty members were promoted to full professor at a somewhat earlier age than had been customary, skewing the intrarank distribution for professors more toward younger faculty and accordingly moderating the rate of improvement in professors' average salaries. Over the last sev-

TABLE 8-2 *Ratios of average compensation*

Year of comparison	Professor to assistant professor	Percent change ratio	Professor to instructor	Percent change ratio
1964–65	1.6000	1.0	1.8868	1.1
1965–66	1.6155	0.3	1.9084	1.2
1966–67	1.6207	0.3	1.9305	1.2
1967–68	1.6260	0.3	1.9531	1.0
1968–69	1.6313	(0.2)	1.9724	0.4
1969–70	1.6287	0.0	1.9802	(0.2)
1970–71	1.6287	(0.5)	1.9763	(0.6)
1971–72	1.6207	(0.3)	1.9646	(1.0)
1972–73	1.6155	0.0	1.9455	0.0
1973–74	1.6155	0.0	1.9455	0.2

SOURCE: Computed from data for institutions reporting comparable information in successive summer issues of the *AAUP Bulletin*.

eral years the promotion rate appears to have moderated slightly, thus depressing the true rate of increase in full professors' salaries if one could standardize for age and seniority. The evidence, therefore, appears to confirm the expectations derived from traditional wage theory.

INTER-INSTITUTIONAL MOBILITY As noted previously, the movement of college teachers from one college or university to another cancels out when one is considering the universe of higher education, but mobility rates are highly responsive to changing market conditions. This observation is supported by anecdotal evidence and experience over the years in higher education, although the supporting data are rather poor. Reviewing the limited evidence available in the mid-1960s, this author concluded that in 1963 about 8 percent of all college professors moved from one teaching position to another (Cartter, 1965*b*, pp. 266–267; 1974, p. 288). The rapid expansion of enrollments between 1963 and 1968 dramatically increased the demand for teachers, and it was a rare faculty member who did not receive a number of attractive offers from other institutions. It was in this period that college professors were jokingly referred to as "twentieth-century nomads," and many found that more rapid advancement was possible by changing jobs.

The 1968–69 and 1972–73 ACE faculty surveys provide somewhat better evidence of changing interinstitutional mobility rates. In each questionnaire, faculty members were asked to indicate how many years they had been at their present institution and what their status was immediately prior to their present position (for example, a member of the faculty at another institution, a graduate student, an employee in business or industry). In analyzing these data we removed part-time faculty and then reviewed those who had only been at their present institution for one year.[4] Table 8-3 indicates the number of faculty who remained in college teaching but changed institutions the preceding year.

Interinstitutional job changes dropped 60 percent between 1968 and 1972, as demand conditions in the academic job market changed markedly. Interinstitutional mobility, estimated to have been 8 percent in 1962, was 4.5 percent in 1968 and declined to 1.4 percent by 1972. The most interesting change between the two years, however, was the increase in percent of mobile faculty who possessed the doctorate—from 48.7 percent in 1968 to 73.5 percent in 1972.

Comparing these peak and trough employment years, it seems clear that in periods when the demand for new teachers is low relative to the supply of new doctorates, the number of experienced college teachers who are bid away from other institutions drops sharply, and the qualifications of those who move rise markedly. Conversely, in periods of tight labor supply one would anticipate a much higher interinstitutional

[4]It is not clear whether respondents interpreted the question to mean a *completed* year (in which case the data refer to fall 1967 and fall 1971) or the *current* year (in which case 1968 and 1972 are the relevant years). In all likelihood it is a blend of these two. However, 1967 and 1968 were both good employment years, and 1971 and 1972 were both poor years, so the illustration is valid.

TABLE 8-3 *Faculty members who changed institutions, 1968–69 and 1972–73*	1968–69	1972–73
Number of faculty changing institutions	15,022	6,221
Changers as percent of total faculty	4.5	1.4
Changers as percent of new hires	33.4	36.1
Percent changers with doctorate	48.7	73.5

SOURCE: Computed from ACE faculty survey data.

mobility rate and a corresponding decrease in degree qualifications of those changing teaching positions.

These data, although only covering two recent periods, confirm what would have been expected from traditional labor market analysis and assist in making projections of future faculty flows under changing market conditions.

THE MOBILITY OF EXPERIENCED PH.D.'S
In an early article on the supply and demand of college teachers, this author concluded that, in addition to interinstitutional job changes, about 3 percent of doctorate teachers in the 1952–1964 period left higher education for other (nonacademic) employment and an approximately equal number of senior doctorate personnel entered higher education from nonacademic jobs (Cartter, 1965b, p. 272). Although there were no hard data to corroborate the speculation, it was concluded that the change in faculty size and composition over the decade ending in 1964 could only have come about if the annual net outflow of senior college teachers with the doctorate had been approximately 0.11 percent annually (ibid., Table 3, p. 272).

More recently, Freeman (1971) has used National Research Council data to analyze the mobility of experienced Ph.D.'s between academic and nonacademic sectors. Table 8-4 shows his estimated annual rates of flow by period, from 1935 to 1963. In the late 1930s and from the late 1950s on, relative salaries in higher education were quite good, and there was a modest annual inflow of experienced doctorates. In the post-World War II decade, however, teaching salaries lagged far behind salaries in government and industry, and there was a steady net outflow of senior staff.

TABLE 8-4
Estimated annual percentage of experienced doctorate holders leaving and entering academic employment

	Percent entering	*Percent leaving*	*Net flow (percent)*
1935–1940	4.4	3.5	0.9
1940–1945	3.2	7.9	−4.7
1945–1950	5.7	7.1	−1.4
1950–1955	2.4	5.0	−2.6
1955–1960	4.2	3.5	0.7
1960–1963	4.1	3.4	0.7

SOURCE: Freeman (1971, Table 9.6, p. 178). See also National Academy of Sciences (1968, Ch. 3).

Thus, the gross flows of experienced doctorates into and out of higher education are evidently quite sensitive to labor market conditions, and the net flow is either positive or negative depending upon the relative attractiveness of academic employment.

The 1968 and 1972 ACE faculty surveys provide a glimpse of one side of this market—the inflow from nonacademic employment. Table 8-5 shows the estimated number of senior entrants to college teaching by degree status. Apparently, the number of teaching hires from other employment sectors was only about half as large in 1972 as in 1968, and in each category the percent holding the doctorate was greater in the later year. These data support the theses that the flow of senior personnel (teachers with some employment experience between graduate study and their present job) into college teaching is highly market responsive and that hiring standards also rise and fall under varying academic labor market conditions.[5]

[5]In Tables 8-3 and 8-5 one can have a reasonably high degree of confidence in the percent of new hires with the doctorate, and in the percent distribution of new hires by prior employment status. However, the absolute numbers hired and new hires as a percent of total faculty are subject to a somewhat wider margin of error. The absolute numbers were determined by blowing up the sample data to accord with the NCES estimate of faculty added in 1968 and 1972, plus the estimated number of full-time faculty who died, retired, or otherwise left academic employment. As indicated in Chapter 6, the NCES faculty estimates for recent years have been substantially revised in subsequent years. To this observer's eye the NCES estimates of increments of full-time faculty for 1971 and 1972 appear to be conservatively low, thus total number of faculty hired for these years may be underestimated.

TABLE 8-5 *College faculty hired from nonacademic employment sectors, 1968 and 1972 faculty surveys*

Previous employment	Estimated number	Percent of all new hires	Percent of total faculty	Percent with doctorate
1968				
Elementary and high schools	4,925	11.0	1.5	9.6
Government and industry	7,250	16.1	2.2	35.2
Other	1,640	3.6	0.6	13.9
1972				
Elementary and high schools	1,580	6.0	0.4	13.3
Government and industry	3,165	12.0	0.8	37.6
Other	2,480	9.4	0.7	31.6

SOURCE: Computed from ACE faculty survey data.

Projections in earlier chapters of the number of junior instructional positions open each year have assumed that the *net* flow of experienced staff was zero. The variability of the gross inflow rate demonstrated by the ACE faculty surveys, plus the historical data of flows into and out of higher education over the last 30 years provided by the NRC data, indicate that it is inappropriate to assume a constant zero net flow. In peacetime years, both inflow and outflow gross rates range between about 1 and 4 percent, and the net flow is likely to range between zero and ± 2 percent. In the recent 1971–1974 period, when hiring rates in higher education were considerably below their 1960s levels and the outside economy was somewhat depressed, it seems likely that the gross flows in both directions dropped significantly. Given the projected plentiful supply of new doctorate holders over the next 5 to 10 years, the inflow rate is likely to remain low for the foreseeable future. A much lower proportion of new hires for college faculties are likely to be drawn from other employment sectors than has been customary in past decades. On the other hand, if the economy reestablishes its earlier growth pattern, the outflow rate can be expected to rise again. Thus, in projecting the future demand for college teachers, it seems likely that, over the long run, academic salaries will decline relative to alternative employment opportunities in government and industry and that the net flow of experienced personnel will be away from higher education.

The expected short-run supply response of a decline in relative salaries in higher education will be twofold: first, one can anticipate a modest net outflow of senior personnel, which in turn will create additional teaching openings for junior staff coming directly from graduate schools; second, one would also expect the decline in relative salaries over time to induce a larger proportion of new doctorates to seek initial employment in nonacademic sectors. In the longer run, a decline in relative salaries would also tend to have a dampening effect upon graduate enrollment, thus adjusting the supply of new doctorates to available job opportunities. In a pure market system, where prices and salaries were fully flexible, these equilibrating adjustments would occur fairly rapidly. In the actual world, where only slight adjustments in the average rate of salary increase is likely, where rank differentials are well established and relatively fixed, and where approximately 70 percent of full-time faculty have tenure, the adjustment process is much more gradual.

In our current state of knowledge it is not possible for us to construct a sophisticated predictive model of the academic labor market, but it is possible to estimate the likely response over time to changes in certain key independent variables such as tenure, promotion, hiring, and retirement policy.

A FACULTY FLOW MODEL Several surveys provide benchmark data on faculty composition. Table 8-6 shows the results of the 1963 U.S. Office of Education survey of college faculty (Dunham, Wright, & Chandler, 1966) and of the 1968 and 1972 ACE surveys. The Office of Education survey only reported faculty in four-year colleges and universities, while the ACE surveys cover the universe of higher education. The 1963 survey only reported faculty by 10-year age groups; in Table 8-6 we have estimated the division into five-year groupings similar to the ACE format.

Although the Office of Education and ACE surveys are not precisely comparable, if one assumes that the age distribution of two-year college faculty is similar to that of the four-year

TABLE 8-6 *Age distribution of college and university professors*

Age group	1962–63 Office of Education survey		1968–69 ACE survey		1972–73 ACE survey	
	Number	*Percent*	*Number*	*Percent*	*Number*	*Percent*
30 and under	17,820	10.3	50,975	15.4	27,650	7.2
31–35	27,160	15.7	56,265	17.0	68,355	17.8
36–40	30,970	17.9	54,285	16.4	65,665	17.1
41–45	27,160	15.7	47,665	14.4	62,590	16.3
46–50	23,530	13.6	42,700	12.9	53,760	14.0
51–55	18,170	10.5	31,775	9.6	44,930	11.7
56–60	13,670	7.9	22,510	6.8	31,870	8.3
61–65	9,690	5.6	17,545	5.3	21,500	5.6
Over 65	5,020	2.9	7,280	2.2	7,680	2.0
TOTAL	173,190	100.0	331,000	100.0	384,000	100.0

SOURCES: 1962–63 data from Dunham, Wright, and Chandler (1966); 1968–69 and 1972–73 computed from ACE faculty survey data.

sector, some trends are evident.[6] The rapid expansion of college faculties in the mid-1960s increased the proportion of faculty in the younger age groups and decreased the estimated median age by about three years. The deceleration in hiring in 1971 and 1972 appears to have significantly reduced the numbers in the age-30-and-under range once again, making the 1972–73 distribution more like that of a decade earlier. It is also apparent that the expanded hiring in the mid-1960s brought in (or brought back) to higher education a considerable number of teachers in the middle and upper age groups.

As the beginning point for a faculty flow model, 1972 ACE survey data for full-time faculty has been used to provide age, rank, and tenure distributions, as shown in Table 8-7. One then needs to know the corresponding distribution for entrants and departers from the academic labor market. Table 8-8 gives age distribution estimates for new entrants from graduate school, experienced persons entering college teaching from other employment, senior teachers leaving the academic sector, and teachers who changed institutions but continued teaching.

For all categories of entrants, the distributions are based on ACE survey data. Respondents were asked to indicate how many years they had been at their present institution, and what their prior student or employment status had been. The age distributions in columns 1 and 2 of Table 8-8 are based on the respondents who had been at their present institution one year or less. The interinstitutional mobility group is shown in column 3. Since movements between institutions cancel out, when aggregated, this age distribution is only of passing interest. Column 4 indicates the estimated age distribution of those leaving academic employment for jobs in other sectors of the economy. It is based partly on the distribution of persons intending to leave higher education (not of retirees) as reported in the 1963 Office of Education study (Dunham, Wright, & Chandler, 1966), adjusted in light of the age distribution of

---

[6]The ACE surveys report distributions for university, four-year college, and two-year college sectors separately. In 1972, the two-year colleges had a slightly higher concentration of faculty in the 41-to-50-year-old age range, and somewhat smaller proportions at both ends of the age distribution. The differences were minor enough, however, that it can be presumed that the comparisons in Table 8-6 indicate significant changes.

TABLE 8-7 Age, rank, and tenure distribution of faculty, 1972

Age group	Faculty total		Professor		Associate professor		Assistant professor		Instructor or other		Faculty with tenure	
	Number	Percent	Number	Percent	Number	Percent	Number	Percent	Number	Percent	Number	Percent
30 and under	27,650	7.2	130	0.1	1,350	1.2	16,800	14.3	9,370	31.0	5,845	2.2
31–35	68,355	17.8	1,155	1.0	17,445	15.2	41,145	34.9	8,610	28.5	25,760	9.7
36–40	65,665	17.1	8,315	7.0	29,275	25.4	24,350	20.7	3,730	12.3	42,785	16.1
41–45	62,590	16.3	20,215	16.7	26,250	22.8	13,540	11.5	2,585	8.5	49,690	18.7
46–50	53,760	14.0	26,175	21.6	16,220	14.1	9,015	7.7	2,345	7.8	46,240	17.4
51–55	44,930	11.7	25,605	21.1	12,055	10.5	5,820	4.9	1,445	4.8	40,125	15.1
56–60	31,870	8.3	19,300	15.9	7,175	6.2	4,210	3.6	1,185	3.9	28,700	10.8
61–65	21,500	5.6	14,340	11.8	4,120	3.6	2,405	2.0	640	2.1	19,665	7.4
Over 65	7,680	2.0	5,830	4.8	1,115	1.0	420	0.4	320	1.1	6,910	2.6
TOTAL	384,000	100	121,065	100	115,005	100	117,705	100	30,220	100	265,730	100

SOURCE: Computed from ACE faculty survey data for 1972–73.

TABLE 8-8 *Age distribution of faculty entering and leaving higher education (in percentages)*

Age group	Entrants from other employment (1)	Entrants with doctorate from graduate school (2)	Entrants without doctorate from graduate school (3)	Experienced out-migrants (4)	Mortality and retirement rate (5)
30 and under	20	44	49	20	0.16
31–35	33	29	35	28	0.18
36–40	17	14	9	24	0.28
41–45	14	8	8	15	0.44
46–50	8	4	1	7	0.69
51–55	4	1	0	4	1.07
56–60	3	0	0	1	1.66
61–65	1	0	0	1	6.53
Over 65	0	0	0	0	33.74
	100	100	100	100	

SOURCE: Computed from ACE faculty survey data.

current interinstitutional job changers.[7] Column 4 is the most speculative of the estimated distributions. As in the 1963 Office of Education study, this distribution suggests that those who leave academic employment are somewhat more clustered in the 35–45 age category than are those experienced individuals who enter (or reenter) higher education from nonacademic employment.

Given these estimated age distributions, the composition of college instructional staffs can be analyzed over time under a variety of different assumptions. By developing a computerized simulation model, it is possible to assess the impact of various market conditions and institutional policies on the number of junior faculty openings and on the resulting age distribution of the faculty year by year. We have carried these analyses only as far ahead as 1990, but the sensitivity of hiring levels to different conditions and institutional policies becomes quite apparent.

[7]The implicit assumption is that there are somewhat similar characteristics for those willing to sever their current academic jobs whether or not they remain in teaching or are mobile outside the academic sector.

As noted above, the estimates of likely new faculty positions open in Chapter 6 and 7 assumed a zero net flow of senior personnel into and out of higher education. This seemed to approximate the actual experience of the 1952–1962 period (Cartter, 1965*b*). Freeman's analysis (1971) of National Research Council data, indicating the historical flows of doctorates between academic and nonacademic employment sectors (see Table 8-4), reveals several shifts in the direction of the net flow of doctorates between 1935 and 1963. In the World War II years, and again during the Korean conflict, there was a significant net outflow due chiefly to calls to military service. Between 1945 and 1955, academic salaries also lagged considerably behind comparable salaries in government and industry, contributing to a net outflow of doctorates. Beginning about the time of Sputnik, however, the net flow reversed. The improvement in relative academic salaries beginning in the late 1950s brought about an increase in gross in-migration and slowed the out-migration rate. Although post-1963 data are not available, it is likely that the net flow into higher education approximated 1 percent annually for the 1960s and turned negative again about 1970.

If the net flow of experienced faculty responds to market forces, changes in that flow can be expected to have a significant impact on the level of hiring of junior faculty. On the assumption that the net flow in the foreseeable future is likely to be outward from academe, because of the anticipated declining demand for college teachers, Table 8-9 estimates the impact of various out-migration rates. The figures in column 1 show the anticipated hiring level for junior faculty with zero net flow of senior personnel between academic and nonacademic employment sectors. Five other columns show the expected number of junior faculty openings under alternative assumptions ranging from 0.5 percent to 2.5 percent annual net outflow. Judging from past experience, 2.5 percent is about the highest market-induced net outflow rate that can be expected— exceeded only in the wartime years of the early 1940s.

With a full-time faculty of approximately 400,000 in the mid-1970s, a 1 percent net outflow represents an additional 4,000 job openings. If, as seems likely in the middle and late 1970s, there is a net exodus of approximately 1 percent per year, this would increase the anticipated number of junior faculty openings by

TABLE 8-9 *Estimated demand for new junior faculty under alternative assumptions of net outflow of experienced teachers (in thousands)*

Year	Net outflow of experienced teachers (percents)					
	0.0 (1)	0.5 (2)	1.0 (3)	1.5 (4)	2.0 (5)	2.5 (6)
Actual						
1966	34.5					
1967	26.0					
1968	37.3					
1969	23.6					
1970	24.8					
1971	16.9					
1972	10.9					
Projected						
1973	13.5	15.4	17.3	19.2	21.2	23.4
1974	11.6	13.5	15.5	17.3	19.0	20.9
1975	15.7	17.6	19.6	21.6	23.6	25.5
1976	15.9	17.9	20.0	22.0	24.0	26.0
1977	16.8	18.8	20.8	22.9	25.0	27.0
1978	17.3	19.4	21.4	23.6	25.7	27.8
1979	19.6	21.7	23.8	26.0	28.1	30.2
1980	18.8	20.9	23.1	25.1	27.1	29.2
1981	14.4	16.6	18.8	21.1	23.3	25.5
1982	11.9	14.1	16.3	18.6	20.9	23.1
1983	6.9	9.1	11.4	13.6	15.9	18.1
1984	5.2	7.4	9.6	11.8	14.0	16.2
1985	1.7	3.8	6.0	8.1	10.3	12.4
1986	2.1	4.2	6.3	8.4	10.5	12.6
1987	8.3	10.3	12.4	14.4	16.5	18.5
1988	13.1	15.1	17.1	19.1	21.1	23.1
1989	14.8	16.8	18.8	20.8	22.8	24.8
1990	6.8	8.7	10.7	12.7	14.7	16.6

SOURCE: Computations by the author.

about 25 percent. A net outflow of experienced teachers ordinarily assumes the presence of attractive job opportunities outside academia—a situation that was more evident in the mid-1950s than it was in the mid-1970s recession years. Thus, anything larger than about 1 percent may have to await a more prosperous economy. However, the rate may be increased somewhat by more stringent tenure conditions—that is, institutions fearful of a top-heavy age and rank distribution of faculty may fail to renew nontenure contracts. Young instructors with several years teaching experience may find it increasingly difficult to move laterally to another institution if the job market worsens, and thus depart the academic scene as the result of involuntary termination rather than the enticement of a more rewarding job.

As noted in Table 8-4, since World War II only in the 1950–1955 period has the net outflow of senior doctorates risen as high as 2.5 percent. The early 1950s were years when faculty salaries lagged far behind comparable rates in government and industry and were also years of considerable growth in scientific activities outside the university sector. In today's uncertain world, college teachers appear to be even more job-security conscious than they were 20 years ago, and thus it may take an even greater incentive to induce them to depart from the campus.

In the 1960s, when the gross inflow and outflow of senior doctorates was 3 to 4 percent per year, a policy decision of hiring institutions to hire only at the beginning steps on the promotion ladder would have created a substantial net outflow rate. As Table 8-3 suggested, the hiring rate of experienced personnel in 1972 was apparently less than half the rate in 1968. Simultaneously, however, job opportunities in nonacademic sectors worsened, reducing flows in both directions, but having little impact on the net flow. Although hard data are not available to substantiate the statement, it is the author's impression that in the 1971–1975 period the net outflow rate has ranged between 0.5 and 1.0 percent. If the enrollment projections in Chapter 6 are approximately correct and if the economy resumes its long-term growth pattern, a net outflow of about 1.5 percent would seem likely in the 1980s. Such a rate, judging from Table 8-9, would mean an additional 6,000 job openings annually for junior faculty, compared with an assumption of zero net flow of experienced doctorates.

While this suggests a somewhat more optimistic academic job market for new doctorates than the total enrollment picture might suggest, it should be stressed that it would result from a fairly significant deterioration in the relative compensation of college teachers. While data are not available to estimate long-run mobility response elasticities, it seems likely to be in the order of magnitude of a 1 percent annual net outflow resulting from a 10 percent deterioration in relative salaries and perhaps a 2 percent annual net outflow resulting from a 20 percent deterioration (using 1970 as a benchmark). In actual practice, such a decline in the relative attractiveness of academic careers is likely to occur partly through a compression of rank differentials over the next 10 to 15 years, with senior grades affected more than those in junior ranks.

Different assumptions concerning the net outflow of experienced staff also have an impact over time on the age distribution of the faculty. Because of the rapid expansion of the teaching faculty in the mid-1960s the age distribution became skewed toward the younger end of the distribution, with median age dropping to approximately 40. Table 8-10 shows the distribution for full-time faculty in 1972, as derived from the ACE faculty survey (see Table 8-6). Using the faculty simulation model, columns 2 and 3 of Table 8-10 show the estimated distribution for 1980 and 1990 assuming a zero net flow of senior personnel (2 percent gross flows in either direction), constant student-faculty ratios, 60 percent new hires with the doctorate, and no change in current (1972) retirement policy. Under these conditions the median age of full-time college teachers would rise from age 43 in 1972 to 45 in 1980, and to 49 in 1990. Teachers 35 and under would decline from 25 percent in 1972 to 12.5 percent by 1990, while those over 60 would rise from 7.6 percent to 14.8 percent. As the bottom line indicates, the combined death and retirement rate would be expected to rise from 1.56 percent to 2.88 percent by 1990.

Columns 4 through 6 illustrate the age distributions that would result if the net out-migration rate became 1, 2, or 3 percent annually. As can be seen, larger out-migration rates have little impact upon the over-60 population (for most out-migrants are typically in their 30s and 40s), but the higher

TABLE 8-10 *Age distribution of full-time college teachers, actual 1972, and projected to 1990 (in percentages)*

Age group	Actual 1972 (1)	Zero annual net migration		1990 with annual net out-migration of (percent):		
		1980 (2)	1990 (3)	1 (4)	2 (5)	3 (6)
30 and under	7.2	7.5	4.3	5.2	6.2	7.3
31–35	17.8	13.2	8.2	9.0	9.9	10.8
36–40	17.1	15.0	10.8	11.3	11.4	11.4
41–45	16.3	16.3	14.1	14.2	13.7	13.3
46–50	14.0	15.5	16.3	15.9	15.3	14.8
51–55	11.7	13.2	16.5	15.8	15.4	14.9
56–60	8.3	10.4	15.0	14.3	14.1	13.8
61–65	5.6	6.2	10.2	9.8	9.6	9.5
Over 65	2.0	2.8	4.6	4.4	4.4	4.3
Death and retirement rate	1.56	1.91	2.88	2.77	2.73	2.70

SOURCE: Computed by the author.

outflow rates boost representation in the 40-and-under groups significantly. Thus, while rising out-migration rates may be a symptom of an unfortunate relative deterioration in the attractiveness of academic careers, they produce the side effect of a somewhat more desirable age and rank distribution than would otherwise occur.

If, as suggested above, out-migration rates hold at about 1 percent in the 1970s and rise to 1.5 percent or above in the 1980s, the likely distribution in 1990 would be somewhere between the illustrated 1 and 2 percent rates in Table 8-10.

IMPACT OF TENURE AND PROMOTION POLICY There is one other point of control in the hands of institutions— deciding whether or not a young, nontenured teacher should be promoted to tenure rank. Ordinarily, this decision occurs within the first six years of full-time teaching, but negative decisions are often reached in the first three or four years of teaching.

According to the 1972 ACE faculty survey, 69.2 percent of full-time faculty had tenure, up from 53.7 percent in 1968. With the slowing down of hiring projected for the 1970s and 1980s, and the resulting upward shift in the age distribution of the faculty, higher education is likely to experience a continuing "tenuring-in" phenomenon.

To address this question and to assess its likely effect, we have divided the faculty into tenured and nontenured groups and attempted to estimate the likely attrition and addition rates that might result from differing promotion and out-migration assumptions. On the one hand, some faculty are hired with tenure (usually after prior teaching service), and others reach tenured positions by promotion from nontenure ranks. Departures from tenure rank result from death, retirement, or out-migration. In the case of the nontenured faculty, additions come from new hires, and departures come from the above-mentioned causes plus promotion to a tenured position. Departures, however, in the case of nontenured teachers, may result from terminations (involuntary) as well as from voluntary decisions to seek employment outside of higher education. Involuntary terminations, while not uncommon in the case of individual institutions, were relatively rare for the system of higher education in the growth period of the 1960s. In the 1970s and 1980s, however, it is likely that a higher proportion of young instructors may fail to achieve tenure at one institution and find it difficult to compete successfully with the new doctorate emerging from graduate school to obtain a nontenured position in another college.

Each of these flows into and out of both the nontenured and tenured faculty exhibits a unique age distribution. Table 8-11 shows these distributions, based on analysis of the 1972 ACE faculty survey data. For the purposes of the model, it is assumed that these distributions remain fixed over time—that the age pattern of mobile college teachers is relatively constant even though the magnitude of the flows may vary considerably over time.

Approximately 7.5 percent of new hires in 1972 came in at tenure rank. This figure does not include any teachers who merely changed institutions (intrasystem migration), and thus is concerned only with new entrants to the system of higher education. (However, it includes some individuals who left college teaching in earlier years to take positions in government or industry and are now returning to academic employment.) The median age of such appointees is approximately 36, while

TABLE 8-11 *Age distributions for tenure model (in percentages)*

Age group	New hires tenured	New hires nontenured	Promotion to tenure	Tenured out-migrants	Nontenured out-migrants	Death and retirement rate
30 and under	10.0	32.9	3.0	4.9	21.1	.0016
31–35	24.3	35.3	20.6	19.1	34.3	.0018
36–40	19.9	14.4	26.4	25.1	22.0	.0028
41–45	21.8	8.2	21.6	25.0	12.5	.0044
46–50	12.6	4.5	13.1	11.4	4.9	.0069
51–55	8.7	2.0	7.7	6.9	3.0	.0107
56–60	2.3	2.0	5.5	2.7	2.2	.0166
61–65	0.4	0.5	2.1	4.0	0.0	..0656
Over 65	0.0	0.2	0.0	1.0	0.0	.3374

SOURCE: Computed from ACE faculty survey data for 1972–73.

the median age of tenured out-migrants is about 40½. Nontenured new hires have a median age of about 33, and out-migrants have a median age of about 35½. By contrast, promotion to tenure commonly occurs at about one's 41st birthday. Lacking any evidence to the contrary, death and retirement rates are assumed to be identical for the two faculty populations.

In Table 8-12, the percentage of the full-time faculty with tenure is projected for several combinations of likely rates for gross out-migration of tenured faculty and for new hires at tenure rank. For these calculations, it was assumed that 12 percent of the nontenured faculty were out-migrants and another 20 percent were promoted to tenure each year.[8] Thus the nontenured faculty is pictured as a group whose composition is constantly in flux, although one-fifth each year are assumed to be granted tenure.

Given these assumptions, the tenure percentage ranges from 76.1 percent with high out-migration of senior faculty and a low

[8]The former rate includes a sizable number of junior faculty each year who return to graduate school to complete their degrees, as well as those who teach for several years and then pursue a career outside higher education. The age distribution of entrants and departers is close enough, however, that this assumption has little effect upon the proportion of the faculty with tenure. The promotion rate assumption, however, is critical to the tenure outcome.

TABLE 8-12 Projected proportion of full-time faculty with tenure in 1990	*"Gross" percent annual out-migration of tenured faculty*	*Percent new hires with tenure*		
		10	7.5	5
	1.0	86.0	85.4	84.8
	2.0	82.8	82.2	81.5
	3.0	79.9	79.2	78.5
	4.0	77.2	76.4	76.1

ASSUMPTIONS: (1) Rate of promotion = 20 percent; (2) Rate of attrition of nontenured faculty = 12 percent.

SOURCE: Computed by the author.

fraction of appointment with tenure to 86.0 percent under the reverse condition. It is clear that the out-migration rate is much more influential than is the percent hired with tenure.

In Table 8-13 the out-migration and hiring rates for tenured faculty are kept constant, and the nontenured out-migration and promotion rates are varied. In this case, the promotion rate is seen to have the largest impact upon the resulting tenure proportion. In fact, the lower the promotion rate, the larger the out-migration rate is likely to be, for nonpromotion at the end of the instructor's trial period is akin to termination.

Table 8-14 illustrates possible faculty age distributions under several different sets of alternatives. The most likely outcome would appear to be somewhere between alternatives A and B—alternatives that differ only in the out-migration rate of tenured faculty. With the higher out-migration rate, the distribution tends to become bimodal as a result of departures hitting the 41-to-45 age group most severely. Alternatives C and D are quite

TABLE 8-13 Projected proportion of full-time faculty with tenure in 1990	*Gross flow of nontenured out*	*Promotion rate*		
		20.0	15	12
	10	82.7	78.2	74.2
	15	83.0	78.8	74.9
	20	83.4	79.4	75.7

ASSUMPTIONS: (1) Gross out-migration of tenured faculty = 2 percent; (2) Percent annual new hires with tenure = 10 percent.

SOURCE: Computed by the author.

TABLE 8-14 *Possible age distribution of full-time faculty in 1990 under alternative assumptions*

	Low out-migration (A)	High out-migration (B)	Extreme out-migration (C)	Low promotion, high out-migration (D)
30 and under	5.1	7.0	11.1	8.3
31–35	9.2	11.8	16.6	13.7
36–40	10.0	10.9	11.7	12.4
41–45	11.4	10.3	8.0	11.6
46–50	14.5	13.1	10.8	12.6
51–55	16.4	15.1	13.0	13.2
56–60	16.2	15.4	13.8	13.4
61–65	11.7	11.1	10.0	9.9
Over 65	5.6	5.3	5.0	5.0
Percent with tenure	86.0	79.9	70.8	70.7
Percent new hires with tenure	10	10	10	10
Promotion rate	20%	20%	20%	11%
Gross out-migration tenure	1.0%	3.0%	7.0%	3.0%
Gross out-migration nontenure	12%	12%	20%	20%

SOURCE: Computed by the author.

speculative, illustrating the distributions if the overall proportion of faculty with tenure is kept at approximately 70 percent, either as the result of an extremely high out-migration rate for senior faculty (a most unlikely condition unless there were a severe decline in relative salaries) or a very low promotion rate from nontenure to tenure rank. Both alternatives favor young faculty 40 and under at the expense of those in the 40-to-60 range. Alternative D has the effect of flattening out the distribution curve, while C accentuates the saucer shape noted in B.

In general it can be concluded that the proportion of the faculty with tenure is most sensitive to the promotion rate, while the age-distribution pattern is influenced significantly by both the promotion (retention) rate and the out-migration rate of senior faculty. The former is subject to policy decisions on the part of institutions, while the latter variable depends almost entirely upon impersonal market forces.

Given the slower rate of growth in total teaching faculty (and the possibility of a negative rate in the 1980s if enrollment contracts) and the more severe budgetary constraints of the mid-1970s, it seems likely that (1) the percent of new hires with tenure will fall as institutions more commonly fill full-time vacancies with junior faculty, (2) the promotion rate will decline as institutions become more chary about granting tenure, and (3) the net out-migration rate of senior faculty will tend to rise. Each of these factors will tend to cushion the "tenuring-in" effect of a reduced overall growth rate and will partially compensate for the tendency for the age distribution to shift toward the upper age groups. While it is not possible to predict the resulting distribution, it is likely to be considerably more favorable to junior faculty than would be the case if the patterns of the 1960s continued unchanged.

RETIREMENT PRACTICES The rate at which junior faculty enter higher education is obviously related to the rate at which senior faculty retire. Retirement policy varies widely among American colleges and universities with mandatory retirement age ranging from 65 to 70 with few exceptions.

In a study of annuitants of the Teachers Insurance and Annuity Association (TIAA) it was found that the median age at retirement was somewhat over 65, and that only 18 percent of men and 30 percent of women retired prior to age 65, while 51 percent had retired at ages ranging from 66 to 70 or above (Ingraham, 1974). Some fraction of those who retired prior to age 65 took other employment, and therefore would appear as senior out-migrants in our model. Slightly over half of the TIAA respondents had retired at the mandatory age, another 9 percent gave ill health as the cause, and 5 percent had pressing family obligations. Forty-eight percent took other work after their academic retirement, one-fifth of them on a full-time basis. Teaching, consulting, and research were the most common activities of postretirement (as defined by annuity benefit rules).

During a period of rapid employment growth, such as the 1960s for higher education, the age distribution of college teachers became increasingly skewed toward the younger age groups. Thus, the proportion of full-time faculty at or near retirement age fell, and the retirement rate of college teachers (retirees as a percent of all full-time teachers) dropped from an estimated 1.09 percent in 1962 to only 0.82 percent in 1972.

With the current and projected slowing down in the growth of college faculties, the process will be reversed, and the age profile will gradually shift toward the older age groups. Eventually this will produce a significant rise in the retirement rate (even with no change in policy or practice), but not for at least another decade.

The expected decline in the number of job openings for junior faculty has stirred interest in early-retirement programs as institutions seek ways of maintaining a desirable inflow of young faculty. In several instances colleges have lowered their retirement age,[9] and in a number of other cases early-retirement programs have been instituted on a voluntary basis.[10] Our faculty flow model may be useful in simulating the age distribution and retirement rate under several different types of retirement policy.

Table 8-15 reproduces alternatives A and B from Table 8-14. The column for alternative A assumed a low-rate of out-migration (preretirement) of senior faculty, and the one for alternative B assumed a 3 percent gross (2 percent net) outflow. It was suggested that these seemed to be likely boundary conditions if current institutional practices remained unchanged. Judging from the 1962–63 Office of Education survey of college faculty (Dunham, Wright, & Chandler, 1966) and from the 1973 TIAA survey of annuitants, the common pattern of retirement appears to be such that about 4 percent of those 61 to 65 years old retire annually, as do about 30 percent of those in the over-65 age group. Our estimates of retirement rates for 1972 and 1990 alternatives A and B are based on these assumptions.

Alternatives C and D in Table 8-15 are speculative illustrations of the effect of significant steps to lower the retirement age. Each model assumes a 1.5 percent net out-migration of senior faculty from 1975 to 1990 (assuming a deterioration in the relative salary of college professors). Alternative C assumes the introduction of attractive voluntary early retirement policies

---

[9]For example, in 1972 New York University, whose mandatory retirement age had been raised from age 66 to 69 about 1960, announced a reduction to age 65 effective in 1976. In another case, an attempt to lower the retirement age in New Jersey was reversed by court action on the grounds that the previous arrangement was in the nature of a contractual obligation for those first employed under its terms. This issue will need further judicial review before the authority of institutions to lower mandatory retirement age is clear.

[10]One of the most attractive such programs is that of the City University of New York, which parallels city provisions for firemen and policemen.

TABLE 8-15 *Age projections, 1990*

	Unchanged retirement policy		Early retirement policy	
Distribution	Low out-migration (A)	High out-migration (B)	Voluntary (C)	Mandatory (D)
30 and under	5.1	7.0	8.9	9.6
31–35	9.2	11.8	14.6	15.7
36–40	10.0	10.9	12.9	13.7
41–45	11.4	10.3	12.6	12.8
46–50	14.5	13.1	15.8	15.7
51–55	16.4	15.1	17.6	17.2
56–60	16.2	15.4	12.1	11.8
61–65	11.7	11.1	4.4	3.7
Over 65	5.6	5.3	1.0	0.0
Percent with tenure, 1990	86.0	79.9	77.5	76.0
Percent retirement, 1990	2.15	2.03	3.26	3.32

SOURCE: Columns A and B from Table 8-14; columns C and D computed by the author.

such that in successive five-year periods beginning in 1975, the percentage of teachers 55–60 years old who retire become 5, 10, and 20; for 61-to-65-year-olds, the percentage rises to 10, 20, and 30; and for the over 65 group it moves to 40, 60, and 75. Under those conditions, the overall retirement rate would rise to 3.26 percent, and the percent of faculty with tenure would be 77.5 percent in 1990. As contrasted with alternatives A and B, the percent of faculty age 56 and over would be only about one-half as high; 37 percent of full-time faculty would be 40 and under, compared with 24 percent in A and 30 percent in B.

Alternative D is an even more extreme example where age 65 becomes the mandatory retirement age by 1980, and early retirement rises to 25 percent in 1980–1985 and to 50 percent in 1985–1990. (This would be akin to establishing age 62 as the customary retirement age and permitting overage appointments for up to three years for the most effective teachers.) The combination of early retirement and net out-migration is most favorable to the younger faculty, and results in a retirement rate of 3.32 percent by 1990.

The most critical parameter in attempting to estimate future faculty demand, given likely enrollment patterns, is the ratio in which students and faculty are combined in the educational process. In Chapter 6 we saw how volatile the year-to-year incremental ratio has been over the last 15 years, but that the long-term trend appeared to be reasonably constant at an average 17:1 ratio—the ratio assumed in projections of junior faculty appointments and of the age distribution of the full-time faculty in this and the preceding chapter.

Conflicting pressures today and in the coming decade may alter this ratio, although it is difficult to predict which way the balance may turn. Problems of inflation, economic recession, and the resulting budgetary constraints imposed on colleges and universities will tend to push the ratio upward. The changing enrollment mix, which is likely to see lower-division, vocational, and nondegree enrollments expand relative to upper-division and graduate enrollments, can also be expected to exert upward pressure on the average ratio. Typically, lower-division and nondegree programs have student-faculty ratios of 20:1 or more, while upper-division programs average about 15:1 and graduate study 10:1 or less. On the other hand, slower enrollment growth—perhaps even a modest decline—over the last quarter of the century will increase the ratio of the employed labor force to college students, and may mean that public and private resources can increasingly be devoted to the enrichment of education. In addition, if enrollments contract in many institutions faster than the rate for which ordinary faculty attrition can compensate, the average student-faculty ratio may drop because of the inability of colleges and universities to respond sufficiently.

While it is impossible to predict which direction student-faculty ratios may move, it is possible to illustrate the effects of such movement on hiring and resulting age distributions. The impact on junior staff hiring is obvious: for a typical year in the 1970s, when a 17:1 ratio predicts a need for about 10,000 new faculty (apart from replacements for deaths or retirement), a 15:1 incremental ratio would require 11,333 and a 20:1 ratio would require only 8,500. Judging from history, it seems likely that the incremental ratio for periods of five years or more are likely to remain within this range of 15:1 to 20:1—even though for any single year the marginal ratio may be above or below this range.

In Table 8-16 the predicted age distribution of the faculty in 1990 is shown for incremental ratios of 15, 17, and 20 to 1, assuming a zero net migration of senior faculty. Because the 1972–1990 period encompasses predicted periods of both expansion and contraction, no significant differences are evident in these distributions. The lower faculty-response alternative (20:1 ratio) has a slightly larger fraction of the faculty at both ends of the spectrum (35 and under, 61 and over) and slightly reduced numbers in the mid-range.

Alternatives C, D, and E illustrate the result of a steady movement over the 1972–1990 period either toward a higher or lower ratio than the current 17:1. In the column for alternative D, a 2 percent net out-migration of senior faculty is posited to indicate the joint effect; in E and F a zero net migration rate is assumed.

What would seem to be the most likely pattern for the future? There seems little basis for prediction, but one may be permitted an intuitive speculation. For the next several years, it seems likely that the incremental student-staff ratio will remain considerably above the average ratio. Community college and non-

TABLE 8-16 *Projected faculty age distributions in 1990 under alternative student-faculty ratios*

	Constant ratios			Sliding ratios		
	15:1 (A)	17:1 (B)	20:1 (C)	17:1 to 15:1 (D)	17:1 to 15:1 (E)	17:1 to 20:1 (F)
30 and under	4.2	4.3	4.5	7.1	5.1	4.0
31–35	8.1	8.2	8.3	11.5	9.5	6.8
36–40	10.9	10.8	10.6	13.0	11.9	8.6
41–45	14.3	14.1	13.9	14.6	14.7	12.5
46–50	16.4	16.3	16.1	15.1	16.1	16.0
51–55	16.5	16.5	16.4	14.2	15.6	17.5
56–60	15.0	15.0	15.1	12.5	13.8	16.9
61–65	10.1	10.2	10.4	8.2	9.2	12.0
Over 65	4.5	4.6	4.8	3.7	4.1	5.7
TOTAL	100.0	100.0	100.0	100.0	100.0	100.0
Assumed annual net out-migration rate (percent)	0	0	0	2	0	0

SOURCE: Computations by the author.

degree enrollments are likely to continue to grow relative to other sectors during the 1970s, and continued tight budgetary constraints seem probable for the immediate future. After 1980, a declining ratio seems probable, partly through a conscious policy of enrichment and partly because the author suspects that the enrollment mix will gradually shift in favor of upper-division and postbaccalaureate study again.[11] If this were to occur, and if the net out-migration of faculty were to rise to 1.5 percent in the 1980s due to a modest erosion of relative salaries for college professors, the age distribution would be likely to be between those in alternatives D and E in Table 8-16 in 1990. Such a distribution is more favorable to junior faculty and provides a fairly even distribution between ages 30 and 60. The total number of faculty in 1990 would be slightly smaller in the column for alternative B than in the one for alternative A because the ratio is higher in the former alternative during the remaining expansion of enrollment in the late 1970s and is lower in the contraction period of the late 1980s. But the rising net out-migration rate would increase the number of openings for junior faculty.

COMBINED EFFECTS ON JUNIOR FACULTY If mobility, tenure, and retirement patterns and student-faculty ratios remain unchanged over the next decade or two, it is likely that the proportion of college teachers with tenure will rise above 80 percent, the average age of teachers will rise by at least five years, and the fraction for the faculty not over 35 years of age will decline significantly. A growing imbalance can be expected between the demand for new junior faculty with the doctorate and the supply of new Ph.D.'s seeking academic positions. If these parameters remain constant the proportion of new Ph.D.'s taking college teaching positions, as high as 60 percent in the mid-1960s, might drop to only 15 to 20 percent in the 1980s. This shortfall of academic openings would be felt most severely by those disciplines that have few attractive job alternatives outside higher education.

[11]The 1960s and 1970s might be viewed as periods when public policy has been primarily concerned with the issue of access, and, accordingly, the community college sector has expanded disproportionately. The long-term historical trend, however, is toward increased years of schooling, and it may be anticipated that an increasing proportion of youth in the 1980s and beyond will pursue at least four, and perhaps six or more years of postsecondary education.

However, a combination of normal market responses and institutional policy decisions may moderate these conclusions and make the situation somewhat less gloomy for the young Ph.D. seeking an academic position in the 1980s. The continued presence of a larger number of qualified college teacher candidates than of attractive new positions, which first emerged in 1971 and which is likely to become more pronounced in the 1980s, can be expected to have a dampening effect upon academic pay scales and contribute to an erosion of relative salaries. As is illustrated by past experience, such a decline in relative salaries almost assuredly will bring about a modest net out-migration of senior faculty to government and industry. Even a 1 percent annual net outflow is sufficient to employ an additional 10 percent of new doctorate holders at projected output levels. Thus, ordinary market responses tend to initiate one form of corrective behavior.

Another form of expected response, to offset the higher unit cost of instruction implied by a more senior faculty, is the effort by deans and department heads to replace experienced personnel who depart with junior instructors just emerging from graduate school. In a growth period such as the 1960s, when new young faculty were constantly being added to meet enrollment expansion, departments were more tempted to replace departing full professors with senior faculty drawn from other institutions, or from outside the academic sector—this action helped to maintain a desirable distribution between young and old, tenured and nontenured staff. In a no-growth context, by contrast, this balance can be maintained only if openings created by senior departures are filled by junior staff. Normal departmental response, reinforced by pressures from top administrators who may be more conscious of budget constraints, tends to favor junior staff hiring when growth rates decline. Tables 8-3 and 8-4 illustrate this effect between the peak growth period of 1967–68 and the much slower growth period of 1971–72, when interinstitutional mobility and hiring of senior staff from outside academia sharply declined.

Other institutional policy responses can also be expected to have an impact on hiring rates. It seems likely that retirement age will be reduced in many institutions—particularly those which currently have mandatory retirement ages between 68 and 70—and that early (voluntary) retirement programs will become more common. While such moves are favorable from the standpoint of expanded junior faculty openings, beyond their initial one-time impact the annual effect is relatively minor given today's age distribution. For example, if age 65 had become the mandatory retirement age in 1972, it would have immediately opened up only 7,700 positions (2 percent of total full-time faculty) and thereafter raised the estimated annual retirement rate by one-fifth of one percentage point (approximately 750 openings annually). The annual effect would be about twice as great in 1990 as the proportion of all college teachers over age 60 is projected to increase.

Institutional tenure policy will also affect hiring rates at the point of entry. While a predicted tighter tenure policy is likely to have a favorable effect upon new hires right out of graduate school, a sharply reduced promotion-to-tenure rate would also boost the out-migration rate of junior faculty. Thus a lower promotion rate is not an unmixed blessing for the new Ph.D., who might find it easier to get a first job in higher education only to find reduced opportunity for advancement and continuation. In the last 10 to 20 years, if a young instructor was not granted tenure or contract renewal at his or her first institution of employment, the usual pattern was to move to a somewhat less prestigious institution where the odds of ultimately receiving tenure were higher. Indications are, however, that lateral or even downward mobility will become increasingly difficult in future years, most particularly in the 1980s when many institutions may be reducing the size of their total faculty. The sharp reduction in interinstitutional mobility between 1968 and 1972, indicated by the ACE surveys (see Table 8-3) may be a precursor of the new pattern.

Viewed in concert, these anticipated institutional and market responses will probably make the hiring outlook for junior faculty somewhat more optimistic than the initial projections in Chapters 6 and 7. If one were to estimate the magnitude of these effects the author would be tempted to speculate that in the 1980s these factors might have a combined effect of creating between 5,000 and 7,500 additional junior faculty positions a year. This would result from a predicted rise in the senior faculty out-migration rate to 1 percent or more annually, a gradual downward adjustment in mandatory retirement age, and a decline in the promotion-to-tenure rate from approximately 20 percent (of the nontenured faculty) in the late 1960s to perhaps 10 percent. Thus junior faculty hiring from the graduate schools might average between 8,000 and 12,500 annually during the 1980s rather than the initially projected 3,000 to 5,000 indicated in the estimates of Chapters 6 and 7.

The sharp turnabout in academic job market conditions between 1968 and 1972, indicated by the behavior patterns revealed in the ACE faculty surveys, provides a short-term illustration of what the transition from a rapid growth decade of the 1960s to a no-growth decade in the 1980s may be like. To understand better the adjustment process at the point of job entry, Chapter 9 concentrates on this same time period for new Ph.D.'s first entering the academic labor market.

9. First Job Placement of New Doctorates

Traditional wage and employment theory pictures employee and employer units as relatively homogeneous, so that market influences evidence themselves chiefly in salary levels and in employment or unemployment situations. The academic labor market, however, is highly differentiated on both the supply and demand side. There are exceptional, good, and mediocre doctorate holders seeking jobs in institutions that vary widely in quality and attractiveness. Ordinarily, the market works relatively well as a sorting device, so that the most promising Ph.D.'s from the most distinguished graduate programs are placed in the most-preferred job openings, and less promising Ph.D.'s from the less outstanding graduate schools find initial positions in institutions of less distinction and prestige. Only one-half of 1 percent of the labor force are college professors, and Ph.D.'s have many alternative employment opportunities outside of higher education. Thus, unemployment is seldom the fate of a person holding the highest earned degree— although he or she may face short-term unemployment during a job search. Instead, one might think of a kind of hierarchy of academic jobs where new doctorates begin the job search near the top of the pyramid and work their way gradually down as the best positions are filled. Within the academic labor market, there are obvious degrees of attractiveness as one proceeds from the most sought-after positions in the distinguished universities and colleges down through the middle range of senior institutions, and then to the less prestigious senior institutions and the superior community colleges, and finally to the more ordinary two-year colleges and secondary schools.[1]

---

[1]There are always exceptions that prove the rule. Some young men and women enter graduate school hoping eventually to take positions in two-year colleges or secondary schools. The great majority of Ph.D.'s, however, seek positions in

Each academic job aspirant ordinarily has a reasonably good assessment of his or her own abilities and a fairly realistic view of job prospects based on a general knowledge of the placement pattern of earlier generations of Ph.D.'s from their graduate institution. Thus, every new Ph.D. does not anticipate a call to Harvard, Berkeley, or Amherst, but begins the search with sights initially set on a range of attainable jobs. In addition, it is reasonable to suppose that the typical Ph.D. job seeker has some "reservation price"—which may be expressed as a salary or a job prestige level—below which he will ordinarily not go. Reservation levels differ for each individual, and the patterns differ for various disciplines. Thus, one individual may decide to consider only jobs in universities; another may hold out for an elite college, and, barring such an offer, may go into banking or government service; still another may decide that he or she will consider a job only in New England. Scientists and engineers, who have a wider variety of employment opportunities outside of academia, frequently have high academic reservation prices (or status levels); humanists and social scientists more often were attracted to doctoral study by the desire to be teachers and therefore commonly have lower academic reservation prices.

In the two previous chapters it was seen that when higher education was expanding rapidly and there were many job openings, college teachers had greater mobility as institutions competitively bid for their services, and academic salaries rose more rapidly than compensation in other professions. When hiring declined, salaries tended to lag behind comparable rates in the nonacademic sectors and interinstitutional mobility diminished. In a time of academic affluence one would anticipate that a high proportion of new Ph.D.'s would take their first teaching positions in institutions of high prestige and that low-prestige institutions would have to resort principally to non-doctorate faculty to fill their ranks. By contrast, when the academic job market is depressed, one would expect a larger

---

high prestige collegiate institutions, and graduate departments pride themselves on placements of their new doctorate holders in departments of high repute. Thus, the hierarchical picture presented here is a reasonably accurate description of the way in which typical graduate students and their professors view the academic labor market.

proportion of Ph.D.'s to filter down through the academic hierarchy and take positions that were formerly held by non-doctorate teachers.

In an interesting article analyzing 1967–68 and 1971–72 first job placements of Ph.D.'s, John Niland (1972) argued that academic salaries are relatively inflexible and that short-term changes in academic labor market conditions are reflected principally by the types of institutions to which new Ph.D.'s go. Grouping universities into quality classes, he calculated the percentage of Ph.D.'s from each class whose first employment was in an institution of the same or higher prestige rank. He concluded that in periods of "market loosening" new doctorate holders will "trickle down" through the system and be employed at less prestigious institutions and that the manpower inflow from abroad would diminish markedly and perhaps reverse. Niland's framework for analysis is further elaborated in this chapter by a finer classification of employing institutions, extension to 1973 data from the Doctorate Records File, and distinction by sex.

PH.D. JOB PLACEMENT BY EMPLOYMENT SECTOR

Over the last decade or two, about half of all new Ph.D.'s have gone into college teaching, and about one-fourth have been employed in research and development activities. In the 1957–1967 decade, both employment sectors expanded rapidly as college enrollments and federal expenditures for research and development more than doubled. From 1967 on, however, real federal expenditures for research and development leveled off, and, beginning about 1970, the rate of enrollment growth diminished sharply.

Since 1920, the Doctorate Records File, maintained by the National Research Council (NRC), has collected information on new Ph.D.'s at the time they received their degrees. For the last 15 years information has been collected on employment plans immediately after receipt of the degree, and Table 9-1 summarizes this information for those with known plans who intended to remain in the United States (this includes between 85 and 90 percent of all new Ph.D.'s).

The percentage of Ph.D.'s employed by educational institutions peaked in 1962–63, while the industrial employment share has declined significantly since 1958–1960. Government employment increased significantly between 1968 and 1973,

TABLE 9-1 *Postgraduation plans of doctorate recipients, 1958–1973 (in percentages)*

Year	Educational institution	Industry	Government	Nonprofit	Other employment	Postdoctoral study
			Employment			
1958–1960	63.8	16.2	8.3	3.8	2.0	6.0*
1962–1963	65.6	13.7	7.7	4.2	2.4	6.4
1964–1966	64.5	12.0	6.4	3.9	2.4	10.8
1967	62.0	12.6	5.4	3.2	5.3	11.5
1968	63.2	12.6	5.3	3.1	4.4	11.3
1969	58.6	13.0	7.4	2.6	3.5	14.8
1970	59.1	12.3	7.6	3.0	2.7	15.3
1971	59.5	9.9	7.9	2.6	4.2	15.9
1972	60.6	8.4	9.5	3.0	3.5	17.0
1973	58.3	9.8	9.0	3.6	4.3	16.9

*Estimated.

NOTE: Percentages include only those doctorate recipients with known affiliation at time of receiving the doctorate, and exclude those taking positions in foreign countries. The unknown affiliation totals varied from a high of 10.4 percent in 1968 to a low of 4.9 percent in 1970. Doctorates taking positions in foreign countries averaged about 8 percent.

SOURCES: National Research Council (1967*a* & 1967*b*–1973).

after declining between 1958 and 1968. Nonprofit employment has maintained a steady share of the total, and other employment has increased by two percentage points. Postdoctoral study has apparently climbed dramatically since the early 1960s. This would seem to confirm the general impression that a rising percentage of new Ph.D.'s, particularly in the scientific fields, are remaining in a "holding pattern," continuing at their universities for a year or two in a postdoctoral research capacity while awaiting satisfactory job offers from other potential employers.

A careful review of successive NRC reports, however, suggests some reinterpretation of the data concerning educational institutions. Until 1969 the respondent had a choice of indicating an employment area or the possession of a postdoctoral fellowship. In 1969 the postdoctoral category was refined to permit designation of "postdoctoral study" under the subheadings of "fellowship," "traineeship," or "other." The latter category included 5.4 percent of doctorates in 1969, 6 percent in 1970, and 6.7 percent in 1971. In 1972 and 1973, a fourth category of "research associate" was added, accounting for nearly 6 percent of Ph.D.'s and leaving only about 1 percent in the "other" group. Thus, it appears that 5 or 6 percent of new doctorate recipients who were classified as employed by educational institutions prior to 1969 were reclassified as engaged in postdoctoral study from 1969 through 1973. This interpretation implies a high degree of constancy in the educational institutions category and a more modest rise in the percentage engaged in postdoctoral study as defined in the pre-1969 years. The major shifts over the 15-year period, therefore, seem to be a decline of about five percentage points in industrial employment, and a corresponding increase in postdoctoral appointments.

Considering the fact that the academic labor market has gone through periods of rather substantial shortages and surpluses of Ph.D.'s in this 15-year period, the high degree of constancy in the proportion of new Ph.D.'s employed by academic institutions may seem surprising. The data suggest that academic institutions have been able to absorb a nearly constant proportion of the growing number of Ph.D.'s whether college enrollments were growing rapidly or slowly. The implication is that while the proportion of doctorates entering (or continuing in) academic employment may be a relative constant, the number of new academic staff employed each year from the ranks of those without the doctorate must vary considerably depending upon the total demand for faculty. The data in Chapter 8 (Tables 8-3 and 8-5) indicate a marked variation in the fraction of new faculty with the doctorate between 1968 and 1972, peak and trough years in hiring by the colleges and universities, and Table 9-1 confirms that variation.

Table 9-2 compares the primary work activity of new Ph.D.'s between 1962 and 1973. The proportion engaged principally in teaching gradually rose throughout the 1960s and early 1970s, dropping only in 1973. Correspondingly, the share of doctorate recipients entering research and development employment had averaged about 32 percent in the 1962–1968 years, but dropped by one-third over the next five years. Those engaged in administrative activity steadily increased, as did those performing professional services.

To some extent, these trends result from different growth rates for the number of doctorates in different fields of study.

TABLE 9-2 *Primary work activity of new doctorate recipients, 1962–1973 (in percentages)*

	Teaching	Research and development	Adminis-trative	Professional services	Other	Total
1962–63	46.6	34.7	8.3	5.3	5.1	100.0
1964–1966	50.0	30.6	8.8	4.6	6.0	100.0
1967	51.6	32.1	8.9	4.5	2.9	100.0
1968	53.0	32.0	8.3	4.7	1.8	100.0
1969	54.6	30.8	8.3	5.2	1.1	100.0
1970	55.6	27.9	9.1	6.1	1.3	100.0
1971	56.9	24.7	9.9	6.9	1.6	100.0
1972	57.0	23.1	10.5	7.6	1.8	100.0
1973	55.8	23.3	11.1	9.1	1.7	100.0

SOURCE: See Table 9-1.

For example, the more rapid growth in education and psychology partly accounts for the rise in the administrative and professional services activities. However, the increase of approximately 10 percentage points in those engaged in teaching reflects a significant change within the scientific fields over the last decade. Table 9-3 compares work activities for 1962–63 and 1972–73 for seven major areas of study, and it can be seen that in each of the science areas there was an almost matching increase in teaching and decrease in research.

The decline in the share of research employment fits well with the observed leveling off in the constant-dollar volume of research and development by the federal government beginning about 1968. The increase in the proportion of doctorate holders entering teaching up through 1969 is explainable by the high level of demand for new college teachers as enrollment expanded rapidly. Since 1969, however, the continued high proportion of doctorates entering teaching must reflect an enrichment of teaching faculties, for the rate of net hiring has declined sharply. The only ways in which the number of doctorates indicated by the NRC surveys could have entered teaching in 1972 and 1973 are if the fraction of new hires with the doctorate were unusually high (in contrast to the 1960s), if many non-doctorate holders already in teaching completed the

TABLE 9-3 Comparison of primary work activity of new doctorate recipients, 1962–63 and 1972–73 (in percentages)

| | Primary work activity | | | | | | | | Doctorates awarded by each area | |
| | Teaching | | Research and development | | Administration | | Other | | | |
	1962–63	1972–73	1962–63	1972–73	1962–63	1972–73	1962–63	1972–73	1962–63	1972–73
E. M. P. fields*	28.8	36.3	62.5	54.3	1.3	2.6	7.4	6.8	33.0	26.4
Life sciences	31.0	43.2	60.4	43.3	1.8	3.8	6.8	9.7	16.4	15.1
Social sciences	45.9	59.7	28.0	17.8	4.7	4.5	21.4	18.0	16.3	17.3
Arts and humanities	88.4	91.1	3.8	3.4	3.0	2.6	4.8	2.9	13.6	15.1
Professional fields	70.1	71.7	7.3	9.1	7.3	9.4	15.8	9.8	4.1	4.5
Education	50.3	49.8	4.9	7.4	33.4	31.4	11.4	11.4	16.6	21.6
All fields	46.6	56.9	34.7	23.2	8.3	10.8	10.4	9.1	100.0	100.0

*Engineering, mathematics, and physical sciences.

SOURCE: See Table 9-1.

degree, or if doctorate holders actually displaced non–doctorate holders in teaching positions. To some degree each of these phenomena has probably occurred.

PLACEMENT BY PRESTIGE OF EMPLOYING INSTITUTIONS It was suggested earlier in this chapter that new doctorate recipients taking teaching positions filter down through the higher educational system from higher- to lower-prestige institutions depending upon academic labor market conditions. Thus, when Ph.D.'s are scarce, it is likely that a high proportion of new Ph.D.'s from the high-prestige universities will take first jobs in institutions with equal (or superior) standing to the ones from which they received their doctorates; when Ph.D.'s are more plentiful, an increasing proportion are likely to take positions in colleges and universities of lesser rank than the ones from which they earned their degrees. Niland (1973) demonstrated this phenomenon for the years 1967–1971 using ACE (Cartter) quality ratings of universities. However, the ACE study only included 106 major universities, while the other 2,500 institutions of higher education were lumped in an "other" category by Niland. For the purposes of this chapter, a prestige-rating scheme has been developed that separates educational institutions into 12 groups, and the NRC data from the Doctorate Records File have been reanalyzed and extended to include 1972 and 1973. (The first job placement of new doctorate recipients has also been separately analyzed by sex, discussed in the following section.)

The institutional groups used here are a rough measure of prestige as seen through the eyes of doctorate recipients seeking faculty positions. Any such measures are imprecise, and they may not reflect the true quality of education provided to students, but it is likely that a more accurate picture of the academic labor market can be obtained by such a measure than if one assumed that all institutions were alike and interchangeable.

In developing the prestige groupings, the 1964 and 1969 ACE ratings of graduate programs (Cartter, 1966*a*; Roose & Andersen, 1970) have been utilized to divide doctoral-granting institutions into five categories. Group I includes the 10 top-ranked universities. Group II includes the next 20. Group III includes universities ranked 31 through 65. Group IV includes all other

ACE rated institutions (69), and group V is made up of 118 universities which were not ranked in the ACE study.[2]

The non-doctoral-granting senior institutions were similarly grouped into five classes, based on an unpublished study by the author in 1965. In this study, five quantitative measures were used in an attempt to find proxies for prestige—no one of which is a very adequate measure, but which in concert appeared to give a reasonably good rank ordering of colleges. The five indices, based largely on U.S. Office of Education, AAUP, and ACE data, were: educational and general expenditure per FTE student, books per student in the college library, average compensation per faculty member, percentage of B.A.'s who obtain a Ph.D.,[3] and percentage of the faculty whose highest degree was the doctorate. Colleges were scored on a five-point scale for each index, and the average of the five scores determined the rank position. Included in the study were 767 accredited senior colleges. After the institutions had been grouped into five classes, the author reviewed each group to see if there were obviously misplaced institutions. In the author's judgment, 17 colleges were rated too highly by this scoring (perhaps due to inadequate or incorrectly reported data), and 4 institutions were scored too low. These 21 colleges were moved down or up one group on a judgmental decision. Particular attention was paid to the approximately 15 percent of institutions for which only four scores could be computed, and the nearly 10 percent for whom only three indices were available. While there undoubtedly are a few institutions that are incorrectly grouped by these quantitative measures, the dubious cases appeared to be small enough in number as to be statistically insignificant.

Group VI, the elite four-year colleges, includes such institutions as Amherst, Claremont Men's College, Wellesley, and Hamilton among the 36 so classified. Group VII, consisting of

---

[2]Included in the ACE surveys were all universities which had averaged at least 10 Ph.D.'s per year for the preceding decade. Thus, group V institutions were either quite small or relative newcomers to the doctoral scene.

[3]As in the earlier studies by Knapp (1964), in calculating this percentage the number of women baccalaureates was multiplied by .2 to allow for the fact that women B.A.'s are much less likely to attain the Ph.D. Thus, institutions with a high proportion of women students were not unduly penalized in the scoring.

TABLE 9-4 Employment plans of 1968 doctorate recipients by class of doctorate and employing institution

Class of employing institution	Class of doctoral-granting institution										Total	
	I		II		III		IV		V			
	Number	Percent	Number	Percent	Number	Percent	Number	Percent	Number	Percent	Number	Percent
I University (10)	214	69.1	75	24.2	15	4.8	5	1.6	1	0.3	310	100.0
II University (20)	218	26.6	426	52.0	131	16.0	34	4.1	11	1.3	820	100.0
III University (35)	155	17.6	308	34.9	328	37.2	79	8.9	12	1.4	882	100.0
IV University (69)	180	14.2	400	31.5	292	23.0	353	27.8	44	3.5	1,269	100.0
V University (118)	84	7.9	275	26.0	300	28.4	263	24.8	136	12.9	1,058	100.0
VI College (36)	61	34.1	79	44.1	23	12.8	13	7.3	3	1.7	179	100.0
VII College (153)	108	15.7	224	32.5	197	28.6	130	18.9	30	4.3	689	100.0
VIII College (249)	61	8.6	227	32.2	202	28.6	175	24.8	41	5.8	706	100.0
IX College (466)	41	3.7	214	19.0	286	25.4	440	39.1	144	12.0	1,125	100.0
X College (617)	19	5.5	83	24.2	82	23.9	125	36.5	34	9.9	343	100.0
XI Two-year colleges	12	10.5	26	22.8	34	29.8	29	25.5	13	11.4	114	100.0
XII Elementary and secondary schools	10	8.1	34	27.4	32	25.8	33	26.6	15	12.1	124	100.0
Total known institutions	1,163	15.3	2,371	31.1	1,922	25.2	1,679	22.0	484	6.4	7,619	100.0

Unknown institutions	89		280		237		211		97		914	
Total teaching in U.S. educational institutions	1,252		2,651		2,159		1,890		581		8,533	
Foreign teaching	144		255		146		108		32		685	
Other teaching	22		56		51		52		21		202	
Total teaching	1,418	15.1	2,962	31.4	2,356	25.0	2,050	21.8	634	6.7	9,420	100.0
Total postdoctoral study	495	20.0	811	32.4	623	25.0	410	16.4	155	6.2	2,494	100.0
Total research and development employment	934	17.0	1,665	30.3	1,421	25.8	1,109	20.2	370	6.7	5,499	100.0
Total in teaching, research and development, and Postdoctoral	2,847	16.3	5,438	31.2	4,400	25.3	3,569	20.5	1,159	6.7	17,413	100.0

NOTE: Unknown professional services, administration, and other categories omitted here comprised 5,421 in 1968, or 24 percent of total Ph.D.'s awarded.

SOURCE: Computations made for the author by the Doctorate Records File Office of the National Research Council.

153 colleges, includes such institutions as Franklin and Marshall, Drew, Sewanee, Alfred, Kalamazoo, Sweet Briar, and Brooklyn College (CUNY). Group VIII includes 249 institutions, of which Adelphi, Rollins, Whittier, Shimer, San Diego State, and Western Michigan University are examples. Group IX includes all other accredited four-year institutions (466 in number), and group X is reserved for unaccredited four-year institutions (a surprising 617).

Group XI includes all two-year colleges in the country. Ideally, one would have wished to separate this category of institutions into two or three subgroups, for there is probably as much differentiation among two-year colleges as there is among four-year institutions. However, sufficient data were not available, and such a small proportion of doctorate recipients traditionally have become junior college teachers that this distinction is of less importance.

Finally, group XII includes all doctorates taking positions in elementary and secondary schools. Presumably, this group consists largely of graduates from schools of education.

The data used for classifying universities and colleges were drawn from the 1962–1965 period. This is probably an appropriate period when first job placements in the 1967–1973 years are being analyzed, especially in view of the expected time-lag in the reputation of institutions.

Tables 9-4 and 9-5 show the class of doctoral-granting institutions across the top (group I being the highest ranking and V the lowest). The rows show the number of new doctorate recipients employed by each group of institutions from each class of doctoral institution. 1968, the highest academic employment year in the 1967–1973 period, is shown in Table 9-4, and 1973, the poorest employment year in the last 15 years, is shown in Table 9-5.

As can be seen from these tables, each category of university tends to hire heavily from its own level of institutions. In Table 9-4, for example, in 1968 the top 10 universities hired 69 percent of their new doctorates from universities within the top 10, and did not draw significantly from universities in groups III through V. The next 20 universities hired 52 percent of their new doctorate faculty from within their own group, 27 percent from group I, and only 16 percent from group III. Only in groups IV and V is there a tendency to draw the majority of faculty from superior universities.

The most elite four-year colleges draw almost entirely from group I and II universities, while lower-prestige colleges increasingly draw from lower-ranked universities. Community college and secondary school Ph.D.'s come primarily from the middle-ranked universities.

The interesting point in comparing Tables 9-4 and 9-5 is that the pattern of where each group of institutions draws its new faculty with doctorates hardly differs between good and bad employment years. On the other hand, the numbers indicate that the higher-ranked institutions employed fewer new doctorate recipients and the lower-ranked institutions more doctorate recipients in 1973 than in 1968. Thus, in a looser labor market there is a downward movement—relatively greater employment in less prestigious institutions—but not a shift to the left—higher-ranked groups did not tend to hire more doctorate recipients from more prestigious institutions than previously. Hiring patterns for each class of institutions remained remarkably stable, although the rate of Ph.D. hiring altered significantly between 1968 and 1973.

Comparing the total entering teaching in known institutions, it is interesting to note that between 1968 and 1973 the number of doctorate recipients from group I universities increased less than 3 percent and group II nearly 10 percent. By contrast, Ph.D.'s from the next three classes of universities increased by 28 percent, 38 percent, and 115 percent, respectively, over the five-year period. These are somewhat greater differences than in total doctorates awarded by those classes of universities, indicating that the lower-prestige universities did less well in placing their Ph.D.'s in nonteaching positions.

Tables 9-6 and 9-7 provide another way of looking at the same data. Here the university and college groups are placed in overlapping order. It is assumed that from the viewpoint of institutional prestige, group VI colleges are approximately the equivalent of group III universities in the preference scale of the average new doctorate recipient weighing employment alternatives. That is to say, it is assumed that job offers from Smith, Bowdoin, or Grinnell have about the same appeal to a young Ph.D. as would equivalent offers from Florida State, New York

TABLE 9-5 *Employment plans of 1973 doctorate recipients by class of doctorate and employing institution*

	Class of doctoral-granting institution											Total	
	I		II		III		IV		V					
Class of employing institutions	Number	Percent	Number	Percent	Number	Percent	Number	Percent	Number	Percent	Number	Percent
I University (10)	130	62.2	55	26.3	13	6.2	9	4.3	2	1.0	209	100.0
II University (20)	150	24.0	341	54.4	87	13.9	36	5.8	12	1.9	626	100.0
III University (35)	156	19.8	252	32.1	297	37.8	61	7.8	20	2.5	786	100.0
IV University (69)	185	15.5	344	28.8	269	22.5	340	28.4	57	4.8	1,195	100.0
V University (118)	112	9.6	229	25.7	272	23.4	285	24.5	195	16.8	1,163	100.0
VI College (36)	73	39.7	64	34.8	27	14.7	15	8.1	5	2.7	184	100.0
VII College (153)	99	11.4	272	31.2	258	29.6	173	19.9	69	7.9	871	100.0
VIII College (249)	116	16.2	316	27.9	348	30.8	252	22.3	100	8.8	1,132	100.0
IX College (466)	84	4.5	367	19.7	441	23.6	684	36.6	292	15.6	1,868	100.0
X College (617)	37	6.0	125	20.4	154	25.2	194	31.7	102	16.7	612	100.0
XI Two-year colleges	26	4.7	86	15.4	180	32.3	156	27.9	110	19.7	558	100.0
XII Elementary and secondary schools	24	5.9	78	19.0	110	26.8	120	29.3	78	19.0	410	100.0
Total known institutions	1,192	12.4	2,599	27.0	2,456	25.6	2,325	24.2	1,042	10.8	9,614	100.0
Unknown institutions	204		548		627		596		236		2,211	

Total teaching in U.S. educational institutions	1,396	11.8	3,147	26.6	3,083	26.1	2,921	24.7	1,278	10.8	11,825	100.0
Foreign teaching	188		367		257		198		57		1,067	
Other teaching	34		90		116		136		67		443	
Total teaching	1,618	12.1	3,604	27.0	3,456	25.9	3,255	24.5	1,402	10.5	13,335	100.0
Total postdoctoral study	884	16.8	1,505	28.6	1,317	25.0	1,119	21.2	440	8.4	5,266	100.0
Total research and development employment	826	15.1	1,450	26.4	1,396	25.5	1,297	23.7	508	9.3	5,479	100.0
Total in teaching, research and development, and postdoctoral	3,328	13.8	6,559	27.2	6,169	25.6	6,671	27.7	2,350	9.7	24,080	100.0

NOTE: Unknown, professional services, administration and other categories omitted here comprised 9,647 in 1973, or 28.6 percent of total Ph.D.'s awarded.

SOURCE: See Table 9-4.

TABLE 9-6 *Percentage distribution of teaching employment among classes of institutions for each class of doctoral-granting institution, 1968*

Class of employing institutions	Class of doctoral-granting institution					All universities
	I	II	III	IV	V	
A (I)	18.4	3.2	0.8	0.3	0.2	4.1
B (II)	18.7	18.0	6.8	2.0	2.3	10.8
C (III and VI)	20.6	16.3	18.3	5.5	3.1	13.9
D (IV and VII)	24.7	26.3	25.4	28.8	15.3	25.7
E (V and VIII)	12.5	21.2	26.1	26.1	36.6	23.1
F (IX and XI)	4.6	10.1	16.7	27.9	32.4	16.3
G (X and XII)	2.5	4.9	5.9	3.4	10.1	6.1
	100.0	100.0	100.0	100.0	100.0	100.0

SOURCE: See Table 9-4.

TABLE 9-7 *Percentage distribution of teaching employment among classes of institutions for each class of doctoral-granting institution, 1973*

Class of employing institutions	Class of doctoral-granting institution					All universities
	I	II	III	IV	V	
A (I)	10.9	2.1	0.5	0.4	0.2	2.2
B (II)	12.6	13.1	3.5	1.5	1.1	6.5
C (III and VI)	19.2	12.2	13.2	3.3	2.4	10.1
D (IV plus VII)	23.8	23.7	21.5	22.1	12.1	21.5
E (V plus VIII)	19.1	23.7	25.2	23.1	28.3	23.9
F (IX plus XI)	9.2	17.4	25.3	36.1	38.6	25.2
G (X plus XII)	5.1	7.8	10.7	13.5	17.3	10.6
	100.0	100.0	100.0	100.0	100.0	100.0

SOURCE: See Table 9-5.

University, or Case Western Reserve. Similarly, group VII colleges and group IV universities, and group VIII colleges and group V universities are paired off. Group IX four-year colleges and group XI two-year colleges are placed on a par, and the unaccredited colleges and secondary school teaching are placed together in the last group. This pairing off provides seven broad categories of institutions by prestige level, and is a more satisfactory way of treating the universe of higher education than Niland's alternative of placing all non-doctoral-granting colleges in a single group below the lowest-ranked university.

With this seven-classification grouping, Tables 9-6 and 9-7 show where the Ph.D.'s produced by the five groups of universities took their first teaching jobs in 1968 and in 1973. In both tables there is a flow of Ph.D.'s downward and to the right—the lower-prestige graduate schools tend to place their Ph.D.'s in somewhat lower-prestige institutions. However, in 1973 the filtering-down process is much more marked than in 1968. The top 10 universities placed 58 percent of their Ph.D.'s in teaching positions in A, B, and C institutions in 1968, but only 43 percent in 1973. The group II universities placed 38 percent in these top three groups in 1968, but only 27 percent in 1973. Most graduate schools placed nearly twice as large a proportion of their Ph.D.'s in institutions in classes F and G in 1973 as in 1968.

One way of viewing the difference in market effects is to measure the proportion of doctorate recipients who take first teaching positions in institutions of superior, equal, or lower prestige than their Ph.D.-granting school. Table 9-8 shows the comparative figures for 1968 and 1973. Doctorate recipients from the lower-quality universities appear to have suffered most from the market deterioration, with groups IV and V having the largest percentage point increase in doctorates going to institutions of lower prestige.

Reviewing the 1968 and 1973 data for two quite different job market years, several themes emerge. First, it is evident that Ph.D.'s from any given class of graduate schools tend to spread themselves out through the job market, but principally in a downward direction. Only about 5 percent of doctorates move upward to superior-prestige institutions. Second, regardless of the labor market tightness or looseness, institutions tend to hire from the same array of graduate schools. Hiring probably is

TABLE 9-8 *Percentage of doctorate recipients who took teaching positions in institutions of superior, equal, or lower prestige ranking, 1968 and 1973*

Class of doctorate institution	1968			1973		
	Superior	Equal	Lower	Superior	Equal	Lower
Group I		18.4	81.6		10.9	89.1
Group II	3.2	18.0	79.2	2.7	13.1	84.8
Group III	7.6	18.3	74.1	4.0	13.2	82.8
Group IV	7.8	28.8	63.4	5.2	22.1	72.7
Group V	20.9	36.6	42.5	15.8	28.3	55.9
All groups	5.1	21.7	73.2	4.6	16.7	78.7

SOURCE: See Tables 9-4 and 9-5.

influenced by school ties of present faculty and personal relationships built up over the years between graduate departments and chairmen in employing institutions. Third, apparently the most flexible market factor is the proportion of new faculty with the doctorate in the lesser-prestige institutions. When Ph.D.'s are relatively scarce, these colleges tend to hire a larger proportion of nondoctorates; when Ph.D.'s are more plentiful, the quality of faculty (as measured by highest degree) tends to rise rapidly. In the higher-prestige colleges and universities, hiring patterns remain relatively constant, with change in the number of new faculty hired the chief variable. Thus, quantity is the main variable for the high-prestige institutions, and quality of faculty hired is the key variable for the lesser-prestige colleges, as academic labor market conditions vary.

SEX DIFFERENCES IN FIRST JOB PLACEMENT For 1967 and 1968, and 1971 through 1973, the Doctorate Records File data have distinguished between men and women doctorate recipients. These data cover an interesting period between peak and trough hiring and also includes the period when equal employment pressures have been brought to bear on colleges and universities. Unfortunately, data on doctorate recipients are not available by ethnic origin, but the sex distinction provides some insight on the impact of affirmative action programs.

The last five years have seen a dramatic increase in the proportion of women earning the doctorate. As Figure 9-1 illustrates, in the late 1920s and early 1930s about 16 percent of Ph.D.'s were women. Between 1932 and 1954 (with the excep-

FIGURE 9-1 *Percentage of doctorates awarded to women*

SOURCES: National Research Council (1973; 1974).

tion of the war years), the percentage dropped steadily to a low of 9.1 percent in 1954. Modest increases appeared in the late 1960s, and then a sharp increase appeared in the early 1970s. Table 9-9 indicates the growth rate of the number of doctorates awarded to men and to women over the last decade. With the end of the draft in 1969 and the less-than-rosy job prospects in the early 1970s, the rate for men has dropped sharply and even turned slightly negative in 1973. The rate of increase in women Ph.D.'s, however, rose significantly in 1966 and has remained high through the last eight years. Between 1971 and the end of the decade, if current trends continue, the entire increase in annual doctorates awarded could come from the expanded enrollment of women.

Many studies of sex discrimination in colleges and universities have appeared in recent years.[4] While the difference in

[4]Bayer and Astin (1968); Bayer and Astin (1975); Cartter and Ruhter (1975); Lester (1974); and Solmon (1973).

Year	*Men*	*Women*	*Combined total*
1963	10.4	12.5	10.7
1964	12.6	12.2	12.6
1965	14.2	12.7	14.1
1966	8.8	18.8	9.9
1967	13.1	16.7	13.5
1968	11.4	20.1	12.4
1969	12.8	15.6	12.3
1970	14.2	17.2	14.6
1971	6.9	15.7	8.0
1972	1.7	15.0	3.6
1973	−0.3	15.1	2.2

TABLE 9-9
Annual growth rates of doctorate recipients, by sex, 1963–1973 (in percentages)

SOURCES: National Research Council (1972; 1973, p. 2; 1974).

average salary between men and women is in the neighbor-hood of 20 percent at present, there is evidence that this differ-ential is narrowing (Bayer & Astin, 1975). When one corrects for differences in degree held, years of employment, academic discipline, research productivity, and rank, the salary differ-ences between men and women are significantly reduced although they do not entirely disappear. Recent studies also indicate that differentials today have been almost eliminated at the point of entry into college teaching, due, at least in part, to affirmative action programs, but that they persist among the older members of the profession. As Bayer and Astin con-cluded: "The amount of differential in rank which could be attributable to sex was halved during the period (1968–69 to 1972–73), and salary differentials by sex were all but eradicated for faculty members in junior ranks" (ibid., p. 9).

A persistent difference between young men and women doc-torates up through the 1960s was the type of institution in which they took their first jobs. Initial job placement is proba-bly the most important factor in the long-term career develop-ment of the new Ph.D. The work patterns of a lifetime are usually formed in those first several years of college teaching, and visibility in one's discipline and potential mobility are markedly affected by the type of institution at which one begins his or her career.

Until recently, women Ph.D.'s have been at a disadvantage in first job placement. A much higher proportion of women than men doctorate recipients have entered junior college or public school teaching, and, among the more prestigious colleges and universities, women have been underrepresented on the faculties of all but the predominantly women's institutions. Only in the last year or two, when equal employment policies enforced by the U.S. Department of Health, Education, and Welfare have prodded institutions of higher education, have women significantly improved their first-job placement performance.

Analysis of Doctorate Records File data on employment plans of new doctorates reveals the significant change that has taken place in the last year or two. Table 9-10 shows the percentage of teachers with doctorates who were women, hired by each class of employing institution from 1967 to 1973. The most dramatic improvement has taken place in the university sector, and most

TABLE 9-10 *Percent of new teachers with doctorates who were women, by class of employing institution, 1967–1973*

Class of employing institution	1967	1968	1971	1972	1973
I	4.4	10.0	15.0	15.4	27.8
II	12.8	13.7	16.4	18.5	25.2
III	13.7	12.9	18.3	19.6	22.5
IV	9.3	10.8	13.9	15.6	17.9
V	10.7	12.2	15.0	15.8	18.4
Total, universities	10.7	12.2	15.5	16.9	20.6
VI	22.1	10.0	16.0	28.8	27.2
VII	19.4	16.4	19.1	17.4	21.1
VIII	17.6	16.9	17.1	18.0	21.6
IX	16.1	16.1	16.6	18.6	18.1
X	28.1	22.7	22.4	20.3	20.4
Total, four-year colleges	19.0	16.7	17.9	18.8	20.1
Two-year colleges	27.0	23.7	21.3	26.0	22.2
Elementary and secondary schools	35.8	29.5	29.4	26.4	26.6
All educational institutions	14.7	14.5	17.3	18.5	20.8

SOURCE: Computations made for the author by the Doctorate Records File office of the National Research Council.

particularly among the high-prestige universities. Compared with 1967 and 1968, 1971 and 1972 showed an improvement of almost 50 percent in the proportion of women hired, while 1973 represented an approximate doubling of the proportions of five years earlier. Considering that women received about 18 percent of all doctorates awarded in 1973, all classes of educational institutions did as well or better than the overall proportion of women in the total Ph.D. pool, indicating that nonteaching employment fared somewhat worse than academic employment. It has been reported that affirmative action compliance pressures have been applied more heavily to the more outstanding colleges and universities, on the assumption that this would have greater impact on the total educational system. Judging from the data in Table 9-10, such efforts have apparently had a significant effect on the universities in groups I and II and the colleges in group VI.

As a corollary to the improved performance in the hiring of women Ph.D.'s in the high-prestige senior institutions, the fraction of new teachers with doctorates hired by the two-year colleges, the public schools, and the least prestigious four-year colleges has declined since the late 1960s. When it is recalled that total Ph.D. hiring has increased substantially in these latter categories relative to the slower growth in the high prestige senior institutions, it is apparent that men doctorates have fared considerably less well in the last year or two both relatively and absolutely in the prestige colleges and universities.

Table 9-11 provides a comparison of the percentage of male

TABLE 9-11 *Percent of new teachers with doctorates hired, by class of employing institution and by sex, 1967–1973*

Class of employing institution	1967	1968	1971	1972	1973
Men					
I	5.6	4.3	2.7	2.3	2.0
II	11.3	10.8	8.7	8.3	6.1
III	12.1	11.8	8.7	8.9	8.0
IV	18.5	17.3	15.7	14.6	12.9
V	14.6	14.2	13.3	14.1	12.5
Total, universities	62.2	58.5	49.0	48.3	41.5

TABLE 9-11 *(continued)*

Class of employing institution	1967	1968	1971	1972	1973
VI	2.4	2.5	1.8	1.6	1.8
VII	8.5	8.8	8.9	8.8	9.0
VIII	9.0	9.0	11.6	11.0	11.7
IX	11.5	14.5	17.4	17.6	20.0
X	3.2	4.1	4.8	5.6	6.4
Total, four-year colleges	34.5	38.9	44.5	44.5	48.9
Two-year colleges	1.3	1.3	3.1	3.8	5.7
Elementary and secondary schools	2.0	1.4	3.3	3.4	3.9
TOTAL	100.0	100.0	100.0	100.0	100.0
Women					
I	1.5	2.8	2.2	1.9	2.9
II	9.6	10.2	8.2	8.3	7.9
III	11.2	10.4	9.3	9.6	8.9
IV	11.0	12.5	12.1	11.8	10.7
V	10.1	11.8	11.3	11.7	10.7
Total, universities	43.5	47.7	43.2	43.2	41.1
VI	3.9	1.6	1.6	2.8	2.6
VII	11.8	10.3	10.1	8.1	9.2
VIII	11.2	10.9	11.4	10.6	12.2
IX	12.9	16.5	16.5	17.7	16.9
X	7.3	7.1	6.7	6.2	6.3
Total, four-year colleges	47.0	46.5	46.3	45.5	47.2
Two-year colleges	2.9	2.5	4.1	5.9	6.2
Elementary and secondary schools	6.6	3.3	6.5	5.4	5.5
TOTAL	100.0	100.0	100.0	100.0	100.0

SOURCE: Computations made for the author by the Doctorate Records File office of the National Research Council.

and female doctorates hired by each class of institution. Between 1967 and 1973 the university sector declined from being the first employer of 62.2 percent of men doctorates to only 41.5 percent; for women Ph.D.'s, a more modest decline from 43.5 to 41.1 percent was recorded. By 1973 a larger percentage of women than of men doctorates was being placed in universities in groups I, II, and III and colleges in groups VI, VII, and VIII. In the late 1960s, the first job placement pattern was quite different for women than for men; by 1973 there was no appreciable difference. This equality has been achieved, however, by a steady deterioration in the job opportunities for men, while the women reasonably well held their own in a declining job market. For both men and women, there has been a steady upward movement in the proportion taking first jobs in two-year colleges.

Reviewing the data in the Doctorate Records File, three disciplines were selected as being reasonably representative of the sciences, social sciences, and humanities. Biology was chosen for the sciences because it had a larger representation of women than did physics or chemistry. Under this logic, sociology should have been selected in the social sciences, but the author's identification with economics and a limited data-processing budget dictated a different choice. English was selected to represent the nonscience fields.

Table 9-12 shows the average percentage of new teachers with doctorates who were women in 1967–68 and 1972–73 for the three disciplines. For the group I universities, a marked improvement in the proportion of women hired is evident in all three subject areas. For other classes of institutions, the performance is mixed; only universities in groups IV and V and group VII senior colleges showed improvements in all disciplines. For all educational institutions, only English among these fields showed a significant increase. The absolute numbers shown in parentheses on the subtotal lines indicate that English showed the most substantial absolute, as well as relative, gains for women.

Tables 9-13 and 9-14 show the relative performance of men and women Ph.D.'s in first job placements in research and development. For those working in educational institutions the table gives the distribution of these researchers by class of employing institution. Universities have provided the most

TABLE 9-12 *Percent of new teachers with doctorates who were women, by class of employing institution, 1967–68 and 1972–73 in biology, economics, and English*

Class of employing institution	Biology		Economics		English	
	1967–68	*1972–73*	*1967–68*	*1972–73*	*1967–68*	*1972–73*
I	14.3	25.0	2.5	10.7	14.3	35.7
II	22.2	16.3	8.3	2.8	20.4	34.2
III	25.6	24.6	6.8	7.8	20.6	37.1
IV	10.4	12.2	2.7	7.6	19.9	25.5
V	9.4	12.6	1.4	4.0	18.0	26.9
Universities	15.0	16.4	4.3	5.9	19.2	30.1
	(34/227)	(48/293)	(16/368)	(23/393)	(107/557)	(198/658)
VI	27.3	30.8	13.3	10.5	18.2	51.3
VII	21.8	13.4	3.2	8.8	22.1	30.9
VIII	17.2	18.6	8.6	11.5	27.4	30.2
IX	8.6	11.1	7.0	6.1	24.5	30.8
X	28.6	23.0	8.3	0.0	38.5	35.6
Four-year colleges	16.1	15.8	7.4	7.7	25.8	32.3
	(54/335)	(61/386)	(10/136)	(26/337)	(117/454)	(274/849)
Two-year colleges	5.9	24.6	0.0	25.0	45.4	44.1
	(1/17)	(15/61)	(0/1)	(1/4)	(10/22)	(41/93)
Elementary and secondary schools	0.0	23.5	0.0	0.0	58.3	60.7
	(0/1)	(4/17)	(0/1)	(0/1)	(7/12)	(17/28)
All educational institutions	15.3	16.5	5.1	6.8	24.0	32.6
	(89/581)	(128/771)	(26/511)	(50/734)	(251/1,045)	(530/1,628)

SOURCE: Computations made for the author by the Doctorate Records File office of the National Research Council.

important source of research positions for women, while industry has been most important in the placement of men. Differences by employer and by sex in each employment sector over the six-year period reflect more the change in mix among fields of study than in changing propensities of members of these fields to take first jobs in one employment sector or another.

Among the doctorates hired in research and development work at educational institutions the general pattern is a decrease in the proportion hired at the most prestigious universities and an increase in the less prestigious institutions,

TABLE 9-13 *Percent of new researchers with doctorates who were women, by employing institution, 1967–1973*

Employing institution	1967	1968	1971	1972	1973
Educational institutions	9.7	10.2	11.2	14.3	18.2
Class					
I	12.1	9.8	15.3	12.4	21.6
II	9.2	12.2	13.8	18.9	22.7
III	8.1	10.9	10.6	17.8	16.1
IV	7.8	8.4	7.7	10.8	15.2
V	5.5	7.1	9.0	7.1	10.7
VI and below	16.7	11.6	13.5	14.9	22.1
Government	5.0	6.6	16.2	5.3	9.1
Industry and business	1.4	1.8	1.9	2.1	3.7
Other	7.5	11.1	7.6	19.8	25.2

SOURCE: Computations made for the author by the Doctorate Records File office of the National Research Council.

although (except for the group I universities) the change is not very great. The men show a fairly substantial increase in government employment (but with great year-to-year variation), while the pattern for women did not change appreciably over the six years.

Tables 9-15 and 9-16 show the situation of Ph.D.'s taking positions as postdoctoral students. The pattern did not alter greatly over the six-year period, although the women slightly improved their relative position. Improvements were most marked for women in the universities in groups I and III. Table 9-16, however, indicates that there was considerable variation from year to year. Over the six years, the pattern of postdoctoral appointment did not differ greatly for men and for women Ph.D.'s, although postdoctoral appointments were most common in the hard sciences, where the number of women was relatively small.

Based on the placement information for these three postdegree activities, it appears that declining demand for Ph.D.'s relative to the supply since 1967 has adversely affected opportunities for both men and women with the larger adjustment burden being borne by men. Additional insight on the differ-

TABLE 9-14 *Percent of men and women with new doctorates employed in research and development, by type of employer, 1967–1973*

Employing institution	1967	1968	1971	1972	1973
Men					
All educational institutions	20.1	24.6	13.2	19.9	21.0
Class					
I	23.6	20.0	9.7	11.0	10.7
II	23.8	23.3	19.4	19.4	18.9
III	19.9	20.0	21.4	19.6	19.7
IV	19.0	22.7	23.3	26.6	25.6
V	6.9	7.1	13.8	10.1	10.8
VI *and below*	6.8	6.9	12.4	13.3	14.3
Government	16.9	16.6	4.5	30.2	24.2
Industry and business	52.8	49.8	53.7	42.4	47.2
Other	10.2	9.0	28.6	7.5	7.6
TOTAL	100.0	100.0	100.0	100.0	100.0
Women					
All educational institutions	47.8	48.5	29.8	45.4	44.3
Class					
I	30.0	19.0	13.9	9.3	13.3
II	22.5	28.6	24.5	27.1	25.0
III	16.2	21.4	20.0	25.6	17.0
IV	15.0	18.3	15.4	19.4	20.8
V	3.8	4.8	10.8	4.7	5.9
VI *and below*	12.5	7.9	15.4	13.9	18.0
Government	18.6	18.8	12.9	21.8	20.9
Industry and business	16.8	15.4	18.3	12.4	16.5
Other	16.8	17.3	39.0	20.4	18.3
TOTAL	100.0	100.0	100.0	100.0	100.0

SOURCE: Computations made for the author by the Doctorate Records File office of the National Research Council.

TABLE 9-15 *Percent of postdoctoral students who were women, by class of resident institution, 1967–1973*

Class of employing institution	1967	1968	1971	1972	1973
I	10.3	9.9	11.6	13.1	16.4
II	13.9	14.3	11.6	11.9	13.5
III	9.7	10.5	10.1	9.3	15.5
IV	12.9	12.4	10.6	8.6	11.5
V	11.4	9.4	5.7	6.2	13.9
VI and below	15.4	23.8	15.0	15.5	20.2
All educational institutions	11.9	12.2	10.9	10.8	14.7

SOURCE: Computations made for the author by the Doctorate Records File office of the National Research Council.

TABLE 9-16 *Percent of men and women with doctorates engaged in postdoctoral study, by class of resident institution, 1967–1973*

Class of resident institution	1967	1968	1971	1972	1973
Men					
I	30.0	25.9	21.2	20.7	20.5
II	31.0	34.2	30.9	31.0	26.1
III	20.7	21.4	22.4	22.9	22.6
IV	11.2	13.0	16.7	16.9	19.4
V	3.4	3.3	5.8	5.9	7.7
VI and below	3.5	3.2	3.0	2.6	3.8
TOTAL	100.0	100.0	100.0	100.0	100.0
Women					
I	25.6	20.5	22.8	25.8	23.2
II	37.2	40.9	29.9	34.6	24.8
III	16.5	18.1	20.8	19.4	24.1
IV	12.4	13.1	16.3	13.1	14.7
V	3.3	2.5	2.9	3.2	7.3
VI and below	5.0	4.9	4.3	3.9	5.9
TOTAL	100.0	100.0	100.0	100.0	100.0

NOTE: Totals may not add due to rounding.

SOURCE: Computations made for the author by the Doctorate Records File office of the National Research Council.

ential consequences of these changes in the doctoral labor market is provided in Table 9-17, which shows employment prospects for new degree holders for alternate years since 1965. The percent of Ph.D.'s who had already signed employment contracts at the time of receiving the doctorate was higher in 1967 than in later years, although this may reflect the practice in the tighter labor market of hiring doctoral candidates prior to the completion of their degrees with the understanding that the remaining degree work would be completed during their new employment. Between 1967 and 1973, however, the percent of men who had signed employment contracts at the time they completed degree requirements had fallen by 8 percentage points while the percentage of women who had signed had fallen by 10 percentage points. The loosening of the market appears more strongly in the percentages of doctorates who were still seeking prospective employers. Data on percentages who have already signed contracts and who are negotiating is admittedly susceptible to several interpretations—not all of which imply a depressed market. Alternative optimistic interpretations, however, can less plausibly be applied when the doctorates report they have not yet begun negotiating. Since

TABLE 9-17 *Employment prospects of men and women with doctorates, 1965–1973 (in percentages)*

	Signed contract	Negotiating	Seeking prospects	Other and unknown
Men				
1965	80	8	5	7
1967	81	7	4	7
1969	79	8	7	6
1971	77	7	12	4
1973	73	8	14	5
Women				
1965	72	9	10	9
1967	73	9	10	9
1969	67	9	16	8
1971	65	9	19	8
1973	63	11	20	6

SOURCES: Data for 1965–1969 from Astin (1973, p. 158); figures for 1971 and 1973 calculated from National Research Council data.

1967 the percentage of women seeking prospects doubled while those percentages for men increased two-and-a-half-fold. However, the certainty attached to future employment was greater each year for men doctorates than it was for women; larger percentages of men had already signed contracts and larger percentages of women were either still negotiating or still looking for a party with whom to begin negotiations.

Table 9-17, however, probably tells us more about changing labor market conditions in general than it does about meaningful sex differentials. Insofar as the practice of wives subordinating their careers to their husband's career development may still be a common pattern, first job placement data would tend to favor the men. In the case of a married man's and woman's completing graduate study in the same year, the husband may make a job commitment first, after which the wife seeks suitable employment in the same area. Thus, the higher proportion of women doctorates still seeking employment at the time they receive the doctorate may be partly an artifact reflecting traditional patterns of family decision making. Unfortunately, the data are not available separately for single and married women (55 percent of women doctorates in 1973 were married) and the extent to which the higher proportion of women reporting no serious job offer at the time of receiving the Ph.D. as a voluntary pattern is not clear.

The preceding tables have observed sex differentials in the first job placement of new doctorate recipients without regard to the institutions from which they received their doctorate; greater insight into changes in the academic labor market can be obtained by viewing the mobility of men and women from and to various classes of institutions. Table 9-18 shows the percentages of doctorates awarded to women by the five classes of graduate schools in the 1967–1973 period. The group II universities (55 percent of which were state universities) were the only ones consistently above the national average in each year. The group I universities (eight of which are private and five of which were essentially men's universities until the 1940s) have recorded a quite dramatic increase over the last few years. Overall the share of doctorates awarded to women has increased by half since 1967.

As in the analysis of all doctorate recipients in the preceding section, the most telling picture of changes in the job market

TABLE 9-18 *Percent of new doctorates awarded to women by class of degree-granting institution, 1967–1973*

Class of doctoral-granting institution	1967	1968	1971	1972	1973
I	9.2	10.4	13.0	14.4	17.4
II	12.3	13.2	15.0	16.6	18.9
III	10.8	12.1	14.6	14.9	18.0
IV	12.1	11.3	13.0	15.4	16.6
V	10.5	11.1	13.7	15.0	16.3
All universities	12.0	12.8	14.4	16.0	18.0

NOTE: "New doctorates" includes doctorates entering teaching, research and development, or postdoctoral study upon graduation. These activities averaged approximately 85 percent of all persons earning the doctorate.

SOURCE: Computations made for the author by the Doctorate Records File office of the National Research Council.

TABLE 9-19 *Placement of teaching doctorate recipients in institutions of equal or superior prestige, 1967–1973 (in percentages)*

Class of degree-granting university	1967	1968	1971	1972	1973
Men					
I	20.1	18.8	13.4	13.8	10.3
II	23.0	21.2	18.8	17.3	14.5
III	25.8	25.6	19.1	19.5	16.0
IV	41.1	36.4	32.3	30.8	26.4
V	60.8	56.1	50.7	48.7	44.3
All universities	29.2	27.6	24.4	23.9	20.6
Women					
I	8.9	15.3	10.0	11.4	12.8
II	19.8	19.6	17.6	15.7	17.9
III	23.8	25.9	22.4	27.4	21.7
IV	27.0	35.6	33.0	31.5	30.5
V	51.6	55.8	46.9	45.6	44.8
All universities	22.8	26.7	24.4	24.9	23.8

SOURCE: Computations made for the author by the Doctorate Records File office of the National Research Council.

and the relative achievements of men and women Ph.D.'s is found in the measure of doctorates who found teaching positions in institutions of equal or superior prestige. Table 9-19 compares these percentages by year and by sex. In 1967 the horizontal or upward mobility of men with doctorates was much more pronounced than for women; by 1973, however, the women graduating from every class of university outperformed the men. The year 1968 appears to have been a reasonably good one for women, but then the deterioration in general academic market conditions caused a decline in high-prestige placements experienced almost equally by the men and the women. In 1972 and 1973 women about held their own in absolute terms, while men continued to experience a downward trend.

Tables 9-20 and 9-21 show the relative performance of men and women with doctorates in research and development and postdoctoral study appointments in institutions of equal or superior prestige. Although a somewhat smaller proportion of women entered these two types of postdegree activity than

TABLE 9-20 *Placement of new doctorates entering research and development in institutions of equal or superior prestige, 1967–1973 (in percentages)*

Class of degree-granting institution	1967	1968	1971	1972	1973
Men					
I	68.0	57.3	47.1	44.4	46.0
II	70.2	65.2	45.3	50.3	43.9
III	68.1	71.5	42.0	58.2	59.0
IV	89.3	89.0	77.7	82.3	73.6
V	92.6	96.7	87.8	94.2	87.1
All universities	73.3	71.1	60.3	61.0	57.8
Women					
I	76.2	59.3	57.1	31.6	45.2
II	60.0	73.3	72.2	63.0	64.6
III	80.0	91.7	61.1	78.1	61.8
IV	37.5	94.7	88.9	95.7	63.9
V	66.7	40.0	100.0	100.0	88.9
All universities	70.8	78.3	72.4	69.6	61.7

SOURCE: Computations made for the author by the Doctorate Records File office of the National Research Council.

TABLE 9-21 *Placement of new doctorates entering postdoctoral study at institutions of equal or superior prestige, 1967–1973 (in percentages)*

Class of degree-granting institution	1967	1968	1971	1972	1973
Men					
I	63.9	58.4	57.4	60.1	58.2
II	76.3	74.7	71.3	72.4	68.7
III	87.4	85.2	82.3	81.3	79.4
IV	92.3	95.0	91.8	93.1	87.0
V	100.0	100.0	97.1	97.3	92.9
All universities	80.6	79.4	77.5	78.1	75.6
Women					
I	69.2	38.9	56.6	63.3	59.5
II	75.6	75.9	69.1	81.5	69.9
III	82.1	85.7	84.6	85.1	78.9
IV	93.3	96.7	92.6	92.5	86.9
V	100.0	100.0	87.5	100.0	96.8
All universities	79.0	75.4	75.5	82.7	75.4

SOURCE: Computations made for the author by the Doctorate Records File office of the National Research Council.

entered teaching, those who did fared comparatively well. In the case of research and development placements, a slightly larger proportion of women obtained positions in equal or superior universities in all years except 1967. The advantage enjoyed by women was greatest in 1971, and had narrowed again by 1973. The number of women with doctorates taking research and development positions from each class of doctoral-granting institution was relatively small, however, so the line-by-line comparisons are not very meaningful.

In the case of postdoctoral-study appointments, shown in Table 9-21, the percentages going to, or remaining in, universities of at least equal prestige is nearly identical for men and women in each of the five years.

Reviewing these tables one would have to conclude that, at least for the time span covered by the data, there appears to be no evidence of discrimination against women in the quality of institution for first job placement in research and development and postdoctoral activity, and that what discrimination may have existed in teaching appointments had disappeared by 1973.

Our data do not reveal the terms of employment, only the status of the institutions to which new doctorates went. However, taking into account the Bayer and Astin (1975) conclusion that salary discrimination against women had apparently disappeared by 1972 for young Ph.D.'s, and the evidence in this chapter that first job placement discrimination had disappeared by 1973, one would have to conclude that academic institutions have successfully eliminated sex inequities in the job market for the current generation of young doctorate recipients. Beyond initial job placement, the career advancement of women depends primarily upon peer review within schools and departments. Fair and equal treatment of persons of unequal ability or commitment to their profession is bound to result in unequal rewards in later life. The important measure is whether women with the same qualifications and accomplishments as men are advanced and remunerated in equitable fashion throughout their professional careers. Equity at the point of entry to the job market—a critically necessary first step—had apparently been achieved in the academic arena by 1973.

10. An Overview of Projected Academic Labor Market Conditions

The broad outline of likely future academic labor market conditions is reasonably clear. On the demand side, the number of new college and university teachers hired depends upon four factors: (1) overall college enrollments, (2) student-faculty ratios, (3) faculty retirement policy, and (4) the net migration of experienced faculty. The first two affect the level of expansion demand (which can be negative as well as positive); the latter two determine the level of replacement demand for faculty.

Over the past 10 or 15 years, replacement demand has been relatively steady at about 1½ to 2 percent of total faculty; net migration has stayed close to zero (despite 3 to 4 percent gross flows into and out of higher education), and age-distribution–dependent death and retirement rates have been below 2 percent. It has been argued, however, that the present and likely future decline in relative salaries of academic personnel will give rise to net out-migration amounting to as much as 1½ percent annually in the 1980s and early 1990s. In addition, with a more slowly expanding total faculty, the age distribution will shift toward upper age levels. Consequently, death and retirement rates will rise over the next two decades—to at least 2 percent annually under current retirement policies, and perhaps to 3 percent if positive early retirement policies are implemented. Replacement demand for faculty at the junior entry point can be expected, therefore, to rise from not more than 2 percent in the 1960s to 3½ to 4½ percent by 1990. In 1972 net replacement needs for faculty numbered approximately 6,000; in 1990 the corresponding number is likely to rise to over 9,000 because of the changed age distribution of college teachers, to about 15,000 if a deterioration in relative salaries contributes to a significant net out-migration, and perhaps to 18,000 or 19,000 if the typical retirement age drops by three or four years. Thus, replacement needs are likely to create many additional future job openings, which will cushion any decline in expansion demand for college teachers.

The factors that contribute to the expansion demand are somewhat more unpredictable. The only clearly predictable factor is the decline of about 25 percent in the size of the traditional college-age population. If the ratio of college enrollment to the 18-to-21-year-old age group remains constant in the future, this demographic shift would mean a decline in FTE enrollment of some 1.8 million students between 1980 and 1994. With a constant student-faculty ratio, this would imply a reduction in the total size of faculty by more than 100,000 college teachers. Thus, if college attendance rates remained constant, teaching staffs would be shrinking in the mid-1980s approximately at the rate of normal faculty attrition, and during most of the 1980s there would be predicted zero hiring of junior faculty.

In Chapters 4 and 5, however, undergraduate degree-credit enrollment was projected to decline between 800,000 and 1,300,000, partly offset by more stable enrollments in graduate and professional programs and expanding enrollments in non-degree studies. The most likely magnitude of the net decline (FTE) is about one-half million. However, this projection assumes a modest increase in participation rates. The experience of the early 1970s and the more dire predictions of the impact of declining rates of return for investment in college education by Dresch (1975) and Freeman (1975) may make the author's view appear moderately optimistic.

The other great uncertainty is what will happen to average student-faculty ratios. All immediate evidence suggests that the overall ratio will continue to rise, thus damping down expansion demand for faculty in the late 1970s and contributing to a somewhat worsened market for doctorates in the 1980s. However, today's pessimism appears to be based more on the problems of inflation, recession, and constrained state revenues and private philanthropy than on any detectable long-term shift in the desired proportions in which educational inputs are combined. The very process of enrollment contraction may lower student-faculty ratios (even if unintentionally), since it is difficult for colleges and universities to shrink the size of their teaching faculties as rapidly as enrollment decreases may call for in some institutions.

Overall, the signs suggest that the annual hiring of junior faculty, which averaged about 27,000 between 1962 and 1972, will average not more than 16,000 between 1972 and 1982 and will decline to less than 10,000 in the 1982–1992 period. During this latter period, expansion demand is likely to be negative, but rising replacement needs will more than offset the general contraction as far as new hiring at junior levels is concerned.

The major reason for labor market imbalance is that the nation's graduate schools expanded to meet the requirements of a rapidly growing research and educational market; thus today's capacity is appropriate for the high level of demand for new Ph.D.'s experienced in the mid-1960s, but considerably larger than necessary for the late 1970s and 1980s. Current graduate school capacity could easily turn out 40,000 to 45,000 doctorates annually. If as many as three-fourths of all new faculty hires in the future are doctorate holders (a proportion that has been approached only in the last two or three years and that is considerably above the 45 to 50 percent figure of the 1960s), then the academic sector is likely to absorb only about 12,000 new doctorates annually for the next several years, and average only about 7,500 during the 1980–1995 period. Therefore, academic demand will probably require not more than 35 percent of graduate school capacity output for the next few years, declining to about 20 percent in the 1980s. In most years between the end of World War II and 1970, at least one-half the new Ph.D.'s found teaching positions in colleges and universities; it seems unlikely that anything close to this fraction will do so in the remaining years of this century.

Barring some dramatic increase in educational demand not now foreseen—such as a sharp increase in recurrent education due to a national program of paid educational leaves, or a significant enrichment of higher education through major reductions in class size—doctoral outputs probably will be reduced and much greater attention will be paid to career alternatives to academic employment. The reduction in enrollments and degrees will, to some extent, happen as a natural market response on the part of students, but, increasingly, institutions and funding agencies (particularly state boards and legislatures) are likely to enforce enrollment reductions.

Employment in other than academic activities is today the lot of a rising number of new Ph.D.'s, but is often an involuntary choice. It seems predictable that graduate faculties will give much greater attention in the future to the training of students who have a broader array of skills than just those suitable to the teacher-scholar and will seek out markets for highly trained personnel in a variety of governmental and business sectors.

DIFFERENTIAL IMPACT OF DECLINING ACADEMIC DEMAND Throughout most of the preceding analyses, academic demand and supply have been dealt with in aggregate terms. It is obvious, however, that different disciplines will continue to experience rather different demand conditions.

One important differentiating factor is the reliance of various fields on the academic labor market for employment of their doctorates. A decline in future undergraduate enrollments will have a much more significant impact on the employment possibilities for classicists than it will for biochemists or nuclear engineers. The educational sector traditionally has been almost the only source of demand for classical skills (although archival and curatorial needs are sometimes filled by classicists); in the case of scientists and engineers, industry and public agencies have normally represented a significant fraction of the manpower demand.

Table 10-1 ranks the major fields by the percentage of employment accounted for by the academic sector; a second column indicates the percent for whom teaching was the primary activity of new Ph.D.'s. (Postdoctoral study, rather than employment as defined by the National Research Council in the Table 10-1 data, is the immediate activity of nearly half the physical scientists and bioscientists; it engages less than 10 percent of the social scientists, and less than 5 percent of the humanists.) Of the humanists who take employment immediately after receipt of the doctorate, about 90 percent enter the academic sector; about three-fourths of social scientists take academic positions, while about two-thirds of bioscientists and less than two-fifths of physical scientists take college and university jobs. Thus, assuming enrollment shares remain constant, a change in enrollment is likely to affect the overall demand for humanists most, the social scientists next, the bioscientists nearly as much, and the physical scientists and engineers least of all.

TABLE 10-1
Percent of
employed new
doctorate
recipients in
academic jobs,
and percent
primarily
engaged in
teaching, 1973

Subject area	Percent in academic employment	Percent teaching as primary activity
English	91.7	88.6
Foreign language and literature	91.2	85.1
Other arts and humanities	88.7	82.0
Anthropology	86.0	72.4
History	85.5	78.7
Education	80.6	45.7
Political science	77.7	66.1
Mathematics	77.2	61.9
Professional fields	75.6	66.0
Economics	70.1	60.3
Biosciences	65.5	48.6
Psychology	54.0	35.4
Agricultural sciences	50.1	22.8
Environmental sciences	42.8	30.0
Physics	39.1	30.8
Chemistry	35.9	30.6
Earth sciences	35.9	37.8
Engineering	27.7	10.3
All fields	68.6	51.4

SOURCE: Computed from National Research Council (1974).

Judging from the experience of new doctorate recipients in finding teaching positions over the last several years, this ordering of disciplines predicts reasonably well the relative difficulty in finding suitable employment utilizing graduate skills. In fact, the gap between the humanists and social scientists is somewhat larger than may appear in Table 10-1, for there are many jobs in government and industry for social scientists at less than doctoral levels but for which Ph.D.'s may be considered candidates, while there are few positions that expressly seek humanists at intermediate levels. Thus the spectrum of job alternatives, which tends to be a continuous function for engineers and most scientists, is more commonly a discontinuous function for humanists. New Ph.D.'s with specialization in the romantic poets or in medieval history are likely to find few nonacademic alternatives that will utilize their training, whereas economists in international trade or finance are likely to find that they are reasonably well suited for a wide array of alternative employment possibilities.

A second factor that differentiates among fields is the enrollment growth rates in the various undergraduate subject areas. No field can assume that its enrollment share will remain unchanged over time because fashions, student interest, societal needs, and employment prospects change. An important trend over the last 10 years has been the general relaxation of lower-division breadth requirements. Thus traditional service courses, for example, in modern languages and English, once heavily populated with nonelective enrollees, have suffered sharp enrollment decreases in many institutions. The physical sciences, the glamor area of the late 1950s and early 1960s, lost much of their popularity during the Vietnam conflict—perhaps because of the association of research in physics and chemistry with military and industrial uses. By contrast, the emerging concern with environmental problems has greatly expanded enrollments in many of the biosciences. Economics, a popular field in the 1930s and 1940s, was somewhat eclipsed during the affluent 1950s and 1960s, but in the last several years, probably because of the recession, has experienced renewed student interest. These intracollegiate shifts in undergraduate enrollments have a profound effect on the demand for new faculty in particular disciplines. Institutional adjustments are not very difficult when total enrollment is growing, but in a "steady state" condition adjustment problems are likely to be increasingly severe.

Table 10-2 shows the growth patterns in the number of undergraduate degrees awarded between 1963–64 and 1968–69, and between 1968–69 and 1973–74, and indicates the NCES projection of growth for the next ten years. In the rapid enrollment growth years in the mid-1960s, when humanities and social science B.A.'s grew by 75 percent or more, the biological sciences grew by 55 percent while the EMP fields (engineering, mathematics, and the physical sciences) experienced growth of less than 33 percent. Over the most recent five-year period, only psychology and the biosciences have expanded by a third, followed closely by the humanities and social sciences, with the EMP fields relatively constant.

TABLE 10-2 Percentage change in bachelor's degrees by subject area, 1963–64 to 1973–74, and projected to 1983–84	*1963–64 to 1968–69*	*1968–69 to 1973–74*	*Projected 1973–74 to 1983–84*
Social science	+ 85	+28	+ 1
Psychology	+121	+79	+47
Humanities	+ 75	+28	+ 7
Mathematical sciences	+ 44	+ 8	+12
Engineering	+ 23	+ 4	+ 3
Physical sciences	+ 23	0	−14
Biological sciences	+ 55	+33	+10
ALL FIELDS	+ 56	+34	+ 5

SOURCE: Calculated from U.S. Office of Education (1975, Table 23).

Looking to the future (and remembering that column 3 represents a 10-year change, as contrasted with 5-year changes in columns 1 and 2), if the NCES field projections are even approximately correct, only mathematics is likely to come close to maintaining its 1968–69 to 1973–74 growth (and this not very substantial). All other fields are projected to experience a marked slowing down (and in some instances a reverse) of growth rates. Psychology appears to have further expansion ahead, but the annual rate is projected at less than a third of that recently experienced. In most subject areas, the projected growth (and thus the derived demand for new faculty) is not more than 1 percent annually, and in the physical sciences the prediction is for absolute contraction.

Table 10-2 suggests that the physical sciences, engineering, social sciences, and humanities, in that order, may have the most depressed enrollment growth conditions over the next decade, while the psychologists, mathematical scientists (principally applied and computer specialists), and biological scientists (chiefly basic medical and environmental sciences) may fare slightly better than the norm. The norm, however, represents a growth rate only about one-tenth as great as that of the last five years.

A third differentiating factor, related to the preceding point, is that past differences in rates of growth have produced somewhat different faculty age distributions in various academic disciplines. An early review of age profiles produced the conclusion that in 1960 the expected death and retirement rate for college teachers varied from a high of 3.7 percent in classics to a low of 0.5 percent in biochemistry (Cartter, 1966c, p. 38n). In the former case, enrollment growth had been negligible for several decades, thus, few young faculty had been hired and the median age of classicists was about 52. In the latter case, the discipline was relatively young and rapidly expanding; therefore, few biochemists were over 45 and the median age was about 34. While these cases represent the extremes, there are noticeable differences even in broad subject classifications.

Table 10-3 shows the age distributions of full-time faculty in four broad areas as determined from 1968 and 1972 faculty surveys. Fifty percent of social science professors were 40 or younger in 1972, as contrasted with 47 percent in EMP fields, 42 percent in the humanities, and 38 percent in the biological sciences. At the other end of the age spectrum nearly 30 percent of biologists and humanists were over 50, while less than 25 percent of social scientists and professors in EMP fields were in their fifties or sixties. Estimated retirement rates in 1972 ranged from 0.66 percent for social scientists up to 1.01 percent for humanists.

The marked drop in the percentages 30 years old and under between 1968 and 1972 reflects the slowdown in enrollment growth and the increased budget constraints on hiring. The

TABLE 10-3 *Age distribution of full-time faculty, selected discipline areas 1968 and 1972 (in percentages)*

Age	Biological sciences 1968	Biological sciences 1972	EMP fields 1968	EMP fields 1972	Social sciences 1968	Social sciences 1972	Humanities 1968	Humanities 1972
30 and under	11.1	4.3	16.2	5.8	19.6	10.5	17.4	6.9
31–40	33.1	33.3	37.4	41.2	34.5	39.4	34.9	35.5
41–50	31.5	32.8	26.4	29.5	27.5	27.6	24.6	30.0
51–60	18.5	22.6	13.5	17.4	13.8	17.0	15.7	19.3
Over 60	5.8	7.0	6.5	6.1	4.6	5.5	7.4	8.3
	100.0	100.0	100.0	100.0	100.0	100.0	100.0	100.0
Estimated retirement rate	0.64	0.84	0.79	0.74	0.65	0.66	0.94	1.01
Percent with doctorate		67.4		70.9		78.8		61.7
Percent with tenure	62.9	67.2	57.2	69.0	49.8	58.8	49.8	63.1

SOURCE: Computed from ACE faculty survey data.

social sciences appear to have been least affected by this change in labor market conditions, while the science fields show the most substantial decline. The data suggest that the social science and EMP fields experience a somewhat higher mid-career out-migration of professors, since they have a somewhat smaller percentage of their faculty in the 41- to 60-year-old range but the differences are not significant enough to distinguish whether they merely emerge from past variations in the rate of faculty growth.

The last two lines of Table 10-3 indicate that about 70 percent of all full-time faculty had the doctorate in 1972 (considerably above the 51 percent figure determined in 1963 by the previously discussed Office of Education COLFACS study), and the tenured proportion was approximately two-thirds (up from slightly over half in 1968). The ACE surveys attempted to correct for sampling bias, but some distortions may remain as the result of nonrespondent bias; therefore comparisons across disciplines in any one year are probably more valid than interyear comparisons. In both years, however, a considerably higher proportion of science than nonscience faculty had achieved tenure. The social sciences, by virtue of their somewhat more rapid growth between 1968 and 1972 have a lower tenure ratio than other areas, despite the higher proportion of doctorate faculty.

THE CASE OF PHYSICS Physics is one of the most interesting fields to observe, partly because it has proved to be more market responsive than most academic disciplines and partly because the American Institute of Physics has collected more detailed data on enrollments and employment since the mid-1950s than have other professional associations.

Table 10-4 shows several key enrollment and degree indicators for physics, covering actual data between 1955 and 1974, and doctoral projections to 1980. As column 2 indicates, undergraduate majors in physics as a percentage of male freshmen in four-year institutions peaked in 1961, shortly after Sputnik, then declined steadily until 1972. Baccalaureates, in comparison with junior majors, dipped during the mid-1960s, when there apparently was some out-migration from physics, but the percentage now seems to have stabilized again at about the pre-1962 level. Entrance of B.A.'s into graduate study in physics

TABLE 10-4 *Physics enrollment and degree trends, 1955–1980*

Year	Junior major	As percent of freshmen*	B.A.'s	As percent of Juniors†	First-year graduate students	As percent of B.A.'s	Ph.D.'s	As percent of first year†	As percent of B.A.'s‡
Actual									
1955–56	3,700	NA	2,420	78.1	NA	NA	490	NA	NA
1956–57	4,300	NA	2,883	83.6	NA	NA	446	NA	NA
1957–58	5,301	NA	3,293	82.3	NA	NA	472	NA	NA
1958–59	5,903	1.73	3,891	81.1	NA	NA	501	NA	NA
1959–60	6,504	1.92	4,669	83.3	NA	NA	533	NA	20.7
1960–61	7,161	2.00	5,042	81.3	NA	NA	615	NA	21.5
1961–62	7,934	2.11	5,293	77.5	NA	NA	699	NA	20.8
1962–63	7,873	1.91	5,622	74.5	3,280	58.3	858	NA	21.7
1963–64	7,520	1.69	5,452	69.0	3,362	61.7	792	NA	17.5
1964–65	7,132	1.61	5,611	72.9	3,354	60.0	983	40.9	19.7
1965–66	7,014	1.59	5,517	75.3	3,503	61.7	1,048	39.8	19.7
1966–67	7,345	1.45	5,037	71.2	3,409	67.6	1,233	45.5	22.6
1967–68	7,822	1.33	5,236	73.0	3,251	62.0	1,325	44.2	23.8
1968–69	7,587	1.37	5,522	72.8	2,998	54.3	1,355	44.2	24.5
1969–70	7,480	1.36	5,975	77.5	3,202	53.5	1,545	50.2	28.7
1970–71	6,884	1.16	5,782	77.0	2,658	46.0	1,530	50.2	29.1

1971–72	6,593	1.08	5,755	80.1	2,449	42.5	1,438	53.3	27.3
1972–73	6,012	0.99	5,282	78.3	2,177	41.2	1,445	51.0	25.9
1973–74	5,858	1.00	4,923	78.1	2,169	44.1	1,236	46.5	21.5
1974–75	5,660	1.01	4,652	78.4	2,205	47.4	1,220	44.0	20.9
Estimated									
1975–76	5,735	1.02	4,520	78.5	2,170	48.0	1,020	42.0	18.2
1976–77			4,475	78.5	2,150	48.0	930	41.0	17.5
1977–78							875	40.0	17.7
1978–79							870	40.0	18.5
1979–80							870	40.0	19.1

*Junior majors as a percent of freshmen two years earlier.

†B.A.'s as a percent of average junior majors one and two years earlier.

‡Ph.D.'s as percent of average B.A.'s and first-year graduate students three to six academic years earlier (four to seven calendar years).

SOURCE: Data through 1974 supplied by American Institute of Physics; projections are the author's.

peaked in 1966, and then dropped quite sharply through 1972—probably a Vietnam effect. The percent of first-year physics students who completed the doctorate peaked in 1971 and then dropped by seven percentage points over the next two years. This decline can be assumed to be in large part a labor market effect.[1]

In the lower portion of Table 10-4 an attempt has been made, using fixed coefficients, to project physics Ph.D.'s to 1980. All the physics doctorates in 1980 are already in the pipeline, so undergraduate majors only have to be projected for one year and B.A.'s and first-year graduate students two years beyond actual data. All ratios except the Ph.D.-completion ratio have been assumed to stabilize; in this case, it appears that there is a significant downward trend. This latter movement also is in keeping with the observed decline in federal graduate fellowships in science, and the swelling of postdoctoral study ranks over the last several years in what has come to be known as the "holding pattern" of those awaiting some improvement in job market conditions.[2]

If the doctoral projection is nearly correct, physics Ph.D.'s will have declined by 44 percent between 1969 and 1978; at that point, it appears likely that the numbers will approximately stabilize at about the old 1962 level unless there are further market inducements altering the educational continuation pattern.

American Institute of Physics (AIP) data on the postgraduation plans of college seniors indicate a sharp decline from 1967 through 1973 in the percentage who plan to enter graduate study in physics immediately after graduation, but a more modest decline in the percentage who intend to pursue graduate study regardless of field. Thus the deterioration in the demand for physicists has apparently encouraged an out-migration to other fields of graduate study. Table 10-5 shows the percentage continuing in physics and in all postbaccalaureate fields.

---

[1]See also Freeman (1975). His data suggest "substantial economic responsiveness in the decision to complete the doctorate program" (p. 33).

[2]Freeman's projection for 1979–80 is 731 to 786 doctorates, using his recursive market model (ibid., p. 38).

		Percentage of students planning postbaccalaureate study in:	
TABLE 10-5 *Postbaccalaureate plans of physics bachelor's degree recipients, 1966–1974*	*Graduating class*	*Physics*	*All fields*
	1966	55	75
	1967	57	77
	1968	46	63
	1969	41	59
	1970	42	64
	1971	35	65
	1972	32	60
	1973	33	58
	1974	35	61

NOTE: Students entering military service immediately after graduation are excluded.

SOURCES: 1966–1972 data from American Institute of Physics (1973, Table 16, p. 35); 1973–74 data provided by AIP.

The data for physics show a marked responsiveness to changing market conditions—one might almost conclude that students were better informed than their college teachers. Average salaries for physicists led the academic parade up through the mid-1960s; since that time, with the slowed growth of academic physics and a modest decline in real research and development expenditures by the federal government after 1967, other fields have assumed the leadership. Undergraduate enrollments have been declining as a share of total enrollment since 1961, and doctoral completion rates dropped consistently from 1966 to 1972, yet it was about 1970 before most science faculty realized that there had been a real shift in the demand for physicists. With a lag of one or two years chemistry, mathematics and engineering have nearly duplicated the response in physics. Mathematics doctorates peaked in 1970 and had dropped 25 percent by 1975. Ph.D. enrollments in engineering were down 20 percent in 1973–74 from their peak in 1968–69, although the number of doctorates awarded did not decline until 1973.

The case of physics encourages one to believe that changing market conditions set up their own countervailing forces; Freeman has ably documented the almost classical response pattern of physics and engineering enrollments.[3] As Table 10-5 demonstrates, however, the market has worked to divert many physics students into other graduate specialties which were reasonably complementary. If one or several disciplines are contracting while opportunities in other fields are expanding, the problem may be quite manageable. The real difficulty emerges when the demand for doctorates in all closely related fields is contracting simultaneously; then the only appropriate market response is a reduction in the total number of graduate students seeking advanced degrees. The key difference between the academic sector and private industry, however, is that in the latter the producer has a strong incentive not to overproduce. In the universities, there is no comparable profit incentive, and no responsibility for the manpower counterpart of inventory accumulation. Thus, the adjustment depends primarily upon the good sense (and information) of the students themselves.

THE NSF VIEW OF SCIENCE AND ENGINEERING   Over the last 20 years, the NSF has had the responsibility of assessing the manpower situation for science and engineering as the focal agency for the federal government. Beginning in 1969, with the report (National Science Foundation, 1969) on *Science and Engineering Doctorate Supply and Utilization*, the foundation has attempted to project needs and resources 10 to 12 years ahead. The world has changed so dramatically since the issuance of this first report, however, that the 1975 doctoral projections for 1980 are now 40 percent below their projection of only six years earlier. Table 10-6 shows the NSF projections of doctorates in science and engineering for 1974–75 and 1979–80 from the 1969, 1971, and 1975 NSF reports. Most striking is the more than 60 percent reduction in the outlook for the physical sciences and mathematics for 1979–80 and the 50 percent reduction for projected engineering degrees.

    The 1969 view was optimistic about the future supply and demand for scientists and engineers, although the report noted that "continuation of present trends may produce a problem several decades ahead." While the authors of the report may be faulted for not looking beyond 1980 in terms of the likely downturn in college enrollments (in 1969 the freshmen of 1987

---

[3]Ibid. See also Freeman (1971, Ch. 4) for documentation of the cobweb adjustment pattern in engineering.

TABLE 10-6 *National Science Foundation projections of doctorates in science and engineering for 1974–75 and 1979–80 in successive reports on doctorate supply and utilization*

Year	Physical sciences*	Life sciences	Engi- neering	Social sciences	All science fields
1969 report					
1974–75	7,800	5,500	4,800	5,200	23,300
1979–80	10,400	7,300	6,400	6,900	31,600
1971 report					
1974–75	6,040	5,420	4,440	6,050	21,950
1979–80	6,460	6,470	4,840	8,060	25,830
1975 report					
1974–75	4,950	4,500	3,450	5,750	18,650
1979–80	3,900	4,900	3,150	6,850	18,700

*Including mathematical sciences.

SOURCES: National Science Foundation (1969, pp. 17–20; 1971, p. 26); and table showing annual doctorates, supplied by the NSF Division of Sciences Resources Studies, which was the basis for Table 8, p. 16 of *Projections of Science and Engineering Doctorate Supply and Utilization, 1980 and 1985* (National Science Foundation, 1975).

were already born), the major source of error was one common to most analysts of the late 1960s—assuming a continuation of recent trends in government research and development expenditures. Since about one-third of all scientists and engineers with doctorates in the labor force are employed in research and development activity outside academia, the effect on employment of a projected change in the rate of growth of research and development expenditures is substantial. The 1969 report (ibid., p. 4) projected the real growth rate of research and development expenditure at 5.7 percent annually; the 1971 report (ibid., 1971, p. 228) projected growth at 2.7 percent to 3.0 percent; the 1975 report (ibid., 1975, p. 34) projects real dollar growth at 1.4 percent and employment growth at only 0.8 percent out to 1985. When it is considered that in 1975 the number of doctorate degrees awarded in science and engineering (estimated by NSF at 18,650) is 8.4 percent of the current national stock of doctorates in the labor force (221,000), this means that the supply growth rate, net of deaths and retirements, is currently about 6.8 percent, far in excess of projected nonacademic needs.

The 1975 NSF report projects enrollments in higher education as growing from 8,645,000 in 1975 to a peak of 9,099,000 in 1979, then declining to 8,204,000 in 1985. Thus, over the next 10 years the average annual change in enrollment is projected to be −0.5 percent. Combining this projection with that for research and development scientists and engineers, the message between the lines of the 1975 report seems to be that *no* new doctorate holders are required for the next 10 years for expansion purposes; the *only* elements of demand are for replacement and the upgrading of quality of staffs currently employed. (It should also be recalled, from Chapter 3, that between 1985 and 1993 there will be a larger absolute decline in the size of the college-age population than will occur between 1980 and 1985; looking only 10 years ahead conceals the real magnitude of the adjustment problem facing higher education.) Tables in the 1975 report suggest "growth" needs of 153,500 doctorates between 1972 and 1985; however, a careful reading of footnotes and comparison of tables indicates that most of the incremental utilization attributable to "growth" is in fact anticipated enrichment. Thus, the academic growth estimates for science and engineering doctorate-holder utilization of 31,600 between 1972 and 1985 on closer examination turn out to be an estimated decline of 18,000 positions for growth purposes offset by a projected "enrichment" of some 49,600.

Similarly, the sizable increase in the utilization of science doctorate holders that the NSF report anticipates is found in nonacademic, non–research and development types of employment. Table 10-7, using NSF figures, indicates the expected growth in utilization for four employment categories. As the NSF report notes: "Thus, the Probable Model indicates that by 1985 about one-third of the doctorate S/E labor force might be employed neither by institutions of higher education nor

TABLE 10-7
NSF estimates of utilization of science and engineering doctorates, 1972 and 1985

Employment	Doctorates in labor force (in thousands)		Annual increase (percent)
	1972	*1985*	
Academic	125.6	157.2	1.8
Nonacademic research and development	63.3	95.0	3.2
Other science and engineering	17.1	40.1	6.8
Non–science and engineering	15.0	82.1	14.0
Total in labor force	221.0	374.5	4.1

SOURCE: Computed from Tables 11 and A-11 of National Science Foundation (1975).

engaged in nonacademic research and development. Furthermore, the same model reveals the possibility that over one-fifth of the 1985 doctorate labor force may not be engaged in any S/E activity, compared with less than one-tenth in 1972 (ibid., 1975, p. 2).

If the National Science Foundation estimates are correct, the number of projected new doctorate recipients indicated in Table 10-6, which decline 52 percent in the physical sciences and mathematics and 32 percent in engineering between 1970 and 1985, may still provide about one-third more Ph.D.'s by 1985 than are required for academic and research and development needs, even accepting the enrichment estimates in these sectors envisioned by NSF. The NSF projection of utilization of scientists and engineers may well prove correct; few Ph.D.'s are likely to be unemployed, given their abilities and training. However, it may well be questioned whether the added 90,000 science doctorates expected to be engaged in nonacademic and non–research and development types of employment represent "enrichment" or serious "underutilization." Certainly an increased number of scientists with doctorates who are in top corporate posts, the Congress, or high civil service positions can be interpreted as enrichment, but the projected fivefold increase in employment in nonscience areas (indicated in Table 10-7) will also include the scientist who has returned to the farm, is selling waterbeds in Berkeley, or driving a taxi in New York City. Little meaningful information is gathered by measuring unemployment rates of Ph.D.'s, for, by-and-large, they are resourceful people who will find some form of employment; more important is the development of reasonably accurate measures of underemployment. While the 1975 NSF report is a much less optimistic document than its two predecessors, it provides few clues as to whether a projected stock of doctorate holders in the labor force in 1985, 23 percent larger than anticipated science and engineering needs, is cause for alarm or a matter about which the scientific community can remain comfortably complacent.

SUMMARY ANALYSIS

Perhaps the clearest danger signal of a possible oversupply of doctorates in the future is seen when one compares the projected rate of increase in the stock of doctorate holders with the likely rate of growth in the need for doctorates in the economy.

Current output of Ph.D.'s represents an approximate 7 percent net annual increase in the stock, and projected Ph.D.'s up through about 1982 maintain the net addition rate at 6 percent or greater. The market model of graduate enrollment and Ph.D. output suggested in Chapter 7 suggests that the net annual flow would decline to about 4 percent of the total stock in the late 1980s. By contrast, the projection of enrollments suggests a required addition to college teaching staffs of less than 5 percent annually in the late 1970s (even allowing for some enrichment) and only 1 to 2 percent in the 1980s. In the nonacademic sectors, the National Science Foundation suggests a required increase of less than 1 percent annually in the stock of doctorates engaged in research and development work. Even if one assumes that science and engineering employment needs in government and industry approximate the growth in real GNP, it is unlikely that the long-term requirement for doctorates in these sectors will be much above 2 percent.

Thus, it appears that the graduate education establishment of 1975 is geared to the unusual growth rates of the mid-1960s, and that, in aggregate, it is turning out Ph.D.'s at a rate about one-third above needs in the late 1970s, and is projected to over-produce by about 50 percent or more in the 1980s. Obviously, this conclusion needs to be differentiated by field; in the humanities it is quite apparent that there will be a significant oversupply over the next 5 to 10 years, while in a few fields, such as environmental biology and computer sciences, the surplus is likely to be small or nonexistent. Nevertheless, considerable reduction in the flow of Ph.D.'s will be required if there is not to be a serious employment problem facing new doctorate recipients entering the job market.

Table 10-8 gives an indication of the extent of the problem facing new Ph.D.'s seeking academic employment. Judging from the Ph.D. and junior faculty projections of Table 7-5, the imbalance between doctorate supply and demand stands out in bold relief. Doctorate production is expected to peak between 1981 and 1985, while academic employment is projected to be at its lowest level. Only after 1990 is there likely to be a significant recovery in the number of academic openings available and in the early 1980s probably less than one in five Ph.D.'s are likely to find academic positions. Columns 2 and 3 of Table 10-8 estimate total faculty employment needs; it is unlikely that more than 75 percent of these positions will be filled by Ph.D.'s.

TABLE 10-8 *Comparison of actual and projected Ph.D. output and academic needs for new junior faculty, 1961–1965 to 1991–1995 (in thousands)*

Five-year period	Doctorate output (1)	Academic requirements		Column 2 as per-cent of column 1 (4)	Column 3 as per-cent of column 1 (5)
		Assuming 1972 conditions* (2)	Assuming significant market response† (3)		
1961–1965	66.0	112.9‡	112.9‡	171	171
1966–1970	118.0	147.5‡	147.5‡	125	125
1971–1975	170.5	70.2	80.0	41	47
1976–1980	198.8	79.6	92.0	40	46
1981–1985	220.9	7.0	38.0	3	17
1986–1990	182.0	26.5	66.0	15	36
1991–1995	200.0§	65.0¶	105.0	33	53

*See Table 7-5.

†Column 2, plus author's estimates of increased out-migration and lowered retirement age based on Chapter 8.

‡Actual.

§Estimated by the author beyond the projections of Chapter 7.

¶Based on projections of undergraduate enrollment from Chapter 4 plus assumed stable enrollments in graduate and professional enrollments in 1991–1995.

SOURCES: Table 7-5 and projections by the author.

Column 3 of Table 10-8 assumes that the net out-migration of senior faculty is 0.5 percent in 1976–1980, rising to 1 percent thereafter; it is also assumed that the movement toward early retirement increases the annual retirement rate by 10 percent in 1976–1980, 30 percent in 1981–1985, and 50 percent in 1986–1990. Thus, columns 2 and 3 probably represent outer boundaries within which actual experience will fall.

The last half of the 1970s appears to be an approximate continuation of the 1971–1975 experience—not particularly good, but not a severe oversupply period. The 1980s outlook, however, is bleak by any standard, and only a handful of disciplines are likely to come through relatively unscathed. Considering that the majority of Ph.D.'s of the early 1980s are already in graduate school (and first-time graduate enrollments in most nonscience fields are still increasing modestly) it is unlikely that a severe supply imbalance can be avoided. While most current graduate students recognize that job opportunities in the 1980s will be limited as compared with the recent past, few students or faculty appear to recognize the magnitude of the potential problem. Enrollment-driven academic budgets provide an incentive to campus administrators to maintain graduate enrollment levels, and university departments with substantial undergraduate teaching responsibilities feel a need for a continuing supply of able teaching assistants. Since job placement is not a real responsibility of the university (although department faculty and placement offices assist students to the best of their abilities), the sanctions that are imposed on a business concern for overproduction are absent in the world of higher education. Under these circumstances, the burden for responding to changing market conditions rests almost entirely upon the students themselves.

In a society that holds the principle of freedom of choice in high esteem—and particularly the freedom to choose a career or vocation—this situation is a real quandary for public policy. If, knowing labor market conditions and prospects for new doctorate recipients, bright students still pursue the Ph.D. in large numbers, do universities (and particularly public universities) have the right or responsibility of denying them admission? If the leading graduate departments should determine to reduce admissions, is there any assurance that this will not merely redirect students into smaller and weaker programs that are still attempting to build toward critical mass?[4]

Federal policy over the last 20 years has been to use fellowship and traineeship funds to encourage students to enter selected fields and to turn off funds when supply shortages diminish. This formally preserves individual freedom of choice by merely altering incentives, but it may also have an unstabilizing influence on the universities. In New York State, the board of regents has undertaken to review the quality of existing doctoral programs in both public and private universities and, in view of impending surpluses, to instruct some institutions of marginal quality to close down Ph.D. programs. Despite complaints that this violates institutional freedom, the review program has generally been thought a constructive move.[5]

[4]Studies by the National Board on Graduate Education of the "Gresham's Law" effect seem to indicate that, up to 1973, the leading departments had not experienced a significant decline in their share of either enrollments or doctorates. See Breneman (1975) and Cartter (1975, pp. 77–88).

[5]However, the New York State Board of Regents has greater constitutional powers than statewide boards in other states, encompassing both private and

The first responsibility of both graduate schools and public agencies should be to ensure that students are well informed of likely job prospects in their fields of interest. The popular media performs this role in part, but usually only long after an imbalance has become severe (and often in exaggerated fashion). Given the average six-year lag between entry to graduate school and completion of the doctorate, it is unfair for students to have to wait until near the completion of their studies to be informed of what was predictable at the beginning.

Those who worked closely with graduate students between 1968 and 1971 well remember the angry sense of betrayal that many students felt when it first became evident that desirable post-Ph.D. placement opportunities were becoming scarce. Science students, in particular, felt that they had been induced into graduate school by attractive federal fellowship programs and encouraged by their faculty advisers only to find that their services were superfluous because of reduced faculty hiring and cutbacks in federal research and development expenditure. Today's graduate students are a more sober lot, more cognizant of the risks attached to the significant investment of time and money occasioned by doctoral studies. Nonetheless, current and future students need to be much better informed about job prospects than they have been in the past.

In a little heralded provision recently published in the *Federal Register* the federal government now requires universities to make such information available to entering students. Although the regulation was originally directed principally toward vocational programs in proprietary schools, it is now thought to apply to all programs preparing students for the professions. The regulation states:

Each participating institution shall make a good faith effort to present to each prospective student prior to the time the prospective student obligates himself [*sic*] to pay tuition and fees to the institution with a complete and accurate statement [which] . . . shall include information regarding the employment of students enrolled in such courses, in such vocation, trade or career field. Such information shall include data regarding the average starting salary for previously enrolled students entering positions of employment for which the courses of study

public sectors. Significant state support for graduate programs in private universities (under the "Bundy plan") also gives the regents somewhat greater power of sanctions.

offered by the institution are intended as preparation and the percentage of such students who obtained employment in such positions. This information shall be based on the most recently available data. If the institution, after reasonable effort, cannot obtain statistically meaningful data regarding its own students, it may use the most recent comparable regional or national data (*Federal Register*, 1975, para. 177.64).

In many fields of study, the professional associations may also be faulted for failing to make significant efforts to acquaint apprentice scholars with estimates of current and future job prospects. As noted earlier, the American Institute of Physics (AIP) has been in the forefront in manpower analyses. Their efforts began in 1960 and have resulted in five reports over the 1962–1973 period.[6] Despite the discontinuance of the National Register of Scientific and Technical Personnel in 1971, AIP and the American Physical Society have combined to continue a Register of Physicists and Related Scientists. The fact that physics is perhaps the best example of a field that has been highly market responsive can be largely attributed to the fact that the professional society has placed truth and objectivity for their field above the parochial interests of their local departments. The adjustments of the last five years have been very difficult for physics departments, but, as a result, they are less likely than certain other disciplines to experience a traumatic supply and demand imbalance in the years ahead.

The engineering societies also have a long tradition of manpower assessment through the Engineering Manpower Commission of the Engineers Joint Council. Over the last several years, chemistry, mathematics, and psychology societies have been increasingly active in their concern for manpower prospects and job placement problems.[7] Few of the social science professional associations have yet taken the problem seriously (or, as in the case of the executive committee of the American Economic Association in 1972, have positively refrained on the basis that those who believe in market-response mechanisms should rely upon market-induced adjustments). In the humani-

[6]The most recent report, *Physics Manpower, 1973* (American Institute of Physics, 1973) is an extensive 120-page document with a wealth of data on education and employment.

[7]See, for example, the special issue of the *American Psychologist* (May 1972) devoted to supply and demand considerations.

ties fields the Modern Language Association has become very active as a job market broker, but almost at the expense of bankrupting the society ("Deficits Mount for Scholarly Groups," 1975). The board of officers of the American Philosophical Association issued an open letter to prospective graduate students in September 1974, indicating the severity of the "job crisis" for Ph.D.'s and advising them that job vacancies in teaching are likely to be significantly smaller in number than qualified job seekers for some time to come.

Clearly the professional societies need assistance in coping with the problem, for in the absence of a concerted effort by federal agencies (other than the National Science Foundation, which has performed this service reasonably well for science disciplines), they are left with a substantial burden. Given the increasing seriousness of the problem of imbalance between doctorate supply and demand, it seems inexplicable that the several federal agencies concerned with higher education (National Institute of Education, U.S. Office of Education, National Center for Educational Statistics) have not seriously undertaken a major study of college and university faculty since 1963. The latest U.S. Office of Education report on estimated faculty employed in higher education was for 1968, and even that report has now been superseded by major revisions in faculty estimates in 1969 and 1971. (See Chapter 6 for a discussion of this issue.) Interinstitutional faculty mobility, the migration of senior doctorates into and out of higher education, retirement rates, and changing faculty age distributions have all been ignored by the segments of the Department of Health, Education, and Welfare concerned with higher education since 1963. Clearly, without leadership from Washington little progress is likely to be made on improving information available to current or prospective graduate students.[8] The current situation is reminiscent of the Department of Health, Education, and

---

[8]The author served for three years as chairman of a federal interagency Committee on Scientific and Professional Manpower (a subcommittee of the National Advisory Manpower Committee, chaired by Eli Ginsberg). In 1972 the committee recommended that the Department of Labor attempt to fill the vacuum by devoting attention to the changing job market for Ph.D.'s in both academic and nonacademic sectors of the economy. The committee stressed that this would be an increasingly important issue, requiring the joint attention of the Department of Labor; Department of Health, Education, and Welfare; and the National Science Foundation. No follow-up action was ever taken, despite strong endorsement by the parent committee.

Welfare's affirmative action pressures on faculty hiring at a time when federal data were inadequate to determine the size of available stocks of qualified minority Ph.D.'s by discipline or by region.

Despite criticisms of federal inaction, institutions engaged in graduate education must also bear some of the burden for informing students and ensuring that Ph.D. output does not outstrip the demand for doctorates. Between 1971 and 1973, according to annual reports of the Council of Graduate Schools, the largest increases in Ph.D.'s awarded were in the humanities and in education—two subject areas most likely to experience serious oversupply problems in the future. Granted, students in humanistic disciplines are probably the least well informed and perhaps the least market responsive, but for these reasons university departments may be considered to have a particular obligation to discourage enrollments of marginal students. Too many institutions are accepting students with dubious credentials in order to maintain enrollments. In the face of current job prospects, the late 1970s and early 1980s ought to be a time when admission and retention standards are raised, not lowered. Knowing that academic job prospects are poor for the next 10 to 15 years, departments and university administrations should be asking: How small can graduate enrollment be and still maintain a viable program, in contrast to the common question of five years ago: How large can one get without detracting from the quality of education?

Over the last five years, Harvard has reduced the size of its entering class in graduate school by 20 percent as the result of a 1969 faculty committee report which concluded that the graduate experience was a disappointing one for many students; under the pressure of rising costs and declining external student support further reductions are contemplated.[9] Several other major universities have instituted similar reductions in scale. Judging from the size distribution of the leading graduate departments in the ACE surveys of scholarly reputation, many of the distinguished departments were considerably larger (sometimes by a factor of three) than necessary to achieve critical mass. In a field such as history, for example, the four

---

[9]See the excellent *President's Report, 1972–73* (n.d., pp. 8–28) for a discussion of the problems facing the graduate school at Harvard.

smallest departments in the top-ranked one-fourth of departments in 1964 had 18 FTE faculty, 85 FTE students, and produced 7 Ph.D.'s annually. The average size for all high-quality departments was 32 graduate faculty, 185 students, and 12 Ph.D.'s. The small departments were more efficient in the number of doctorates awarded as a percent of enrollment and in Ph.D. output per faculty member. This experience was duplicated in most fields, suggesting that high-quality efficient doctoral programs could function at about half the size of the average outstanding department in the mid-1960s.

In the physical sciences such enrollment and degree reductions have already occurred; in most humanities and social science fields, however, the adjustments that are likely to be necessary have yet to occur. In Great Britain recently, the minister for higher education has indicated that the government would no longer permit the universities "to produce whatever people they fancied or to relate the number and kinds of places they provided to the applicants that came forward" ("An End to Laissez Faire . . . ," 1975).

"Our concept of meeting the so-called natural demand for further education is even less likely to meet the country's needs for trained manpower. So this government must do something more positive in the manpower planning field to guide its choices in the education field" (ibid.). Such an attitude is increasingly likely to become common among state governments and federal agencies concerned with higher education in the United States unless the universities themselves take the initiative in planning selective cutbacks in fields where Ph.D. surpluses are most likely.

An informed student populace is the number one priority, and some modest tightening of admissions standards and/or post-M.A. continuation standards is of equal importance. Given these two conditions, and recognizing that there will always be a lag of several years in free-choice adjustments to changing market conditions, American graduate schools can probably survive the 1980s without having externally imposed standards for enrollment and degrees placed upon them.

THE IMPROVEMENT OF KNOWLEDGE AND INFORMATION

It has been argued that an informed student population is the first requirement for the market to perform effectively as a regulator of the flow of young men and women through doctoral programs. But an informed demand presumes that faculty, university administrations, and educational funding agencies are well aware of current and prospective trends in the supply and demand for Ph.D.'s. At present, this can hardly be said to be the case, and a concerted effort by federal agencies and the various professional societies is urgently needed.

Through the efforts of the National Center for Educational Statistics, the National Research Council, and the Council of Graduate Schools, reasonably good information now exists on current and recent enrollment and degree trends and first job placement of Ph.D.'s. Recent refinements in Higher Education General Information Survey (HEGIS) reporting requirements promise to provide better doctorate enrollment data, differentiated by level, than has been available in the past. The professional societies, were they all to perform as effectively as the American Institute of Physics and the several engineering societies, could improve our knowledge of short-run (three to five years) supply conditions by monitoring enrollments in their disciplines at several key junctures (for example, freshman entrants and their major field aspirations, junior majors, baccalaureates, and first-time entrants in graduate studies).

On the demand side, knowledge is very limited. The Office of Education has not undertaken a major study of college and university faculties since 1963, and judging by the frequency with which their estimates of full-time and part-time faculty and research personnel employed in higher education have been revised, their annually reported data remain somewhat suspect. The only recent benchmarks are provided by the Carnegie Commission and American Council on Education faculty surveys of 1968 and 1972. The Carnegie Council on Policy Studies in Higher Education has undertaken a follow-up 1975 survey, but its usefulness for economic analyses is somewhat limited because the questions dealing with faculty mobility are not consistent with the earlier surveys.

In analyzing the demand for college teachers, the key elements are an accurate knowledge of retirements, of the flow of experienced personnel between academic and nonacademic employment, and of student-faculty ratios. The first of these can be inferred from information about the age distribution of college teachers, but in a period when retirement policy and practice may be changing, this is inadequate. The last of these elements can be determined ex post if the Office of Education data are reliable, but usually only for broad categories of institutions. Improvements in the HEGIS data, and more current availability of such information, promise better information for the future. Information about the migration of Ph.D.'s into and out of academic employment, and interinstitutional mobility, are sadly lacking. In Chapter 8 an attempt has been made to partly fill this gap and to speculate about future faculty flows, but improved periodic data are badly needed if we are to attain a better understanding of the dynamics of the academic labor market.

Several steps could be taken to rectify our ignorance in these areas. First, periodic surveys, such as the U.S. Office of Education's Survey of College Faculty conducted in 1963 (Dunham, Wright, & Chandler, 1966), would provide the necessary benchmarks for assessing changes in faculty resources in the various sectors of higher education. If supplemented by a survey of a sample of departments inquiring as to the immediate, previous, or succeeding employment (or other status) of faculty hired or separated in the past two years, current information about the critical flow of senior personnel into and out of higher education would be available for the first time.

Second, TIAA data cover about one-half of all full-time faculty in the United States and could be an invaluable source of information on mobility. Many public institutions participate in state pension plans, and thus one would need to carefully weight TIAA samples so as to be reasonably representative, but TIAA-CREF records indicate all changes of employment for participants. At the least, TIAA data could identify a large sample of job-changers in any given year, who could then be followed up by a survey instrument designed to determine the attributes of job changers and the reasons for the change. Entrants to higher education can be identified by other means, but we remain woefully ignorant about those who depart.

Third, professional associations, through their contacts directly with scholars and with college and university departments, could be extremely helpful in studying faculty turnover, promotion, tenure, and retirement statistics. Again, the American Institute of Physics can be cited as performing the most effective service in this regard with its periodic surveys of department heads to determine the changing pattern of academic employment of physicists. Even a carefully selected 20 percent sample of departments in the roughly 1,800 senior institutions, reported annually, would give valuable information on current and prospective accessions and separations, and provide a useful profile of the current professoriate.

If such improved data existed, significant headway could be made both in understanding market-response patterns in the academic labor market and in making the market perform more efficiently through better informed suppliers and demanders of Ph.D.-level talent. As a National Board on Graduate Education report noted (Freeman & Breneman, 1974), adequate public policy making requires an improved mechanism for monitoring trends affecting the labor market for the highly trained, further testing and refinement of estimates of supply and demand elasticities, and more imaginative econometric modeling to improve our ability to make useful manpower projections.

Differences among academic disciplines, both on the supply and the demand side, as noted above, make it imperative that disaggregated labor market analyses be undertaken. Throughout most of the preceding chapters Ph.D.'s have been treated as a single commodity; such an aggregated approach can only be taken as a broad profile of the academic labor market, and policies that might be called for in anthropology or history may be entirely inappropriate for electrical engineering or biochemistry. The present study can only be considered a first step toward understanding academic labor market dynamics; subsequent steps are necessary at the level of individual disciplines.[10]

One caveat must be kept in mind in public policy considerations of graduate education. While severe imbalances between the supply and demand of Ph.D.'s are a matter of broad public concern, it would be an error to attempt to "fine tune" the flow of young men and women through graduate school with only manpower concerns in mind. First, our knowledge of future needs for specialized talent trained at the doctoral level, as

---

[10]The author, in conjunction with Ernest May (Harvard), Lewis Solmon (Higher Education Research Institute), and Dorothy Harrison (New York State Education Department), has embarked on a detailed study of five humanistic disciplines with support of the Mellon Foundation. This study, focusing on English, history, philosophy, French, and Spanish, is due for completion in 1977.

experience indicates, is still rather primitive. Attempts by some central agency to fine tune at entry and post-M.A.-continuation points are likely to do more damage than good. Second, a modest oversupply of Ph.D.'s in terms of traditional employment opportunities may be a good thing for both higher education and the economy. In an analogous case it is hard not to believe that the nation's medical care would improve if there were a more plentiful supply of well-trained medical personnel.[11] Competition, and the luxury of being somewhat more selective in hiring and promotion, often make for more efficient services. Third, and very importantly in the area of scholarship, is the argument that learning and knowledge should not be rationed as though they were only marketable "products." Doctoral education for many participants is not just an avenue to a job or career, but a deeply enriching personal experience that is valuable in its own right. In the economists' terms graduate education may also be thought of as partly a consumer's good—enjoyable and rewarding in itself—not only as an investment in human capital that requires some demonstrable rate of return to justify it. If students are well informed as to likely job prospects and still choose to pursue the Ph.D., the most talented should have that right. Whether or not such students should be heavily subsidized with public funds is another and more serious question; and it seems obvious that in periods of oversupply, special efforts should be exerted to assure that standards for admission and continuation be maintained at high levels.

It has been projected in preceding chapters that the full impact of an excess supply of Ph.D.'s is likely to be felt in the early 1980s, and that any significant recovery of academic demand is not likely to occur before the mid-1990s. If correct, this is likely to mean a period of 15 years or more when graduate education will be sorely troubled by problems of

---

[11]This situation may finally occur within the next few years. The stock of active physicians is projected to grow by 6.5 percent annually over the next 15 years, given the current level of output of the nation's medical schools. Department of Health, Education, and Welfare projections indicate that the number of physicians per 100,000 population, up from 140 in 1960 to 176 in 1975, will reach 220 to 254 by 1990. Thus medical education may face the same type of readjustment in the near future that the nation's graduate schools are currently experiencing. See U.S. Department of Health, Education, and Welfare (1974, p. 54).

enrollment contraction and job placement of new Ph.D.'s. In the past, federal government agencies have played a destabilizing role, encouraging too rapid expansion in the 1960s and too abruptly removing support after 1970. These actions have exacerbated the fiscal problems of the major universities and have been a contributing factor to what has been called "the new depression in higher education" (Cheit, 1971). If the universities do not take the leadership in curtailing doctoral output in those fields where substantial surpluses are emerging, the states are likely to react sharply by reducing resources available for the support of graduate study. Given the time-lags in adjustment, they are likely to do it poorly, causing serious deterioration in the quality of programs and failing to foresee future shortages in some disciplines. Universities are delicate organizations of intellectual activity and scholarship, and blunt instruments are inappropriate for bringing about desired change. If public universities would ward off undifferentiated cut-backs imposed on them from state legislatures and state-wide boards, they must take the initiative themselves. Most of the professional societies are sufficiently alarmed to have initiated efforts over the last several years to better inform their members of likely future trends.

The primary aim of responsible public policy and educational administration must be to retain the health and vigor of American scholarship. The next several decades will require a resiliency on the part of institutions in responding to changed market conditions and imaginative leadership on the part of those responsible for the administration of doctoral programs. In response to national needs, most universities passed, with flying colors, the test of rapid growth in the 1960s. The more severe test of creative responsiveness in a period of declining demand will come in the 1980s.

References

American Association of University Professors: *AAUP Bulletin*, summer issues, various years.

American Institute of Physics: *Physics Manpower, 1973*, AIP Publication R.255, New York, August 1973.

American Psychologist, vol. 27, no. 5, May 1972.

"An End to Laissez Faire for British Higher Education?" *Chronicle of Higher Education*, June 9, 1975, p. 11.

Astin, Helen: "Career Profiles of Women Doctorates," in Alice S. Rossi and Ann Calderwood (eds.), *Academic Women on the Move*, Russell Sage Foundation, New York, 1973.

Bayer, Alan: *College and University Faculty: A Statistical Description*, research reports vol. 5, no. 5, American Council on Education, Washington, D.C., 1970.

Bayer, Alan: *Teaching Faculty in Academe, 1972–73*, research reports vol. 8, no. 2, American Council on Education, Washington, D.C., 1973.

Bayer, Alan, and Helen S. Astin: "Sex Differences in Academic Rank and Salary among Science Doctorates in Teaching," *Journal of Human Resources*, vol. 3, pp. 191–200, 1968.

Bayer, Alan, and Helen S. Astin: *Progress in the Elimination of Sex Discrimination in Academe: Have Antibias Regulation and "Good Faith" Helped?*, 1975. (Mimeographed.)

Berelson, Bernard: *Graduate Education in the United States*, McGraw-Hill Book Company, New York, 1960.

Bezdele, Roger H.: *Long-Range Forecasting of Manpower Requirements*, Manpower Planning Committee, Institute of Electrical and Electronics Engineers, Inc., (E.H.-0101-6), New York, 1974.

Bolt, R. H., W. Koltun, and O. H. Levine: "Doctorate Feedback in Higher Education," *Science*, vol. 148, no. 3678, pp. 918–928, May 14, 1965.

Breneman, David W.: *Graduate School Adjustments to the "New Depression" in Higher Education,* National Board on Graduate Education, Washington, D.C., 1975.

Brown, David G.: *The Mobile Professors,* American Council on Education, Washington, D.C., 1967.

Cain, Glen, Richard Freeman, and Lee Hansen (eds.): *Labor Market Analysis of Engineers and Technical Workers,* The Johns Hopkins Press, Baltimore, 1973.

Campbell, Robert, and Barry N. Siegel: "The Demand for Higher Education in the United States, 1919–1964," *American Economic Review,* vol. 57, no. 3, pp. 482–494, June 1967.

Carnegie Commission on Higher Education: *New Students and New Places,* McGraw-Hill Book Company, New York, 1971.

Carnegie Commission on Higher Education: *Higher Education: Who Pays? Who Benefits? Who Should Pay?* McGraw-Hill Book Company, New York, 1973a.

Carnegie Commission on Higher Education: *Priorities for Action,* McGraw-Hill Book Company, New York, 1973b.

Carnegie Commission on Higher Education: *Toward a Learning Society,* McGraw-Hill Book Company, New York, 1973c.

Cartter, Allan: *Theory of Wages and Employment,* Richard D. Irwin, Inc., Homewood, Ill., 1959.

Cartter, Allan: "Higher Education in the Last Third of the Century," *Educational Record,* vol. 46, no. 2, pp. 119–128, Spring 1965a.

Cartter, Allan: "A New Look at the Supply and Demand for College Teachers," *Educational Record,* vol. 46, no. 3, pp. 267–277, Summer 1965b.

Cartter, Allan: *An Assessment of Quality in Graduate Education,* American Council on Education, Washington, D.C., 1966a.

Cartter, Allan: "Future Faculty Needs and Resources," in Charles Dobbins (ed.), *The Improvement of College Teaching: Aids and Impediments,* American Council on Education, Washington, D.C., 1966b.

Cartter, Allan: "The Supply and Demand for College Teachers," Proceedings of the 1965 annual meeting of the American Statistical Association, reprinted in *The Journal of Human Resources,* vol. 1, no. 1, pp. 22–37, Summer 1966c.

Cartter, Allan: "Academic Labor Market Projections and the Draft," in *The Economics and Financing of Higher Education in the United States,* Joint Economic Committee of the Congress, Washington, D.C., 1969, pp. 357–374.

Cartter, Allan: "Scientific Manpower for 1970–1985," *Science,* vol. 172, pp. 132–140, Apr. 9, 1971.

Cartter, Allan: "Faculty Needs and Resources," *Annals,* vol. 404, pp. 71–87, November 1972.

Cartter, Allan: "The Need for a New Approach to the Financing of Recurrent Education," in *Post-Degree Continuing Education,* Proceedings of the Princeton University Conference on Post-Degree Continuing Education, May 1973.

Cartter, Allan: "The Academic Labor Market," in Margaret S. Gordon (ed.), *Higher Education and the Labor Market,* McGraw-Hill Book Company, New York, 1974.

Cartter, Allan M. (ed.): *Assuring Academic Progress Without Growth,* Jossey-Bass, Inc., Publishers, San Francisco, 1975.

Cartter, Allan M., and John M. McDowell: "Changing Employment Patterns and Faculty Demographics," in Allan M. Cartter (ed.), *Assuring Academic Progress Without Growth,* New Directions for Institutional Research, issue 6, Jossey-Bass, Inc., Publishers, San Francisco, summer 1975.

Cartter, Allan, and W. E. Ruhter: *The Disappearance of Sex Discrimination in First Job Placement of New Ph.D.'s,* Higher Education Research Institute, Los Angeles, 1975.

Cartter, Allan, and M. Salter: "Two-Year College Faculty and Enrollment Projections," in *Graduate Education and Community Colleges,* National Board on Graduate Education, technical report no. 5, August 1975.

Cheit, Earl F.: *The New Depression in Higher Education: A Study of Financial Conditions at 41 Colleges and Universities,* McGraw-Hill Book Company, New York, 1971.

Commission on Non-Traditional Study: *Diversity by Design,* Jossey-Bass, Inc., Publishers, San Francisco, 1973.

"Deficits Mount for Scholarly Groups," *Chronicle of Higher Education,* Jan. 27, 1975, p. 3.

Dresch, Stephen P.: "Demography, Technology and Higher Education: Toward a Formal Model of Education Adaptation," *Journal of Political Economy,* vol. 83, no. 3, pp. 535–569, May–June 1975.

Dunham, Ralph, Patricia Wright, and Marjorie Chandler: *Teaching Faculty in Universities and Four-Year Colleges, Spring 1963,* U.S. Office of Education, Washington, D.C., 1966.

Federal Register, vol. 40, no. 35, Feb. 20, 1975, para. 177.64.

Federal Reserve Bulletin, vol. 60, no. 2, February 1974.

Freeman, Richard: *The Market for College-Trained Manpower,* Harvard University Press, Cambridge, Mass., 1971.

Freeman, Richard: "Supply and Salary Adjustments to the Changing Science Manpower Market: Physics, 1948–73," *American Economic Review,* vol. 65, no. 1, pp. 27–39, March 1975.

Freeman, Richard, and David W. Breneman: *Forecasting the Ph.D. Labor Market: Pitfalls for Policy,* technical report no. 2, The National Board on Graduate Education, Washington, D.C., April 1974.

Haggstrom, Gus: Internal working paper for the Carnegie Commission on Higher Education, Berkeley, Calif., 1970. (Mimeographed.)

Ingraham, Mark H.: *My Purpose Holds: Reactions and Experiences in Retirement of TIAA-CREF Annuitants,* Teachers Insurance and Annuity Association of America/College Retirement Equity Fund, New York, 1974.

Knapp, R.: *Origins of American Humanistic Scholars,* University of Chicago Press, Chicago, 1964.

Lester, Richard A.: *Antibias Regulation of Universities: Faculty Problems and Their Solutions,* McGraw-Hill Book Company, New York, 1974.

Lewis, Justin C., and Naomi Sulkin: "Estimating Higher Education Enrollments and Degrees," National Science Foundation, Washington, D.C., 1972. (Mimeographed.)

National Academy of Sciences: *Careers of Ph.D.'s: Academic versus Nonacademic,* publication no. 1577, Washington, D.C., 1968.

National Academy of Sciences: *Doctoral Scientists and Engineers in the United States: 1973 Profile,* a report by the Commission on Human Resources, Washington, D.C., 1974.

National Board on Graduate Education: *Doctorate Manpower Forecasts and Policy,* Washington, D.C., 1973.

National Education Association: *Teacher Supply and Demand in Colleges, Universities, and Junior Colleges,* (title varies) 1955, 1957, 1961, 1963, 1965.

National Research Council: *Doctorate Recipients from U.S. Universities, 1958–66,* Washington, D.C., 1967a.

National Research Council: *Summary Report: Doctorate Recipients from U.S. Universities,* Washington, D.C., 1967b through 1974.

National Science Foundation: *Science and Engineering Staff in Universities and Colleges, 1965–1975,* Washington, D.C., 1967.

National Science Foundation: *Science and Engineering Doctorate Supply and Utilization,* Washington, D.C., 1969.

National Science Foundation: *Science and Engineering Doctorate Supply and Utilization,* Washington, D.C., 1971.

National Science Foundation: *National Patterns of R&D Resources, Funds, and Manpower in the United States, 1953–72,* Washington, D.C., 1972.

National Science Foundation: *Projections of Science and Engineering Doctorate Supply and Utilization 1980 and 1985,* Washington, D.C., 1975.

Niland, J. R.: "Allocation of Ph.D. Manpower in the Academic Labor Market," *Industrial Relations,* vol. 2, no. 2, pp. 141–156, May 1972.

Niland, J. R.: *Where Have All the Ph.D.'s Been Going?,* 1973. (Mimeographed.)

President's Report, 1972–73, Harvard University, Cambridge, Mass., n.d.

Rehn, Gösta: *Prospective View on Patterns of Working Time,* report no. 1B, International Conference on New Patterns for Working Time, Organisation for Economic Co-operation and Development, Paris, 1972.

Rogers, James F.: *Staffing American Colleges and Universities,* U.S. Office of Education, Washington, D.C., 1967.

Roose, K. D., and C. J. Andersen: *A Rating of Graduate Programs,* American Council on Education, Washington, D.C., 1970.

Solmon, L. C.: "Women in Doctoral Education: Clues and Puzzles Regarding Institutional Discrimination," *Research in Higher Education,* vol. 1, pp. 299–332, 1973.

Stigler, George: *Theory of Price,* 8th edition, Macmillan, New York, 1970.

Strothmann, F. W. (for the Committee of 15): *The Graduate School Today and Tomorrow: Reflections for the Profession's Consideration,* Fund for the Advancement of Education, New York, December 1955.

"Surviving the Seventies: Report on the Economic Status of the Profession, 1972–73," *AAUP Bulletin,* vol. 59, no. 2, pp. 188–258, Summer 1973.

U.S. Bureau of the Census: *Current Population Reports,* series P-20 and P-25, various years.

U.S. Bureau of the Census: *Historical Statistics of the United States, Colonial Times to 1957,* 1960.

U.S. Bureau of the Census: *Census of the Population, 1960: Detailed Characteristics, United States Summary,* final report PC(1)-1D, 1963.

U.S. Bureau of the Census: "Estimates of the Population of the U.S. by Single Years of Age, Color, and Sex, 1900–1959," *Current Population Reports,* ser. P-25, no. 211, July 2, 1965.

U.S. Bureau of the Census: "Projections of the Population of the U.S., by Age and Sex (Interim Revision) 1970–2020," *Current Population Reports,* ser. P-25, no. 448, Aug. 6, 1970.

U.S. Bureau of the Census: "Projections of the Population of the U.S., by Age and Sex, 1972–2020," *Current Population Reports,* ser. P-25, no. 493, December 1972.

U.S. Bureau of the Census: "Undergraduate Enrollment in Two-Year and Four-Year Colleges, October 1972," *Current Population Reports,* ser. P-20, no. 257, 1973.

U.S. Bureau of the Census: "Population Estimates and Projections: 1975–2000," *Current Population Reports,* ser. P-25, no. 541, February 1975.

U.S. Department of Health, Education, and Welfare: *The Supply of Health Manpower,* (HRA 75-38), December 1974.

U.S. Department of Health, Education, and Welfare: *Monthly Vital Statistics Report,* National Center for Health Statistics, Mar. 27, 1975.

U.S. Office of Education: *Projections of Educational Statistics to 1975–76: 1966 Edition,* 1967.

U.S. Office of Education: *Projections of Educational Statistics to 1977–78: 1968 Edition,* 1969.

U.S. Office of Education: *Projections of Educational Statistics to 1979–80: 1970 Edition,* 1971.

U.S. Office of Education: *Teaching and Research Staff by Academic Field in Institutions of Higher Education, Fall 1968, 1972.*

U.S. Office of Education: *Digest of Educational Statistics: 1972 Edition* (prepublication data), 1973*a*.

U.S. Office of Education: *Projections of Educational Statistics to 1981–82, 1972 Edition,* 1973*b*.

U.S. Office of Education: *Projections of Educational Statistics to 1982–83: 1973 Edition,* 1974.

U.S. Office of Education: *Projections of Educational Statistics to 1983–84: 1974 Edition,* 1975.

Weathersby, George: *A Broad View of Individual Demand for Postsecondary Education,* paper delivered at NCHEMS national invitational seminar, May 1974. (Mimeographed.)

Wolfle, Dael: *America's Resources of Specialized Talent,* Harper & Brothers, New York, 1954.

Index